ASTA® Directory of Sail Training Ships and Programs

Edited by
Laura K. Stack
and
Lincoln P. Paine (Consulting Editor)

Eighth Edition, 1995

American Sail Training Association

Newport, Rhode Island

Published by
American Sail Training Association (ASTA®)
365 Thames Street
P.O. Box 1459
Newport, RI 02840

Copyright © 1995 by the American Sail Training Association

All rights reserved. No part of this book may be produced or utilized in any form or by any means, electronic or mechanical, including photocopying, recording, or by any information storage and retrieval systems, without permission in writing from the publisher. For information contact the American Sail Training Association.

ISBN 0-9636483-1-4

Library of Congress Cataloging-in-Publication Data

ASTA® Directory of Sail Training Ships and Programs
8th ed./edited by Laura K. Stack and Lincoln P. Paine

Printed by Ripon Community Printers in the United States of America

American Sail Training Association

Board of Directors

Gail R. Shawe, Chairman
Bart Dunbar, Vice-Chairman
Jeff Parker, Secretary
Per H.M. Lofving, Treasurer
Chris M. Bagley, Canadian STA (ex-officio)
Fred Addis
Peter Ansoff
Richard Bailey
Cdr. C.H. Barber, USN (ret.)
Ernestine J. Bennett
Robert Booth
Arden Brink
Ned Chalker
Steve Cobb
Dawn Curtis
Peter Evans
John Wesley Gardner
Edward Griggs
Melissa Harrington
Nick Horvath
Tom Kelly
Karen Love
Joe Maggio
Mary Sue McCarthy
Phillip McLaren
Jeffrey N. Parker
William Pinkney
Michael Rauworth
Dusty Rhodes
Robby Robinson
Bert Rogers
Walter Rybka
Wallace Stark
Alix Thorne
Robert Walker
Barclay H. Warburton, IV
Mark Wells
John Wigglesworth
Capt. David V. V. Wood, USCG (ret.)

Commodores Council

Henry H. Anderson
David Brink
Pete Hall
Nancy H. Richardson
VADM. Thomas R. Weschler, USN (ret.)

National Advisory Board

D. K. Abbass, PhD
Don Birkholz
James P. Bond
Martha Boudreau
Mary T. Crowley
Capt. Ernst M. Cummings, USCG (ret.)
Henry Dormitzer
James Ellis
Michael Ford
Lars Forsberg
Diane Glennon
Joseph Gribbins
Tim Jones
Linda Jordan
William Ladd
William Lee
Candide Kane-Mays
Michael Naab
Lincoln Paine
Rafe Parker
George Rounds
Ed Rumowicz
Leon Schertler
Avery Seaman
Capt. Richard T. Shannon, USCG (ret.)
John Southam
Peter Stanford
Capt. Hal Sutphen, USN (ret.)
Steve Wedlock
Peter Willauer

American Sail Training Association

Pamela C. Wuerth, Executive Director
Karen Lokay, Membership Secretary
Laura K. Stack, Program Coordinator

Arden R. Brink, Chairman, Publications Committee

Patricia Linn Lussier, Designer/Desktop Publisher

Special thanks to: Jim Gladson, David Higgins, Dan Quinn, Michael Rauworth, Nancy Richardson, Gail R. Shawe, Onne Van Der Wal, John Wigglesworth, David V. V. Wood, and the trainees aboard the *Tole Mour*.

Cover photo by: Onne Van Der Wal/Stock Newport

Back cover: ASTA® file photos

For interior photos designated as "ASTA file photos" we thank the photographers. Special thanks to Nancy Linden who shot many of them.

This 8th edition of The ASTA® *Directory of Sail Training Ships and Programs* was desktop published on a Macintosh IIvc computer utilizing MicrosoftWord 5.1, and QuarkXPress 3.1. Text is set in ITC-Clearface font.

The following service marks are the property of the American Sail Training Association:
- ASTA®
- Tall Ships®
- Tall Ships Are Coming®
- Return of the Tall Ships®

® denotes a service mark of the American Sail Training Association registered in the United States and Canada.

CONTENTS

ASTA Masthead v
ASTA Mission Statement 8
Welcome to ASTA, by Gail Shawe 9
Sail Training in Brief 11
The American Sail Training Association 13
    Publications 15
    Conferences, Seminars, Rallies & Dockside Demos 16
    Billet Bank & Insurance 18
    Sail Training Vessels 19
    Sail Training & Sea Education 20
    Choosing a Sail Training Program 22
    Shipping Out 23

ARTICLES
Sail Training: The Next Century, by David V. V. Wood 27
It's More Than Just a Boat Ride, by James Gladson 33
"Life on the *Tole Mour*", by Cadets 41
Take Charge of Your Sail Training Experience, by M. Rauworth 45

DIRECTORY
Sail Training Ships, United States & Canada 47
Sail Training Programs, United States & Canada 165
International Sail Training Associations 192
Rig Identification 193
Membership & Gift Information 209

American Sail Training Association Mission

To encourage character building through sail training, promote sail training to the American public, and support education under sail.

Welcome to ASTA

On a snowy weekend in January, 1994, a group of loyal representatives of the American Sail Training Association (ASTA®) gathered in Newport, Rhode Island to discuss the organization's future. As the cold wind blew outside, heated discussions were taking place around the table: what is ASTA's mission; what is the vision for ASTA; where have we been; where are we going; and, how do we get there? Who is ASTA's constituency? What is sail training? The group carefully examined all of these questions and more until, in the end, the group reached a consensus and refined ASTA's mission: "To encourage character building through sail training, promote sail training to the American public, and support education under sail."

Throughout all the conversations and planning that accompanied the long-range planning process, it became increasingly apparent that the American Sail Training Association means different things to different groups and organizations. It is precisely this broad and diverse constituency that makes ASTA such an important and dynamic organization. ASTA simultaneously serves as the national trade association for sail training, an events coordinator in concert with port cities, and a vehicle through which people of all ages gain access to the world of sail training. As we look to the future, we all agree that we must preserve this diversity; we must be vigilant in maintaining the rich cultural mix that is the American Sail Training Association.

Phase one of the long-range plan requires implementation of internal structural changes and a revision of the organization's by-laws. While this may sound mundane, it lies at the very heart of what needs to happen so that ASTA will attain its exciting vision for the future. For the remainder of 1994, we will plot the course for the rest of this century. We will continue those programs and services that are successful, refining those which are not up to ASTA standards, all the while keeping a steady watch on the horizon and what the future may bring.

We look forward to the creation of scholarship programs to put students, trainees and educators on licensed member vessels. We will create a stronger presence for ASTA throughout the country by defining and implementing a method for regional representation. ASTA will strengthen its relationship with the worldwide sail training community through broader participation in international events. We will continue to work closely with all American ports that host tall ship events. We have already begun planning celebrations to mark the millennium: TALL SHIPS 2000℠. This is a challenging and exciting time for ASTA and we invite you to actively participate in the organization's evolution and growth.

The annual ASTA *Directory of Sail Training Ships and Programs* is a clear demonstration that sail training is taking place along both coasts as well as on rivers and lakes throughout the United States and Canada. Sail training occurs on large and small ships as well as within programs for young and old. We hope you will use this

Directory to discover your own potential for becoming involved with ASTA, tall ships and sail training.
   Welcome Aboard!

Gail Shawe
Chairman

Sail Training in Brief

Sail training describes challenging and adventurous programs conducted aboard ships under sail, often for the purpose of developing self-reliance, teamwork, responsibility and leadership. Sail training combines a focus on the development of better shipmates with the sailing school objective of training better sailors. Both include participation in the work of the vessel and the development of safety and seamanship skills necessary to effectively handle a vessel in its naturally challenging elements of wind and water.

The American Sail Training Association (ASTA®), with headquarters in Newport, Rhode Island, is a non-profit, national organization dedicated to bringing such opportunities to people of all ages and backgrounds, and to coordinating the activities of the whole community of sail training vessels. We do this for four primary reasons:

- Sail training is an educational and character building experience for all.
- International goodwill results when sail training ships from around the world gather in a spirit of camaraderie and friendly competition.
- Sail training fosters a greater awareness of, and appreciation for, the values of our maritime tradition.
- Environmental stewardship is a natural response to sailing the waters of the world.

Sail training and adventure cruises are the primary means of achieving these ends. International sail races and gatherings were begun in 1956 by the Sail Training Association (STA), the international coordinating body for sail training headquartered in England. The STA organizes annual tall ships races in European waters for sailing craft ranging from full-rigged ships to modern-day sloops. Periodically they also support major transoceanic races such as the Grand Regatta Columbus in 1992.

Sail training cruises are working expeditions with trainees typically organized in three watches or shifts (four hours on and eight hours off while under way) and fulfilling the traditional role of an able bodied seaman on a sailing ship. Sail handling, climbing the rigging, a trick at the wheel and galley, and cleaning duties are all part of the day's work. In addition, many sail training cruises include special components which focus on the marine sciences, maritime history or literature and familiarize trainees with their environment and the historical significance of ships and the sea.

Under sail, trainees confront the challenge of wind and sea and develop the self-discipline and teamwork required to take a vessel to sea. Even though cruises often last less than a week, the effect on the individual can last a lifetime. Although races sponsored by the STA require fifty percent of the ship's complement to be between the ages of fifteen and twenty-six, most cruises are open to "youth of all ages" so that those who missed the opportunity while a youngster have the opportunity to "sign on".

ASTA is dedicated to extending the experience of sailing with particular emphasis on the educational opportunities provided by traditional vessels. The ships are living

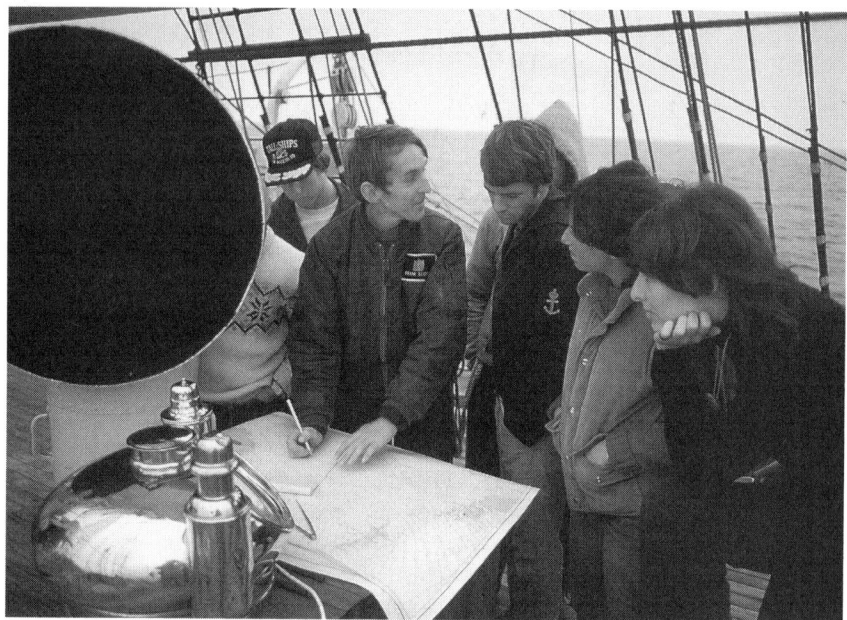

ASTA file photo

Sail training facilitates leadership. A vessel at sea is often described as a microcosm of the world where fresh water, food, fuel and other resources must be wisely used, and respect for others and pulling your share are critical to achieving the greater mission.

symbols of the past and are a bridge to international goodwill and global environmental stewardship.

The American Sail Training Association

The American Sail Training Association (ASTA®)was formed in 1973 by the late Barclay Warburton, owner of the brigantine *Black Pearl*, as an affiliate of the Sail Training Association (STA) to coordinate and conduct sail training activities in American waters. ASTA is one of many national sail training associations that have grown from the STA's success in gathering a small fleet, now grown dynamically, of traditional square-riggers for friendly international exchange and competition. STA's international TALL SHIPS® Races, with designated harbor festivals, bring together the ships and shores of most European countries, Russia and other former Soviet states, Canada, Mexico, and countries throughout South America and around the Pacific Ocean, including Australia, New Zealand, Indonesia and Japan.

At first, ASTA worked primarily to coordinate races and gatherings of sail training ships around the United States. ASTA's interest in helping to establish and codify standards for sail training ships and programs developed rapidly with the formation of the Council of Educational Ship owners, which lobbied successfully for the passage of the Sailing School Vessels Act of 1982. The Sailing School Vessels Council, founded in the following year, worked with the U.S. Coast Guard to develop regulations for sailing school vessels.

In conjunction with the Australian Bicentenary TALL SHIPS® gathering in Sydney, ASTA also organized the first international discussions on safety standards and equipment for sail training programs. This was followed by the first safety-at-sea seminars, in 1989. The seminars modeled on the United States Sailing Association's seminars but adapted for programs on particular aspects of sailing safety. As an alternative to racing, ASTA developed the concept of rallying sail training vessels where various aspects of seamanship can be demonstrated under way and ashore. Rallies occur every year in various locations with a variety of ASTA member vessels participating.

In addition, ASTA has worked with the STA and other national sail training associations in the organization of sail training races and cruises-in-company in connection with international events of major significance. Among these have been:

- 1976 The TALL SHIPS® Races from Bermuda to Newport prior to the celebration of the United States Bicentennial at Operation Sail in New York.
- 1978 The first sail training races in the Pacific rim, held in honor of the voyages of Captain James Cook.
- 1979 The first National Maritime Heritage Week, held in Newport, Rhode Island.
- 1980 The celebration of Boston's 350th anniversary.
- 1984 TALL SHIPS® Races held in honor of the 450th anniversary of Jacques Cartier's first voyage to Canada, coordinated with the Canadian Sail Training Association (CSTA), founded the same year.

1986 Cruises-in-company held in conjunction with transatlantic races to Operation Sail 1986/Salute to Liberty in honor of the Statue of Liberty's centennial.
1990 The first TALL SHIPS® Rally, in Chesapeake Bay.
1992 Rallies in conjunction with the Christopher Columbus Quincentenary.

Over the years, ASTA has also undertaken many other projects to meet the needs of the rapidly growing sail training community. These include publications, conferences and seminars.

ASTA file photo

ASTA member vessels greet members of the international fleet at waterfront events each year. Plans are already under way for the year 2000 when the largest gathering of tall ships ever will visit North America in a series of port visits and races planned by ASTA and the STA of the United Kingdom.

Publications

Running Free is ASTA's bimonthly newsletter and is a benefit of membership for all levels of membership. *Running Free* is the most important forum for reporting on the work of ASTA and its members. Among the standard features appearing in *Running Free* are articles on conferences, rallies, and legislation and regulations affecting sail training, as well as news about ships and announcements of employment opportunities (the Billet Bank).

Sailing into port is a dramatically different way to see the sights.

The *ASTA Directory of Sail Training Ships and Programs* first appeared in 1980, and is now in its eighth edition. The directory provides background about ASTA, its history and aims, and details on scores of sail training ships and programs in the United States and Canada. A copy of the directory is sent free to all ASTA members paying at or above the regular membership level. It is also available for sale and distributed free of charge to school libraries and guidance counselors.

ASTA Guidelines for Educational Programs under Sail explains ASTA standards for sail training education within the framework of the Sailing School Vessels Act. This manual defines criteria and indicators of effectiveness for the design, delivery and evaluation of curricula, instruction and program administration. In addition to the core of safe seamanship education, the guidelines apply to all aspects of sail training: adventure education, environmental science, maritime heritage and leadership development.

The *ASTA Syllabus and Logbook* provides a progression of skill-building activities in nautical science (safety, seamanship and navigation), and in marine science (oceanography) and aquatic science (limnology). This pocket-size outline enables trainees to keep a personal log of their sea time and to document their progress in sail training through three levels of nautical science – level I, deckhand; level II, seaman; and level III, day watch leader/night watch leader. Trainees can also record their progress through two levels of the marine and/or aquatic science programs (including biology, ecology, chemistry, physics and geology). Requirements for the syllabus are carefully spelled out, and completion of the course work and sea time must be certified by either the instructor or the ship's master.

The *ASTA Rally Handbook* explains in detail the various individual and crew events offered at ASTA TALL SHIPS® rallies, how they are scored and how ships can enter the rallies. *(See Safety Seminars and Rallies following.)*

Conferences, Seminars, Rallies & Dockside Demos

From the first, **ASTA's annual conferences** have gathered a broad spectrum of educators, ships' masters, port representatives, public officials, marine suppliers, naval architects, program administrators, festival managers, preservationists, environmentalists and crew. Conference sessions are developed in response to evaluations and input from ASTA members as well as outside trends. Sessions are structured to provide an open forum for information exchange, with a panel of experts to guide the discussion and to answer questions from the floor. In addition to such topics as vessel operations, regulatory issues, educational programming and safety-at-sea, conference sessions have addressed media relations, marketing, funding and other non-profit management issues.

One of ASTA's chief concerns is to ensure that the highest safety standards are met by all those who participate in sail training programs, whether as officers, crew, instructors or trainees. Safety concerns are addressed in a number of ways. ASTA's *Guidelines for Educational Programs under Sail* stresses the various regulations that govern the safe operation of the different classes of vessels that work with sail trainees. **Safety Seminars** focus on safety and survival issues for sail training programs. Through this train-the-trainer approach, ASTA provides opportunities for captains, crew and program developers to improve their operational skills and their effectiveness as instructors. Through the International Safety Forum, initiated in 1992, ASTA also works to expand the international dialogue between ships' masters by collecting and discussing case studies of actual safety-at-sea incidents, and then developing safety strategies.

A more immediate way to encourage the development of safe seamanship skills is through **TALL SHIPS® Rallies.** These gatherings, sponsored by ASTA, provide an excellent opportunity for crews and individual trainees to demonstrate their abilities in a series of friendly shipboard and shoreside competitions designed specifically to promote and develop seamanship and teamwork skills and to foster heightened safety awareness for crews, trainees, officers, instructors and spectators.

ASTA Rallies are comprised of scored events for individuals and for crews, and exercises take place both on vessels under way and ashore in port. Except for the Rally's first "event" – a safety inspection to US Coast Guard standards – all shipboard events are

ASTA TALL SHIPS® Rallies invite healthy competition and a chance for trainees to show off new-found prowess.

scored by the vessel captains themselves on the honor system. Other required shipboard events include precision anchoring, man overboard drill, sail maneuvers and heavy weather preparation. Individual events are navigation and helmsmanship. Optional ship events include getting under way under sail, abandon ship, fire drill, precision navigation under way, sending crew aloft, lowering and recovering small boats and sail handling.

Shoreside crew events include knot tying relay, heaving line and hawser pass, bucket brigade, rigging a fire hose, repairing a leaky pipe, tug of war, rowing and launching, and sailing a small boat around a short course. Individual events are the heaving line toss (separate events for distance and for accuracy), hawser/bollard toss and knot tying.

ASTA file photo

Tall ships events provide opportunities for travel, meeting new friends, and becoming part of an international sail training scene.

The Dockside Demo is an interactive exhibit designed to answer the question, "What is it like to sail a tall ship?" Through hands-on demonstrations, video presentations, simulations, storytelling, music and static displays the exhibit informs the public (children as well as adults) about some of the basics of sailing, particularly on traditional vessels. The Dockside Demo also demonstrates the educational value of sailing and how sail training can have a lasting impact on one's life.

The Dockside Demo includes interactive displays that introduce visitors to four essential components of the sailing experience: handling the wheel, knots and rope work, line handling and mechanical advantage of block and tackle, and navigation and piloting.

This exhibit is designed for the thousands of people who come to TALL SHIPS® Rallies and includes participatory elements for all ages. The exhibit requires 2,400 square feet of space (40' x 60') with a minimum ceiling height of 12'. When the miniature ship *Federalist* is part of the exhibit, as it often is, the ceiling height must be over 22'. The exhibit must be indoors or in a tent, although it is possible for the *Federalist* to be out-of-doors and adjacent to the rest of the exhibit.

ASTA Services: Billet Bank & Insurance

As a service to members, ASTA maintains a **Billet Bank** through which experienced sailors (licensed or not) can be put in touch with ships in need of crew. ASTA members who pay a nominal fee of $5 per year are sent crew requests received from ships. In addition, those enrolled in the Billet Bank are listed as available crew so that ships can reach them. Those members enrolled in the Billet Bank can send a brief description of their qualifications—including preferred positions, such as deckhand or cook, or any licenses and sea time, if any—to the ASTA office, where it is kept on file. The ASTA office will pass on the information to inquiring ships. Any further contact between crews and ships is up to them. ASTA does not endorse any specific program or individual crew, but simply shares information as it becomes available.

The Maritime Heritage Insurance Program was developed by Alexander & Alexander in conjunction with Crawley Warren & Co., Ltd. (a Lloyds of London Broker) for the specific purpose of providing insurance coverage and risk management for ASTA, historic vessels, sailing school operations and other maritime preservation organizations. The program is specifically designed to provide commercial insurance for all hull and liability risks of vessels, whether they are navigating, permanently berthed or under construction.

The Maritime Heritage Insurance Program was developed in 1983 by Alexander & Alexander in conjunction with the National Trust for Historic Preservation. In 1991, the American Sail Training Association (ASTA) became a "co-sponsor" and the program was consolidated into the London market (underwritten with first-class London securities).

Ports provide opportunities for the public to see and access the ships. Each vessel has a special story to tell.

Photo by Lowry Photography

Sail Training Vessels

The sail training mission differs from vessel to vessel according to the type of program offered. While the curriculum taught on any given vessel can vary from year to year, or from voyage to voyage, the scope of an individual vessel's mission is determined in part by the type of vessel it is according to government regulations written and enforced by the U.S. Coast Guard. Some vessels carry dual certification. This section briefly describes the various types of program-related regulations and is taken from the ASTA's *Guidelines for Educational Programs under Sail.*

Sailing School Vessels (SSV) are certified as Subchapter R – Nautical Schools – under Title 46 of the Code of Federal Regulations. An SSV is a vessel of less than 500 gross tons carrying six or more sailing school students or instructors, principally propelled by sail, and operated by a non-profit educational organization exclusively for the purpose of sailing education.

Oceanographic Research Vessels (ORV) are certified as Subchapter U under the U. S. Coast Guard regulations. An ORV is a vessel employed exclusively in either oceanographic (saltwater) or limnologic (fresh water) instruction and/or research. ORVs generally will not hire any instructors without proper scientific credentials.

Passenger vessels are certified according to size and the number of passengers carried. Subchapter C – Uninspected Vessels may operate with no more than six passengers for hire. Subchapter T – Small Passenger Vessels are vessels of under 100 gross tons that carry passengers for hire. Most sail training vessels listed in this directory are certified as Subchapter T vessels. Subchapter H – Passenger Vessels are vessels of more than 100 tons. Because passenger vessels are technically engaged in trade or commerce, they cannot operate under a certificate of inspection as SSVs. However they are required to meet the highest U.S. Coast Guard rules and regulations for the service in which they are engaged. Many offer educational programs and work closely with local community and education groups. They also provide excellent opportunities for sea experience, especially for those experienced trainees qualified to sign on as volunteer or paid crew, as many do.

Attraction vessels Generally speaking, attraction vessels are museum ships tied up to a dock, usually but not always on a permanent basis. Although an attraction vessel's operators are entitled to charge admission to visitors or fees for programs conducted while the ship is at the dock, attraction vessels cannot charge trainees, passengers or guests for any use of the vessel under way.

Sail Training & Sea Education

Sail training experience need not be restricted to the types of vessels described above, and indeed many have benefited from sail training experiences aboard private yachts, military, state school and foreign vessels. Just as there are different types of sail training vessels, there are different types of sail training programs.

Sail training usually takes place aboard vessels large enough to accommodate six or more students, with group-living challenges concentrated by the confined space and a simple, often Spartan — by shoreside standards — setting. Ship operation and daily maintenance are part of the demanding routine, and these often involve the preservation of historic skills and crafts which in turn help the trainee develop a sense of stewardship for our maritime heritage and for the water environment.

By its nature, a complete sail training program includes the following nine elements, in greater or lesser measure depending on the particular thrust and duration of the program. The curriculum requires students, a ship, and a body of water; the instruction offers shipboard living, sailing, and sea experience; and the result is that students become shipmates, sailors and stewards of the environment

Sea education means teaching and research aboard, as well as practical experience in operating, vessels propelled primarily by sail. In addition to such subjects as seamanship and navigation, programs may also offer oceanography and other marine subjects, as well as the study of maritime history and literature, physical science and mathematics. Sea education encompasses the study of the world's aquatic environment in its

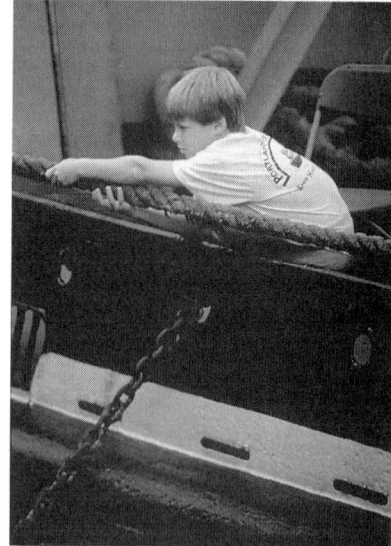

"You don't have to be big to be tall." ASTA member vessels come in all shapes and sizes... and so do their crews!

Introduction 21

Aboard a sail training vessel everyone counts! All hands help to raise and set sail, weigh anchor, stand watch and take their turn at the helm. Sailing a large training vessel takes teamwork, vigilance and the ability to follow directions.

ASTA file photos

totality, including saltwater and fresh, whether in rivers or lakes or on the ocean. These environments create a dynamic theme for interdisciplinary learning and enhance awareness of the importance of a healthy marine environment to global well-being. Several programs are either part of, or are recognized by, educational institutions that grant academic credit for shipboard programs. One of ASTA's primary goals is to provide sail training programs with the guidelines necessary for developing programs that educational institutions will recognize, and to involve educators more in the development of appropriate curricula for shipboard education.

A steadily increasing number of programs are now part of, or are recognized by, educational institutions that grant academic credit for under way programs. One of ASTA's primary goals is to provide shipboard programs with the support and guidelines necessary for recognition by mainstream educational institutions.

Choosing a Sail Training Program

The four essential components of any sail training program are a seaworthy vessel, a competent captain and crew, qualified instructors and a sound educational program appropriate and suited to the trainee's needs.

There are as many sail training programs as there are ships, and choosing the right one depends a great deal on your personal needs and desires. Sail training differs from going on a cruise ship in that you are expected to take part in the running of the ship by handling sail and line, standing watch, and working in the galley (the ship's kitchen). Whether you want a program that specializes in oceanography or adventure training, one that lasts a day, a week or an entire semester, whether you want to ship out in a schooner or want the added challenge and thrill of climbing aloft in a square rigger. All these options will ultimately dictate the kind of program a prospective trainee will choose. As to what sail training programs require of their trainees, beyond an eager willingness to get the most out of their time on the water, the requirements are few.

Safety Trainees should look for vessels that operate under U.S. Coast Guard regulations. Many ships venture no more than twenty miles from a harbor and are rarely under way overnight. Offshore voyaging offers the challenge of distant passages where severe weather and water conditions may be unavoidable. Being under way round the clock requires watch duties night and day, demanding both physical and mental stamina and perseverance. If applying to a foreign flag vessel, look into the international regulations that apply.

Sailing experience With few exceptions, no prior experience is required of trainees, although a high degree of competency must be demonstrated for anyone seeking volunteer or paid crew positions.

Swimming ability Trainees are encouraged to be able to stay afloat for at least five minutes while fully dressed, however most programs have no formal swimming requirements.

Age limits vary from program to program, but most sail training programs start accepting unaccompanied trainees from the age of fourteen (ninth grade).

Academic credit Some vessels are tied directly to academic institutions that grant academic credit to trainees who successfully complete sail training programs as part of a course of study or project in a wide range of subjects. Some educational institutions will also grant credit for on-board independent study.

Co-education Some vessels sail with single-gender crews; others are co-educational.

Cost Prices vary considerably, with the range being from about $25 to $150 per person per day, depending on the nature and duration of the program and the type of vessel.

Financial aid While a few programs have limited financial assistance available for trainees, most trainees find it necessary to seek private, business and/or community support to help defray the cost of sail training. In addition, there are a small number of independent organizations that provide financial aid to trainees, usually through matching grants.

Introduction 23

Shipping Out

As we are in great part defined by the things we use, perhaps the simplest way to conjure up the essence of shipboard life is to describe what you will take with you – and what, by extension, you will leave behind. Each ship has its own rules and requirements, and trainees should inquire about specific arrangements before signing on. For instance, some ships provide foul weather gear for trainees; others do not. What follows is an abbreviated version of a memorandum sent to all trainees who ship out aboard the *HMS Rose*. While the three-masted *Rose* is larger than most training ships, the following gives an excellent idea of the conditions that prevail aboard sail training vessels of any rig or size.

"Some Suggestions for Packing before You Ship Out...

"**Personal space** aboard any vessel is limited, so be conservative in the amount of gear you bring. All your gear must be stowed in your bunk or your allotted shelves. Excessive gear will only mean discomfort for you. A sea bag or other soft luggage is recommended; there is no space to store suitcases or rigid luggage. Temperature

Below: Life aboard traditional vessels offers a glimpse into a past when "sail was king" and provided transportation, movement of goods and the ability to explore far off lands.

ASTA file photos

Above: Meals under way are hearty and often the highlight of the day. Galley duty is a shared opportunity to assist the ship's cook.

Above: Many sail training vessels employ educators to plan and facilitate multi-disciplinary programs at sea.

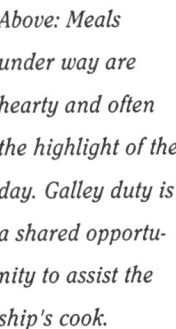

extremes can vary dramatically at sea during all twelve months of the year; sometimes it will be hot and sunny, other times it will be cold and damp. You should carefully select a modest quantity of casual clothing to deal with all possible conditions.

"**Bedding** The ship provides a mattress with cover for each bunk, but your choice of personal bedding is your own. You may bring sheets, blankets, a pillow or sleeping bag.

"**Clothing** Some specific items of clothing are recommended. At least one set of older clothes which you don't mind getting tar on is a good idea. The ship's standing rigging is regularly preserved with tar and as you climb aloft it is likely to get on your clothes. Sneakers are good footwear aboard, so also are topsiders or moccasin-type leather shoes. Shoes with leather soles are slippery and dangerous on board.

"**Foul weather gear** A full suit of foul weather (or rain) gear is a necessity for all hands: coat, pants, hat and boots are recommended. Seafaring continues even if it rains. With proper rain gear you will be able to comfortably perform your duties in all weather conditions.

"**Equipment** Books, cameras and musical instruments may be brought aboard, but be advised that some musical instruments are vulnerable to the dampness at sea. You may wish to bring some sort of rigging knife; most sailors find that a knife to which a lanyard (or tether) may be attached is their most important tool. Only knives on lanyards are allowed aloft.

"**Personal items** You should bring one or two towels as well as whatever shampoo, toothpaste and other toiletries you ordinarily require.

"**Money** You will not be able to cash personal checks aboard. It is recommended that you bring sufficient cash to meet your individual needs. Travelers checks are also recommended.

"**Medical** The ship is equipped with first aid kits. If you have medical idiosyncrasies of which you think the captain should be aware, do not hesitate to inform him. If you are concerned about becoming seasick, speak with your doctor before leaving home; there are a number of effective prescription remedies which you may wish to take advantage of ahead of time.

"**What not to bring** Operating the ship requires everyone's attention and concentration. Do not bring radios, tape players, or other cumbersome electronic devices. The sea is a particularly corrosive environment for such items. Also loud music is too intrusive to others in the confined shipboard environment. It should be unnecessary to point out that illicit drugs, alcohol, firearms or other weapons must not be brought aboard."

Introduction 25

Teamwork...

ASTA file photos

ASTA file photo

SAIL TRAINING: THE NEXT CENTURY

by Captain David V. V. Wood

(This article first appeared in *Sea History*)

In late July of 1972, the U.S. Coast Guard's training barque *Eagle* set sail from her home port of New London, Connecticut on an extraordinary voyage. In what amounted to a Presidential command performance, she was to participate in a TALL SHIPS® Race from the Solent, on England's south coast, to the Skaw between Denmark and Sweden, and then visit Kiel, Germany for the sailing events of the 1972 Olympic Games – the first time she had returned to Germany since being taken over by the Coast Guard at Bremerhaven in 1946, in the aftermath of World War II. There were a number of other "firsts" for *Eagle* in this voyage, but they belong to another story. What stood out for me – and, I believe, for *Eagle's* entire complement of officers, crew, and cadets – were the excitement and adventure of participating in an historic international event, the thrill of pitting our developing skills as square-rigger sailors against those of the other magnificent, cadet-crewed vessels in the race (Germany's *Gorch Fock II* and Poland's *Dar Pomorza*), and the opportunity to mingle ashore with fellow seamen from the fifteen nations and more than sisty sail training vessels participating in the event. None of us had ever experienced anything so exhilarating; we had known some great sailing in *Eagle*, of course, but in isolation. The international camaraderie of seafarers, the challenge and satisfaction of competition, the drama and pageantry of a major international gathering–these were new, and they were wonderfully exciting. It would not be an understatement to say that the experience set my own course for the remainder of my Coast Guard career, and while there were many glorious days during my subsequent tours in *Eagle* and other ships, I would frequently look back to 1972 as a kind of watershed, a benchmark against which such days were to be measured.

Such experiences on the part of the thousands of young people who participate in such events in Europe each year, not to mention the millions of spectators who go to see the ships and share in the excitement in the ports which host them, go a long way toward explaining the remarkable growth in numbers of the world's fleet of large, square-rigged schoolships during the late twentieth century. Given the trend in modern merchant and naval fleets toward ever larger and more complex ships with ever smaller and more technologically sophisticated crews, this development could hardly have been anticipated when the organizers of the first International TALL SHIPS® Race set out in 1956 to bring together what they believed were the last of the great square-riggers still training young men for careers at sea for a race across the Bay of Biscay from Torbay to Lisbon. Five ships entered that race, three of them Scandinavian *(Danmark, Christian*

Radich, and *Sølandet),* one Belgian *(Mercator),* and one Portuguese *(Sagres I).* Eight years later, when the organizers of the first "Operation Sail" in New York Harbor had a similar idea (the race was separately organized), more than twice as many large ships showed up — three of them (Germany's *Gorch Fock II,* Argentina's *Libertad,* and Chile's *Esmeralda)* of post-World War II build[1]. By 1992, when the "Grand Regatta Columbus Quincentenary" visited various U.S. ports in commemoration of Columbus' voyage to the New World, fully ten of the twenty-four naval and merchant schoolships present had been built since 1964.

To those (and I am one) who believe that the modern square-rigged ship represents a pinnacle of human achievement in appropriate technology, and that — notwithstanding the size and complexity of modern oceangoing vessels — training at sea under sail remains the best possible sort of apprenticeship for those aspiring to a seagoing career, this growth in the number of schoolships is indeed gratifying. But it must be acknowledged that the equally remarkable growth in popularity of tall ships *events* has played a significant part in encouraging the increase in large, traditionally-rigged schoolships. Tall ship gatherings on a grand scale, such as 1992's Operation Sail and Sail Boston, are relatively infrequent in North America, for the simple reason that only one large schoolship (the Coast Guard's *Eagle)* is based here, and such ships tend to be tied fairly closely to an academic program that makes the scheduling of transoceanic voyages difficult to coordinate with such events; but more modest gatherings of traditionally-rigged vessels, with an occasional large schoolship, have become a regular feature of such annual festivals as Norfolk's "Harborfest" and similar harbor and waterfront celebrations around the country. In Europe, the annual schedule of such events is almost bewildering, with port cities from Scandinavia to Iberia vying fiercely to host the scores of sailing vessels competing each year in the "Cutty Sark TALL SHIPS® Races"—direct descendants of that first race in 1966.

The popularity of such events is not surprising. For all the obvious reasons — the desire to celebrate a glorious maritime past, nostalgia for an age when human affairs moved at a slower and less bewildering tempo, the romance of the sea and far-off, exotic places, admiration for the craftsmanship and beauty of the ships themselves — people by the thousands and even millions are drawn to the waterfront whenever sailing ships are in harbor. In his foreword to Operation Sail's official program for the 1992 event, OpSail's Honorary Chairman Walter Cronkite suggests that we celebrate ships because they brought our world "to the critical pitch of communication and commerce that has made today's global awareness possible." Whatever the attraction, by bringing visitors to town, tall ships events inevitably provide an economic boost to the cities hosting them, and can even be a catalyst for waterfront redevelopment, improved facilities for tourism, and so forth. The Commonwealth of Massachusetts, for example estimated the overall economic impact of Sail Boston 1992 at something on the order of $500 million, and a study commissioned by the Merseyside Development Corporation, which organized events in the port of Liverpool for the final port call of the Grand Regatta Columbus, found benefits on a comparable scale. For the owners (usually governments) of large schoolships, such events are a marvelous opportunity for showing the flag and generating international goodwill, or even for subtly promoting economic investment in their countries — a fact which may help to explain why much of the recent growth in the num-

The work of sailing a large traditional vessel requires teamwork, vigilance and the ability to follow directions.

ber of large schoolships has been in such places as Latin America and Eastern Europe (including Russia). For the crews and trainees, of course, such events are a wonderful opportunity to meet, compete, and party with people of similar age and interests, and to learn more about other cultures.

The Sail Training Association (STA), established in the United Kingdom in 1956 to carry on the idea embodied in the International TALL SHIPS® Race of that year, deserves much of the credit for these developments. As the races (and the in-port events that attended them) grew steadily in popularity, they provided a stimulus to the growth of numerous sail training projects within the UK, most of which – unlike the big schoolships – had little or nothing to do with training professional seafarers. Rather, they grew more or less directly out of the idea embodied in the first Outward Bound school established at Aberdovey, Wales in 1941, that an experience of seafaring under sail is ideally suited to develop qualities of courage, endurance, discipline, self-reliance, resourcefulness, teamwork, tolerance, and humility (to name only a few) in young people. In short, it is a nearly-ideal character molding experience. In the words of Lawrence Holt, the British shipping magnate who funded the Aberdovey project in collaboration with the legendary Kurt Hahn, father of the Outward Bound movement, it was to be "less a training *for* the sea than *through* the sea, and so benefit all walks of life[2]." This has continued to be the prevalent model for sail training programs in England, most of which stress the aims of character development and adventure rather than seamanship, and most of which, incidentally, operate much smaller vessels than the big schoolships.

Many ships offer "hands-on" programs for school children to experience history, marine and physical science.

Providence file photo

The Ocean Youth Club, for example, sails a fleet of twelve ketches up to 72' in length, with berths for a dozen trainees each on week-long cruises; the largest vessels in the UK are the STA's own schooners, *Malcolm Miller* and *Sir Winston Churchill*, 150' in length with berths for thirty-nine trainees each on cruises of two to three weeks[3].

Originally biennial events, the STA races are now held annually, and regularly rotate between the Baltic, North Sea, the Bay of Biscay, and occasionally the Mediterranean. The stated aim of the Races – called the Cutty Sark TALL SHIPS® Races since 1972, in recognition of the STA's long and happy relationship with its corporate sponsor, Berry Bros. and Rudd– is "to enable young people of all nations to race together at sea, under sail," and the genius of the STA has been to consistently keep the focus on the young people on board the ships. Using its proven ability to bring large numbers of ships – most of them small-to-medium in size, but generally with a liberal handful of the big schoolships – together for the races, the STA has steadfastly held host ports to strict conditions regarding provision of services to ships and wholesome activities for crews and trainees, and has done its utmost to prevent commercialism from overshadowing the ideals of sail training during the in-port events of each race series.

Another result of the STA's phenomenal success, and a heartening validation of its ideals, has been the establishment of sail training associations in other countries. These retain strong ties to the STA, but tend to focus more broadly on coordinating and encouraging the development of sail training programs and less on the narrower role of organizing annual races. The first of such associations was the American Sail Training Association (ASTA®) established in 1973 and initially modeled quite closely on the STA, with the idea of organizing races among the relatively few sail training vessels then operating in U.S. waters. In the more than 20 years since its founding, however, ASTA – and sail training in the US – have evolved in ways that reflect our own geographic and cultural characteristics, and respond to American needs. The same is, of course, true in the other countries where sail training has taken root.

While sail training in the UK is generally understood to mean a seagoing voyage of a week or more in duration and involving young people between fifteen and twenty-five who have little or no prior sailing experience, ASTA's member organizations include a wide range of programs involving cruises from a few hours to six weeks or more in length, "trainees" from elementary school age to adults, and objectives ranging from pure adventure to serious scientific research. What ASTA members have in common is a shared belief that, no matter what other objectives may be served, bringing people together on a sailing vessel and involving them in the work of sailing the ship can often be a life-changing experience. This belief is reflected in ASTA's stated mission, which very much embodies the traditional ideals of sail training: "to encourage character building through sail training, promote sail training to the American public, and support education under sail."

Recognizing the popularity of tall ships events and their enormous potential value in bringing to the American public a greater awareness of the ideals of sail training, ASTA has devoted increasing energy to organizing a series of TALL SHIPS® Rallies each summer in conjunction with harbor or waterfront festivals. Originally conceived as an alternative to races, rallies involve crews in various forms of competition, both at sea and ashore, emphasizing seamanship, safety, and teamwork. In the process of developing this concept, ASTA has cultivated close relationships with port cities from the mid-Atlantic states to New England and the Great Lakes, and in 1993 held its first West Coast rally in San Francisco Bay. The effort to extend this idea to other regions, and thus stimulate public interest in and support for local sail training programs, will continue.

As the end of the twentieth century approaches, what is the future of sail training, both at home and around the world? On one hand, it seems doubtful that the fleet of big square-rigged schoolships will continue to expand; properly maintained, those now in existence will sail for many years to come, but whether they will be replaced when they come to the end of their useful lives seems unlikely. Some, after all – like the great Russian barques *Sedov* and *Kuzenshtern* – are more than sixty years old, and many, like the superb sister ships *Eagle*, *Sagres II*, and *Tovaritsch*, are nearly so. On the other hand, the number of relatively smaller vessels providing youth (and adult) sail training for adventure, education, and character development seems very likely to continue to grow: vessels like Australia's *Young Endeavour*, England's *Lord Nelson*, Japan's *Kaisei*, and the United States' *Corwith Cramer* and *Tole Mour*, as well as many others—not to mention the traditional, but smaller, schoolships like Poland's *Ishra* and Bulgaria's *Kali-*

akra. All of these vessels are under 200 feet and were built within the last ten years; they serve a remarkable variety of "trainees:" naval midshipmen, high school and college students, disadvantaged and adjudicated youth, disabled youth and adults. This, I believe, gives us a glimpse of the future of sail training: fewer big schoolships training professionals, but more and more smaller vessels providing a seagoing experience to a greater variety of people.

To celebrate the beginning of the new century, the STA is already planning a transatlantic TALL SHIPS® Race to be called TALL SHIPS 2000[SM] — that promises to be the largest-ever assemblage of sail training vessels. Following a course similar to that followed by the "Grand Regatta Columbus" in 1992, this magnificent fleet will originate in Europe and sail across the Atlantic to visit ports on the eastern seaboard of North America during the first summer of the new century; similar events are under consideration in the Pacific. Unlike such gatherings in 1976, 1986, and 1992, this fleet will not come to help celebrate a historic anniversary of past events; rather, it will bring the message of the energy and idealism of young people from around the world-the hope of the future. ASTA will be working closely with the STA and with US port cities during the next few years to help plan events on this side of the Atlantic, and to insure that the message of sail training remains at the forefront — a message that seems more valid today than ever before. Training *for* the sea in big square-riggers may gradually disappear over the horizon, but training *through* the sea, in tall ships both large and small, can continue to help the nations of the world develop the leaders and citizens they will need to meet the challenges of the twenty-first century.

As operations officer aboard Eagle, *Captain Wood participated in the 1972 Cutty Sark TALL SHIPS® Races; he returned to command* Eagle *in 1988, and was at the helm during the Grand Regatta Columbus Quincentenary in 1992. Retired from the Coast Guard, he now serves as a member of ASTA's Board of Directors and is U.S. National Representative to the STA's International Racing Committee.*

---

[1] Information on ships participating in the 1956 and 1964 TALL SHIPS® Races comes from Hans Freiherr von Stackelberg's Rahsegler im Rennen: Reisen und Regatten der *"Gorch Fock"* published by Verlag Duburger Bucherzentrale, Flensburg, Germany, 1965. Captain von Stackelberg was an officer of *Gorch Fock* in 1964 and later commanded the ship during the 1970s.

[2] Quoted in Outward Bound USA by Joshua L. Miner and Joe Boldt, New York, William Morrow and Co., 1981.

[3] Information on British sail training programs, and on the history of the STA, is derived from John Hamilton's Sail Training: The Message of the TALL SHIPS®, published by Patrick Stephens Ltd., Wellingborough, UK, 1988. John Hamilton was the STA Race Director from 1976 to 1992.

IT'S MORE THAN JUST A BOAT RIDE

By James Gladson, Los Angeles Maritime Institute

As a sail training teacher since 1972, I have often been asked to justify "taking the kids sailing when they really ought to be in school." It's easy to understand the concern. The general public, even casual recreational boaters, tend to view sailing as a recreational activity indulged in by the leisure class. Yacht racing is seen as an elitist pastime, epitomized by the recurrent America's Cup spending extravaganzas. Sail training, however, is as different from these impressions as night is from day. Robby Robinson, in his article "School Houses Under Sail," praises sailing vessels as:

learning platforms, as observation posts, as transportation systems for awareness, and as delivery systems for understanding. Anonymity, distraction, absence, and other ills that attend regular school are addressed quite simply when every one is 'in the same boat.' The unified mental and physical nature of sail training, the learning community that it sets up, and the 'clean slate' mentality that comes when you cast off, makes sailing an effective learning structure. Kids learn to take responsibility for the ship, for learning how to work it, for their shipmates, and ultimately for themselves. They learn to trust themselves as well as others.

Sail training aboard a sailing school vessel provides an educational venue that is rich in potential for the development of knowledge, skills, and attitudes that are necessary for the education of today's youth but difficult to teach in the confines of the classroom. The sailing school provides a challenging yet nurturing environment that readily meets the needs of the adolescent and young adult learner. It is notably effective with young people who can not cope well with the demands of society and are at risk of dropping out of school or otherwise abandoning the quest for a successful and productive life. Such youth often see themselves as being incapable of living in harmony with mainstream society and destined for a lifetime of failure. Sail training programs endeavor to reverse these tendencies. The sailing school experience enriches, validates, and challenges the conventional school curricula. In this real-world classroom, science, mathematics, physics, biology, geography, history, literature, and even poetry suddenly come to life.

In addition to bringing these academic subjects "to life," sailing school vessels provide a forum in which students can learn many disciplines not easily conveyed in the classroom. One example is problem solving. Even the most successful teachers will tell

The traditions of the sea and all it has to teach are preserved for future generations aboard tall ships.

---

you that while it is relatively simple to teach about problem solving skills, it is very difficult to teach skillful problem solving, even to bright, eager, enthusiastic students in well equipped classrooms. And yet acquiring these skills is commonplace, if not inevitable, on board sailing school vessels. As Captain David Wood, former commanding officer of the USCG *Eagle,* said: "Sail training vessels present real problems, that require real solutions, that you can't walk away from." In such an environment, you see the results of your decisions.

Nearly all of the students come aboard the Los Angeles Maritime Institute's *Swift of Ipswich* are ignorant of the ways of a sailing vessel and only a very few have had any prior sailing experience. As newcomers to the sailing world, their street status and/or classroom pecking orders are not in effect. Thus, they are not burdened with the baggage of previous reputations. This is true to a large extent even with kids who know each other. From the start, the kids enter immediately into an environment that is composed of an integrated array of systems that must be operated with both mind and muscle engaged. Some of the tasks, such as raising sails, require a coordinated team effort, physically pulling together, whereas other tasks, such as steering the vessel, may only be done by one person at a time, acting alone yet in concert with the whole ship. The rules under which these systems function are both simple and demanding. They are not the rules of the teacher or the school board or the government, but rather, rules of nature. The competition is with ignorance, ineptitude, and fear. By conquering these enemies, sail training enables us to produce winners without the usual need to produce a matching set of losers.

Once under way, students begin the never-ending task of learning to work the vessel in the interaction of two infinitely variable, yet inter-related realms of fluid dynamics, the atmosphere and the ocean. As more time is spent on board, the trainees learn to communicate precisely with a language born of the pragmatism of a thousand years of seafaring. They become comfortable with cause and effect, as well as sequencing, persistence, endurance, patience, and courage; all of which are very difficult traits to teach in a classroom.

Much is being said today about the importance of self-esteem. Without a doubt, strong positive self-esteem is essential for personal maturity. Many remedies for low self-esteem have been offered to parents, teachers and others who work with youth. Most of these, if properly applied, do have some positive effect. However, the bottom line seems to be that positive self-esteem comes from knowing that you can do something that not everyone else can do and that you can do it well. It's not just learning to sail, it's what you learn from sailing.

Let me tell you about Jay. I first met Jay when he came to our Mid City Alternative School as a second or third grader with a truly tragic personal background. He was so consumed with rage that he had been mis-diagnosed and placed in an autism program at his former school. Now enrolled at the Mid City Alternative School, only time could tell what would become of this troubled boy.

Since I worked primarily as a secondary school teacher, I had little formal contact with Jay during his early years at the school. I only knew him through the occasional "enrichment" programs offered to the "little kids" such as model-making, videodrama, and gardening. By the time Jay entered the seventh or eighth grade, he was a gruff, explosive, stocky, muscular, clumsy introvert, whose spoken vocabulary consisted mostly of "shut up!", "go away!" and "leave me alone!" shouted with the helpless intonation of a kid who saw himself as a loser, a victim of life's circumstances.

It was this explosive, troubled young man whom I invited to participate in the school's sailing program. Frankly, I felt some trepidation when he finally accepted my invitation and signed up for a one quarter, one afternoon a week, sailing class. Fortunately, about half of the students on board had been enrolled previously in the sailing class for one or more quarters, and thus abided by the "number one rule": "No matter how you really feel about it, you will always treat every other member of the class as though you were best friends. No teasing, no 'bagging', no favorites." I knew that no matter what Jay might say or how he might act, the students on board would accept him.

Jay had a heck of a time that first day. It seemed as though he could not move about the boat without bumping into things. He appeared unable to heave on a line in sync with the other kids. Steering by sight was far beyond his abilities, not to mention steering by compass. Jay even spilled his cup of cocoa and dropped his piece of cake that afternoon. At the end of that first day I thought that Jay would never want to come on board again. The fact that he returned the next week truly surprised me. (I had yet to discover his stubborn streak.)

Jay continued to attend the sailing sessions. It took him nearly a year to learn to coil a halyard and hang it securely on a belaying pin, a task that most kids master on their second or third try. Despite such difficulties, Jay signed up for the class every quarter, and when the time arrived, he signed up for the annual week-long trip to Catalina. One of the landmark days that first year occurred on one drizzly afternoon daysail, when we presented Jay with a rather crudely decorated birthday cake we had baked aboard. "What's this for?" he demanded. "It's your birthday, you fool!" one of his new friends replied, with a big grin. After a very long pause, Jay, with moist eyes and a very soft voice, said "Thanks."

Another landmark day occurred during Jay's second year in the sailing program. One of the new kids was having trouble coiling a halyard and Jay startled all of us by jumping up from across the boat and shouting "Let me show him. I know how." Jay, the boy who once had struggled so hard to learn how to coil a halyard, now had the confidence to teach someone else.

Jay continued to grow into a confident and competent young man both aboard and ashore. One of my most treasured photos is one of Jay, taken in the eleventh grade, smiling confidently from the helm of a 100' schooner off the coast of Catalina. When Jay graduated, he asked me to present his diploma. I introduced him with these words: "I am proud to present this fine, handsome young man . . . a gentleman and a scholar . . . a poet and a good sailor . . . and my friend, Jay." I assure you that these words came from my heart. They had to: I could not read my notes through my tears.

I do not mean to suggest that the sailing program brought about all of the wonderful changes that took place within Jay. Sailing was only a part of it. The Mid City Alternative School was, and still is, a fine school with a strong and dedicated staff. However, the sailing program did offer Jay a demanding yet impartial environment. The vessel and the sea did not know whom Jay used to be or what some one else thought of him. The rules of nature never change on you or favor the other guy. Jay is who he is today because he decided who he wanted to be and took charge of his own life. The sailing school teaches an individual to understand the systems, adapt to the circumstances, plot a course, and take command. The lessons that Jay and other students learned from the sail training program often changed their outlooks. As an educator, I also learned that, despite all the effort I put into developing laboratory to help my students understand the basics of physical science and engineering, nothing compares to the knowledge gained from practical experience. None of my best lab exercises with the finest class of gifted students can hold a candle to that full-size, hands-on, real-life, complicated, dynamic, obdurate contraption called a sailing vessel. So long as my crew and I are careful to use the correct terminology, the kids internalize these concepts in an integrated fashion that will last for a learning lifetime.

In the classroom we try to make the students at least memorize the names of things. We are delighted when some learn the process of doing something. On board, they usually demand to know not only what, but how and why. They wear us out with their numerous questions. While it is not surprising that many similar curricular examples can be found on-board the life sciences and earth sciences, it may be surprising to learn how many street-tough kids "discover" poetry with my on board copy of Masefield, or, how many kids read their first book strictly for the fun of it from the ship's library.

A ship is a microcosm of the world ashore, and as a classroom, it is an unparalleled venue for interdisciplinary learning. For most kids, learning, interpreting and applying the maritime "rules of the road" is their first exposure to a system of regulations that is necessary, logical, beneficial, fair, and uniformly applied to everyone. This may seem triv-

Sailing a tall ship provides unique opportunities to experience immediate results and to practice and take pride in the mastery of skills which are infinitely transferable.

ASTA file photo

ial to some people, but to many of my inner-city kids, who usually see the "law" as the enemy, this is a first.

Learning navigation and piloting is not only important for math and map reading skills, but when did you learn to weigh the options, select a destination, figure out how to get there safely and efficiently, and then do it? The other curricular connections are too numerous to list completely, but consider this example of a discussion which, with variations, is commonly heard on board: It usually starts with questions from the kids about the cargo carrying capacity of a passing ship along with questions about their speed. Next comes "How many crew?" "How much fuel do they use?" etc. If the ship carries 50,000 tons, that's equal to 1,000 railroad cars, which is a train about ten miles long. Or if you would rather visualize it in highway big rigs, that's about 2,500 tractor trailer combinations and that works out to a convoy about fifty miles long. When the discussion branches off to air freight, the kids quickly determine that there probably aren't enough cargo jets in the world to replace the ships we can see from where we are. And further, it couldn't be done at all if the jet fuel had to be delivered by air.

Now just where does all of this fit in the curriculum? Is it math or geography, commerce, science, economics, history or all of these disciplines? The answer of course is that it is education in the round, not just schooling. The sailing vessel is an elegant plat-

The way to command is through mastery of those skills and tall ship captains have years of experience on many different vessels.

form for the study of the planet in its entirety and the human interaction with and within it.

For the purpose of education, we are fortunate to be operating out of Los Angeles/Long Beach harbor, one of the world's busiest harbors – and cleanest – commercial harbors. It is common to see gulls, terns, pelicans, cormorants, grebes and other sea birds feeding in the outer harbor between anchored ships. Sea lions abound and during their northward migration, gray whales are frequently spotted inside the harbor. It's almost as though mama whale is showing her new calf the sights on their way to the Bering Sea. A short distance offshore we generally encounter more species of birds, porpoise, sharks, pilot whales, and jelly fish. The list is endless and different on every trip. And of course the offshore island anchorage truly offers spectacular displays of wildlife.

To be immersed amid such wildlife, while in close proximity to such diverse human enterprises as commercial fishing, sport fishing, manufacturing, cargo handling, bunkering, a naval base, research vessels, pleasure boating and people playing on the beach, is an education in environmental awareness. The kids soon recognize that informed decision making is not easy and uninformed decision making is seldom satisfactory. Is there a more significant step in the development of responsible citizenship?

The on board library is seen to be a valuable collection of references that are both interesting and fun. In most cases, with only a few exceptions, the same books were in my classroom, where they were usually seen as "schoolbooks" of only artificial importance. However, on board the ship, I've seen kids routinely look up a visiting ship in the daily *Marine Exchange* list of "Active Ships in Port" to see where the ship was from, where it was bound, and then dive into the on board copy of *Goode's World Atlas* (a basic college reference) to research not only the geographic locations of the ports, but also the natural resources, the climate types, the economies, and the population distribution of the countries or regions they serve – all so they could speculate and argue about the probable cargo the ship was carrying.

Sail training is neither a new, untested technology, nor is it a quaint, anachronism lingering on only in stagnant, immobile societies. On the contrary, sail training is a vibrant growing field of endeavor throughout the world. Government-supported sail training programs abound in nations as different as Indonesia, India, Brunei, Germany, Japan, and the United Kingdom. Poland, Bulgaria, and several republics of the former Soviet Union have programs as well. In the Western hemisphere, national sail training vessels operate in Argentina, Brazil, Canada, Chile, Colombia, Ecuador, Mexico, the United States, Uruguay, and Venezuela.

In the United States, numerous sail training programs exist along the Atlantic Coast, the Gulf Coast, the Great Lakes, and the Pacific Northwest. While thousands of students have benefitted from programs, there are still too many students who have not had the opportunity to participate in such a beneficial educational opportunity. It has been observed that "the United States is a nation enormously rich in technology and yet desperately poor in experience." As an experiential education endeavor, sail training is a demonstrably cost effective method to improve knowledge, skills, and attitudes. We have the kids, we have the need, we have the know-how. Let's do it!

ASTA member vessels sail from just about every coastal state in the US! Each ship has a program unique to its history and environment.

"LIFE ON THE *TOLE MOUR*"

The following articles were written by five of the twenty-eight young cadets living and traveling on board *Tole Mour*. They are enrolled in OceanQuest Hawaii, a nonprofit joint venture between Marimed Foundation of Honolulu, which owns *Tole Mour*, and VisionQuest National, Ltd. of Tucson, Arizona.

Tole Mour is a 156't, 230 gross ton, three-masted topsail schooner, built in Seattle in 1988. From 1988 through 1992, *Tole Mour* supported primary health care programs in Micronesia, carrying teams of volunteer health care professionals to remote coral atolls in the Marshall Islands to train local community health workers. In 1990, Marimed began to include Hawaii "at risk" youth on its month-long medical trips in Micronesia, offering them a program combining sail training and community service.

At the end of 1992, when the Marshall Islands Health Ministry assumed full responsibility for the health care programs Marimed had initiated in Micronesia, *Tole Mour* was given a new mission: to provide ocean-based treatment and education programs to adolescents who might otherwise be incarcerated or hospitalized.

Today, *Tole Mour* supports OceanQuest Hawaii, an offshoot of VisionQuest's OceanQuest program. Through OceanQuest, VisionQuest has been providing sail training to adjudicated adolescents for the past twelve years on its schooners *Bill of Rights* and *New Way*. ASTA recognized the excellence of the VisionQuest schooner program by naming it "Sail Training Program of the Year" in 1992.

In addition to her twenty-eight cadets, *Tole Mour* is home for a professional crew and treatment staff of twenty-one, some provided by Marimed and some by VisionQuest. Four of the treatment staff are rated AB — they sail and share responsibility for watch standing and sail handling.

Cadets spend from four to six months on *Tole Mour*. Their lifestyle is a demanding one. In addition to watch standing and shipboard maintenance, they average twenty-five hours per week in school, which is conducted in the mess in two sittings. Their life is also full of adventure. A number of cadets who joined the ship in Hawaii in March logged more than 10,000 miles during their time on board, visiting ports in California, Panama, Florida, Virginia, and the Great Lakes.

"Life on the *Tole Mour* begins with an intensive orientation period. All cadets get time to travel, clean, and do other maintenance work. I think that everyone, cadets and staff, get something special for working hard, and for accomplishing something for

Sail training vessels are not just a pretty picture (and they are that!), they offer you the opportunity of a lifetime.

themselves.

You are required to know every line and knot on the ship. You need to know what that line or knot is for in any situation. If a sail becomes fouled up, you need to know which line to pull, before you get thrown off course.

Our boat is clean and neat. We keep the boat clean so that we don't live in a dirty environment. We like to feel clean, and look clean too! We sail often, and try to dock whenever possible. We see many places, and see different cultures and customs. I enjoy it.

I think that whatever you put into the program, you get back doubled. You are suppose to make the best out of every situation? Well, in this case, the situation makes the best out of you." **Anthony Williams**

"As a cadet aboard the *Tole Mour*, it is sometimes hard to get along with the staff and other cadets. Being on a ship that is 150' long, you are going to see people more than you want. But all in all, the cadets take pride in the boat.

In all, we are a good crew and *Tole Mour* is a wonderful boat. Even though I am the only Hawaiian, I am proud to represent the islands of my state.

Some of the responsibilities on the boat include deck washes, hauling sails, and galley detail. We have forty-nine crew aboard. We also have water makers and fishing lines so we can be self-supporting if we have to.

As an addition to the usual duties, there are four watches and four watch leaders to work the various shifts aboard the *Tole Mour*. The watch leaders learn how to navigate the seven seas and how to figure out positions, and cadets that show interest can also take these lessons. All cadets help steer the boat and all sea time is recorded for future use. Overall, *Tole Mour* and the VisionQuest program is helping the future, and hopefully will continue to do so for many years to come." **Josh Knepper**

"Life of the *Tole Mour* is a two way street. The good part is that you get to choose which way you want to go, because it can be whatever you make of it: negative or positive, good or bad, it's all up to you.

If you are the type of person who hates traveling and doesn't like working then maybe you wouldn't like the *Tole Mour*. First of all, life on the *Tole Mour* involves a lot of traveling from one port to the next, and sea sickness is traveling's partner so beware. Secondly, there is a lot of work to be done and the only way to get it done is through teamwork. If you are lazy and don't like working with people, don't come aboard. On the other hand, if you like seeing different places, meeting new people, and do not mind being away from your family, then maybe you and me should trade places.

The Tole Mour can also be a lot of fun. You get to swim in the middle of the ocean, see whales, sharks and different kinds of sea creatures and you get to see the world by sea.

So there you have it. The two way street of the Tole Mour, but don't just take my word for it. See it for yourself and maybe you will have a different opinion." **Kareem Tilghman**

"The *Tole Mour* is a great experience for us youths because this is probably the only chance in our lives to do something like this. And, this is probably the only placement that does something like this, and many of us cadets like being on the boat because we like more freedom. We get to talk and see different people from different places and see a lot of beautiful places and things. I think it is a good experience for me, and we learn a lot of things and get to do a lot of things like go out to see the city and things like that... and go out to a barbecue; well things like that we don't do in camp or the wagon train. Well anyway, the staff and cadets are not respecting one another. It is like being out on the streets treating each other like enemies. But it shouldn't be like that because we live together and see each other every single day that goes by. Well, even though things are a little out of hand, it's okay because many of us make mistakes and get over it so this is like the name of the *Tole Mour:* The Gift of Life and Health." **Luciano Pichardo**

"Life on the *Tole Mour* is very different than my life back home in southeastern Pennsylvania. Hauling on halyards and downhauls is not like pulling on a starter chord to a lawnmower or to my snowmobile, even though it makes both go. It just takes a little longer. Living under the deck of a sailing school vessel is so much different than a roof of a house. The people don't always get along and things don't always go right, but we all live like a family out here. We help each other as much as we need to so that we can try to enjoy most of our time away from our loved ones.

The road we drive on is not smooth and is almost always rough. It reminds me of my sixteen years at home. That is why this place is so great. It lets you look into the future and not into the past. They try to give you the learning as needed for the hustle and bustle of the outside world. Being on a watch from 11:00p.m. to 3:00a.m. doesn't just make us work and sail the ship; it brings us together and shows us teamwork and togetherness.

The main focus of the program is to work on our personal issues, but we all have a responsibility to sail the ship and to take care of her. It is our home and we need to keep it "ship shape". I really enjoy my hard work on the ship, only for the simple fact that it lets me prove that I can do anything if I put my mind to it. I am also glad that I had the chance to be on the *Tole Mour* instead of jail because I had my eyes opened and the kick in the butt to make it in the outside world as I live the rest of my life."
Mike Barnes

TAKE CHARGE OF YOUR SAIL TRAINING EXPERIENCE

by Michael Rauworth

TAKE CHARGE OF YOUR SAIL TRAINING EXPERIENCE! As you think about a sail training experience, it is important to recognize who has responsibility for what, and especially what is your responsibility. One of the most important products of sail training is the development of a sense of judgment about what you can rely on for what, and how much. This applies to: the compass, the weather forecast, your shipmates, the depths on the chart, the strength of the anchor cable, the vigilance of the lookout on that other ship, and many other things. Sail training also builds a reasoned sense of self-reliance. All of this starts from the moment you begin to think about a voyage.

Recognize who you are dealing with and what is included. When you book a sail training trip, you are dealing with the vessel owner or its representative — ASTA is not involved. You must evaluate whether the financial and business arrangements make sense for you. If there is connecting travel involved, for example, find out if you must make arrangements, or if it is somehow tied into those you have made with the vessel. What happens if you miss your ship because your plane is delayed, or vice versa? Do you need trip insurance? Have you confirmed with the vessel owner any possible customs or immigration issues? Will you need a passport or a pre-purchased air ticket? You must seek out the answers to these questions.

Make informed, responsible decisions about risk and safety, level of challenge, physical suitability and other important issues. One of the important reasons to embark on a sail training trip is to engage the world in a different, stimulating, and challenging way — if you wanted to stay warm and dry you should stay at home by the fireplace. Much of the point is to come face-to-face with the elements. At the very least this probably means that you will find yourself wet, or chilled, or tired at some point in a challenging voyage. But everyone's threshold for this is different and you need to find out what you are likely to be experiencing in order to find out if it is well matched for you.

Since the beginning of time, going to sea has been recognized as carrying an element of risk. These days, we more commonly think about risk in connection with highway travel or aviation, but the idea is the same: you get a pre-flight safety brief on an airliner, you get a lifeboat drill on a cruise ship. Part of the value of sail training is addressing these things head on. You need to decide whether you are comfortable with the combination of risks and safety measures connected with your proposed sail training trip.

For example, will you be allowed to go aloft? Will trips in smaller craft be involved? Will you be expected to stand watch at night? Do the physical demands of this ship's experience match with your health and physical abilities? Are you on medication that will (or may) become necessary during the voyage, or do you have a condition (for example, hemophilia or epilepsy) that may need special access to medical attention? If so, does the vessel operator know about this? Will you be able to get up and down ladders, in and out of your berth, and along a heeled-over deck? If there is an emergency, will you be needed to handle safety equipment or to help operate the vessel?

Remember that sail training is often not intended to be like a vacation. Some vessel operators, on the other hand, may offer more leisurely voyages, where very little will be asked of you. You should arrive at a clear understanding of all these things with the vessel operator.

In short, before sailing, you must satisfy yourself that the trip you are looking into is the right thing for you to do, considering safety and risk, suitability, challenge/comfort, convenience, educational value, cost, and any other factors you consider important.

Does ASTA have a hand in any of this? In a word, no! ASTA is your "bulletin board" to introduce you to opportunities. However, ASTA does not operate any vessels, and it has no ability to inspect or approve, nor even recommend vessels or programs because programs are constantly evolving and changing.

ASTA is a nonprofit group with a small staff. It serves as a forum for the sail training community, but it has no authority over what programs are offered, nor how vessels are operated. The information in this directory is supplied by the vessel operators, and ASTA cannot possibly verify all the information, nor visit the ships nor evaluate programs. For these reasons, you must take the information in this Directory as a starting point only, subject to change and correction, and proceed from there directly with the vessel operator. ASTA is not an agent or business partner for the vessel operators, and is not a travel agent; in fact, some of the vessels listed have no relationship at all with ASTA.

ASTA believes in the value of sail training as a concept, but remember, from the moment you take a step beyond looking at this book, the decision and the resulting experiences rest with you!

Directory of
Sail Training Ships
in the United States & Canada

The following list of vessels gives basic data about all ships that hold organizational membership in the American Sail Training Association (ASTA®), as well as a number of vessels that engage in some form of sail training mission but that are not members of ASTA. Member vessels are indicated by the ASTA logo next to their name, and their entry usually includes a narrative description of the program and a photograph of the vessel.

The information here is provided as a service only and no warranty or endorsement of any individual program or vessel by the American Sail Training Association is intended or implied. ASTA is not an agent for any vessel or program and does not control, inspect or approve vessels or programs. All information in this directory is provided by the owners. Before booking or boarding, confirm important facts with the vessel's owner, including the status of safety certificates, equipment, and the suitability of the vessel or program to your abilities and needs.

*A*DVENTURE

Adventure, a National Historic Landmark and a living symbol of Gloucester's great fishing heritage, provides programs and facilities for the pleasure and education of the public. She is a "knockabout" (no bowsprit) schooner. During the 1940s and 1950s *Adventure* was known as a "highliner" (best fisherman) and a champion money-maker. When she stopped fishing in 1953, she was the last of the great Gloucester dory trawlers still in service. Originally fitted with an auxiliary diesel engine, her engine was removed when she became a charter vessel. For twenty-seven years she sailed the coast of Maine as "Queen of the Windjammers."

In 1988 *Adventure* was presented to the people of Gloucester. Much restoration work has been done rebuilding her port side and bow. Plans have been made for rebuilding the starboard side and the stern in order to obtain recertification by the Coast Guard.

Rig Two-masted schooner
Contact Benjamin S. Hersey, Gloucester *Adventure*, Inc., P.O. Box 1306, Gloucester, MA 01931-1306; (508) 281-8079.
Specs Sparred length: 141'. LOA: 121'6". LOD: n/a. LWL: 107'. Draft: 13'9". Beam: 24'6". Rig height: 110'. Freeboard: n/a. Sail area: 6,500 sq. ft. Sail no.: n/a. Tons: 257 grt. Power: none. Hull: wood. Built: 1926; Essex, MA. Designer: Tom McManus. Builder: John F. James & Son.
Coast Guard cert. Attraction Vessel.
Crew n/a. **Trainees** n/a. **Age** n/a. **Sex** co-ed.
Program type Maritime history, music, marine art, geography, marine science, environmental studies and special education.
Affiliated institutions Cape Ann Historical Museum, Essex Shipbuilding Museum and North Shore Community College.
Homeport/waters: Gloucester, MA/ Massachusetts Bay and the Gulf of Maine.
Season Year-round educational program.
Cost Varies according to program.

American Sail Training Association's Mission

"To encourage character building through sail training, promote sail training to the American public, and support education under sail."

ADVENTURESS

With the mission of "Protecting Puget Sound Through Education," *Adventuress* sets sail from March to November carrying a message of care and concern for Puget Sound waters. *Adventuress* is owned and operated by the nonprofit Sound Experience and offers environmental education, marine science and nautical science programs designed for youth and adults, groups and individuals. Scholarships are available. *Adventuress* meets or exceeds all U.S. Coast Guard standards for inspected passenger vessels and is at all times under the command of a licensed captain assisted by a staff of professional mariners, educators and trained volunteers. Safety is our highest priority.

Adventuress was built for millionaire John Borden to gather Arctic specimens for a natural history museum. In January 1913, she sailed from Maine for the Bering Sea via the Straits of Magellan, wintering in Puget Sound in 1913-14. From 1915 to 1952, she faithfully served the San Francisco Bar Pilots off the coast of California. Since 1959, *Adventuress* has provided outstanding educational programs on Puget Sound. She is designated a National Historic Landmark.

Adventuress operates two distinct programs. Sound Exploration consists of two- to ten-day voyages of exploration and self-discovery in Puget Sound, the San Juan Islands and British Columbia. Participants become part of a team learning to "hand, reef, and steer" a tall ship, studying local ecology and history, and discovering skills of living and working cooperatively. Programs emphasize non-competitive hands-on learning, building self-confidence and developing a commitment to caring for each other and the environment. Sound Exploration programs are staffed by five paid professionals and six volunteers, and are open to participants age twelve and older. Elderhostel, teacher training, women's and other special-interest programs are also offered.

Sound Studies are half-day intensive introductions to the marine ecology, history and issues of Puget Sound. Hands-on learning from the decks of a ship under sail stimulates learning by making science and environmental issues real, accessible and exciting. Approximately one hundred three- and five-hour programs are offered each spring from as many as twenty town docks throughout the Puget Sound region. Sound Studies programs carry a paid professional staff of ten, plus two interns and two volunteers, and are open to participants aged eight and older.

Rig Gaff topsail schooner, two-masted.
Contact Sound Experience, PO Box 2098, Poulsbo, WA 98370; (206) 697-6601.

*A*DVENTURESS continued

Specs Sparred length: 135'. LOA: 102'. LOD: n/a. LWL: 71'. Draft: 12'. Beam: 21'. Rig height: 110'. Freeboard: n/a. Sail area: 5,478 sq. ft. Sail no.: TS 15. Tons: 82 grt. Power: 250 hp diesel. Hull: wood. Built: 1913; East Boothbay, ME. Designer: B. B. Crowninshield. Builder: Rice Brothers.
Coast Guard cert. Passenger Vessel (Subchapter T).
Crew 4-5; 8-10 instructors. Trainees 25 (overnight); 45 (day). Age 8- adult. Sex co-ed.
Program type Marine biology and environmental education for elementary school through college level students and youth-at-risk.
Affiliated institutions n/a.
Homeport/waters Seattle, WA/ Puget Sound, into the San Juan Islands, Port Townsend, and Victoria, Canada.
Season March to November.
Cost $20-45 per person for 3-5 hour cruise. $85 per person, per day for youth; $105 per person for adults. $1600 per day for youth groups; $2500.

A. J. MEERWALD/CLYDE A. PHILLIPS

The Delaware Bay Schooner Project is restoring a remnant of the era when prosperity and harvesting the resources of the Delaware Bay went hand in hand. The 1928 oyster schooner *A. J. Meerwald,* expected to be under sail in the fall of 1995, is being returned to her original glory as a representative of the heyday of the Delaware Estuary's productivity. She was one of hundreds of Delaware Bay oyster schooners that participated in the region's multimillion dollar oyster industry and is a product of a shipbuilding industry in South Jersey that served as a mainstay of the local economy.

Once restored, the schooner will sail her native waters carrying "deckloads" of people, providing access to the marine environment, education about the maritime heritage of the region and stressing the need for stewardship of the Bay's environment. The restoration is being undertaken on the banks of the Maurice River where the schooner spent much of her career. Volunteer work parties held on weekends are augmented by a professional team of shipwrights working through the week.

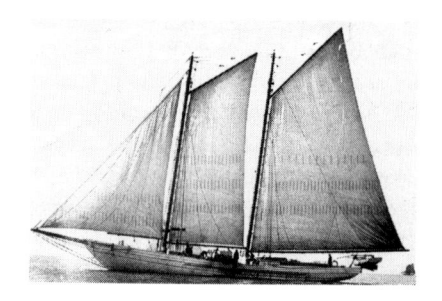

While the vessel is being restored, educational programs related to the resources of the Delaware Bay are being offered to the general public and school groups. An exhibit entitled "Maritime Traditions of the Delaware Bay" is housed at the Schooner Center in Port Norris, and will serve as a land-based introduction to the Bay for people taking a sail on the authentically restored *A. J. Meerwald.*

Rig Gaff schooner (currently undergoing restoration).
Contact Ms. Meghan Wren, Delaware Bay Schooner Project, PO Box 57, Dorchester, NJ 08316; (609) 785-2060, fax (609) 785-2893.
Specs Sparred length: 115'. LOA: 85'. LOD: 85'. LWL: 71'. Draft: 6'3". Beam: 22'1". Rig height: 75'. Freeboard: 2'. Sail area: 4,127 sq. ft. Sail no.: n/a. Tons: 57 grt. Power: 46. Hull: wood. Built: 1928; Dorchester, NJ. Designer: traditional. Builder: Charles H. Stowman and Sons Shipyard.
Coast Guard cert. Passenger Vessel (Subchapter T).
Crew n/a. Trainees n/a. Age Educational programs for students from 3rd grade through high school, as well as adult programs and teacher workshops. Sex co-ed.
Program type Marine biology, environmental studies, maritime history and special education for middle and high school students, youth-at-risk, adjudicated youth, adults and educators.
Affiliated institutions Rutgers University, Stockton State College and Rowan College.
Homeport/waters Bivalve, NJ/ Delaware Bay and coastal New Jersey.
Season Expected to be under sail in the fall of 1995.
Cost Inquire.

ALASKA EAGLE

Alaska Eagle sails approximately 12,000 miles a year as a sailing school vessel. During fall and winter months, *Alaska Eagle* operates off the coast of Southern California and Mexico. The spring and summer months see *Alaska Eagle* sailing in the South Pacific, Hawaii, Alaska, Canada and the West Coast of the United States.

Built of aluminum to race around the world, *Alaska Eagle* won the 1977-78 Whitbread Race as *Flyer*. In the 1981-82 Whitbread, *Alaska Eagle* placed ninth out of twenty-seven. Unlike most Whitbread racers, however, *Alaska Eagle* has a full teak interior, including two heads and four double staterooms.

Since her donation to Orange Coast College twelve years ago, *Alaska Eagle* has sailed more than 90,000 miles with students aboard. Since *Alaska Eagle* is a modern vessel, sail handling, navigation and seamanship techniques taught aboard are current with today's practices aboard offshore yachts. However, the traditions of watch standing, good seamanship, celestial navigation and personal responsibility to the ship and one's shipmates are very much a part of the *Alaska Eagle* experience.

Alaska Eagle will sail for New Zealand in 1994-95, making landfalls at the Marquesas Islands, the Tuamotus, Tahiti, Bora Bora, Tonga, Samoa and Fiji. Arriving in Auckland in the fall of 1994, *Alaska Eagle* will spend the winter

A LASKA EAGLE continued

months exploring New Zealand's cruising grounds. *Alaska Eagle* sails with a complement of twelve aboard, with most students signing on for voyages of ten to twenty-five days. All applicants for positions on board must have intermediate-level sailing experience. For a complete brochure on the *Alaska Eagle* program, call or write the Orange Coast College Sailing Center.

Former name ex-*Flyer*.
Rig Sloop.
Contact Orange Coast College Sailing Center, 1801 West Coast Highway, Newport Beach, CA 92663; (714) 645-9412; fax (714) 645-1859.
Specs Sparred length: n/a. LOA: 65'1". LOD: 65'. LWL: 53'. Draft: 11'. Beam: 16'. Rig height: 90'. Freeboard: n/a. Sail area: 2,800 sq. ft. Sail no.: n/a. Tons: 30. Power: 120 hp diesel. Hull: aluminum. Built: 1978. Designer: Sparkman and Stephens. Builder: Nuisman Shipyard.
Coast Guard cert. n/a.
Crew 3. Trainees 9. Age n/a. Sex n/a.
Program type n/a.
Affiliated institutions Orange Coast College.
Homeport/waters Newport Beach, CA/ coastal California and Pacific Ocean.
Season Year-round.
Cost Inquire.

A LEXANDRIA

The Alexandria Seaport Foundation expanded in the last two years to include a wide range of programs in two general areas: its Boatbuilding School and the Schooner *Alexandria*. While its programs are open to anyone, the organization focuses its sail training, maritime skills building and boatbuilding programs to youth, especially youth-at-risk.

Operated and maintained by a volunteer crew, and originally constructed in Sweden in 1929, the *Alexandria* is benefiting from an extensive renovation begun in 1993. The volunteer crew gained extensive experience with a total down-rig, including masts and spars, and the installation of RADAR, LORAN and GPS provided through BOAT/U.S. in 1993.

Work in 1994 expanded to include a refastening of the hull below the waterline, installation of a new engine provided by Volvo-Penta, and re-installation of its square-top rig.

The ship operated between New Orleans and Boston in 1993 and 1994, with its adult volunteer crew and youth sea cadets. Cadets aboard ship pursue a hands on training program, and receive qualification at the level they attain. Cadets in 1994 participated in the rigging and flying of the square topsails last flown in 1986. Adult crew are encouraged to work towards receiving or upgrading Coast Guard licenses. Timber cutting crews log, mill and dry lumber for future plank replacement, with the intention of pursuing an ambitious sailing schedule with the *Alexandria* for years to come.

A youth crew from the Boatbuilding School is currently constructing a Potomac River Dory Boat, the first of its type built since the early 1950s. At forty-two feet in length, this boat will be used for sail training and environmental studies on the Potomac River. The Potomac River Dory Boat was analogous to the Skipjack on the Chesapeake Bay, and plied its trade in fishing, crabbing, and hauling cargo for decades up and down the River.

The Boatbuilding School maintains a year-round schedule of workshops and classes, including bronze casting and forging, traditional wooden boat construction, lofting, kayak construction, and related topics. Youth/Adult teams continue the construction of Alexandria Class dinghies. These are eleven foot skiffs for rowing and sailing, built and operated by youth with an adult mentor. As well, the Boatbuilding School has completed two 24-foot lapstrake rowing gigs used for on the water shows and rowing competitions.

The Alexandria Seaport Foundation provides speakers for community organizations interested in maritime topics, and acquires artifacts and historic vessels for its collections. The Schooner *Alexandria* is also available for dockside receptions and specialty charters. The *Federalist*, acquired by the Foundation this year, is featured elsewhere in the directory.

Former name ex-*Lindø*, ex-*Yngve*.
Rig Square topsail schooner, three-masted.
Contact Alexandria Seaport Foundation, 1000 South Lee Street, Jones Point Park, Alexandria, VA 22314; (703) 549-7078.
Specs Sparred length: 125'. LOA: 95'. LOD: 92'. LWL: 82'. Draft: 9'. Beam: 22'. Rig height: 85'. Freeboard: n/a. Sail area: 7000 sq. ft. Sail no.: 13. Tons: 195. Power: 235 hp Volvo-Penta Diesel. Hull: Wood, Marstal Stern Baltic Trader. Built: 1929; Pukavik, Sweden. Designer: Albert Svensson, Karl Ogard. Builder: Albert Svensson.
Coast Guard cert. UPV, Coastwise, Registry.
Crew n/a. Trainees 6. Age youth and adult. Sex co-ed.
Program type Sail Training.
Affiliated institutions None.
Homeport/waters Alexandria, VA/ Atlantic and Gulf waters.
Season April to November.
Cost Inquire.

SCHOONER AMERICA

The Schooner *AMERICA* is a re-creation of the world's most famous racing yacht, *AMERICA*, which on August 22, 1851 soundly defeated fourteen British yachts for the 100 Guinea Cup in a clockwise race around the Isle of Wight in the English Channel. The boat will be built entirely of American materials, a showcase for American technology, craftsmanship, and ingenuity. It will be shown worldwide, attend future America's Cup races, and participate in the Sesquicentennial of the 1851 Royal Yacht Squadron Regatta. Great efforts are being made to maintain exacting detail while providing durability to the new

Rig Gaff rigged schooner.
Contact Schooner *AMERICA* USA, Inc., Attn: Dabney Oakley, 100 North Union Street, Alexandria, VA 22314; (703) 683-4654, fax (703) 684-9424.
Specs Sparred length: 130'. LOA: 105'. LOD: 105'. LWL: 92'. Draft: 10'. Beam: 25'. Rig height: 108'. Freeboard: 4'. Sail area: 6,000 sq. ft. Sail no.: 5. Tons: 120 grt. Power: twin 671 Detroit diesels. Hull: wood. Built: 1994-1995. Designer: Steers, modified by Scarano. Builder: Scarano.
Coast Guard cert. Passenger Vessel (Subchapter T).
Crew 5. **Trainees** 50 (day); 8 (overnight). Age n/a. Sex n/a.
Program type Programs are under development.
Affiliated institutions n/a.
Homeport/waters Alexandria, VA/ n/a.
Season Summer and winter schedules to be determined.
Cost Prices not available until '95 launching.

AMERICAN EAGLE

Rig Gaff schooner, two-masted.
Contact Capt. John Foss, Schooner *American Eagle*, PO Box 482, Rockland, ME 04841; (207) 594-8007, (800) 648-4544.
Specs Sparred length: 122'. LOA: 92'. LOD: n/a. LWL: 78'. Draft: 11'6". Beam: 20'. Rig height: 82'. Freeboard: 3'. Sail area: 4,000 sq. ft. Sail no.: n/a. Tons: 70 grt. Power: 193 hp diesel. Hull: wood. Built: 1930; Gloucester, MA. Designer: n/a. Builder: United Sail Loft.
Coast Guard cert. Passenger Vessel (Subchapter T).
Crew 6. **Trainees** 28 (overnight); 49 (day). Age 14+. Sex co-ed.
Program type Maritime history and literature for adults.

AMERICAN ROVER

The *American Rover* operates a rigorous day sailing schedule out of the Norfolk, Virginia waterfront. Cruises are generally 2-3 hour sightseeing and historical tours. Special student educational field trips are also popular.

Rig Three-masted topsail schooner.
Contact Capt. Brook J. Smith, Rover Marine, Inc., P.O. Box 3125, Norfolk, VA 23514-3125; (804) 627-SAIL.
Specs Sparred length: 135'. LOA: 98'. LOD: 96'. LWL: 78'. Draft: 9'. Beam: 24'. Rig height: 80'. Freeboard: 8'. Sail area: 5,000 sq. ft. Sail no.: n/a. Tons: 96 grt. Power: 260 hp diesel. Hull: steel. Built: 1986. Designer: Merritt Walter. Builder Merritt Walter, Panama City.
Coast Guard cert. Sailing School Vessel, Passenger Vessel (Subchapter T).
Crew 4; 2 instructors. Trainees 149 (day sails). Age n/a. Sex co-ed.
Program type Maritime history, marine biology.
Affiliated institutions n/a.
Homeport/waters Norfolk, VA/ coastwise, Chesapeake Bay and tributaries.
Season April through October.
Cost $12.50 for 2-hour cruise, $16 for 3-hour cruise.

ANGELIQUE

The gaff topsail ketch *Angelique* was designed especially for the New England windjamming trade. Built in 1980, her design mirrors the swift, powerful and seaworthy nineteenth-century vessels of the North Sea and English Channel. *Angelique* exceeds Coast Guard specifications for sailing vessels carrying passengers. She has a professional crew of seven and accommodations for thirty-one guests or participants. *Angelique* is available for three- or six-day windjammer cruises as well as group or corporate charters. On her cruises, *Angelique* makes her way with the prevailing winds and tides to such favorite places as Mt. Desert, Isle Au Haut or Swans Island. *Angelique* anchors evenings in snug harbors to enjoy the evening and company of shipmates.

ANGELIQUE continued

Rig Gaff topsail ketch.
Contact Capt. Mike and Lynne McHenry, Yankee Packet Co., Box 736, Camden, ME 04843-0736; (207) 236-8873.
Specs Sparred length: 130'. LOA: 95'. LOD: 95'. LWL: 83'. Draft: 11'. Beam: 24'. Rig height: 100'. Freeboard: n/a. Sail area: 5,269 sq. ft. Sail no.: n/a. Tons: 142. Power: diesel. Hull: steel and wood. Built: 1980. Designer: Imero Gobatto. Builder: Michael Anderson.
Coast Guard cert. Passenger Vessel (Subchapter T).
Crew 7. **Trainees** 31. **Age** n/a. **Sex** co-ed.
Program type n/a.
Affiliated institutions n/a.
Homeport/waters Camden, ME/coastal New England.
Season n/a.
Cost n/a.

APPLEDORE II

The schooner *Appledore II* is an 86' gaff-rigged vessel designed by D. C. McIntosh and built by the Gamage Shipyard of Bristol, Maine, in 1978. Her sail around the world is documented in two books, *Dreams of Natural Places* and *Sailing Three Oceans* by Herb Smith. *Appledore II* sails out of Camden, Maine, from June through October, and Key West, Florida, from November through May. She offers two-hour day sails for up to forty-nine passengers and will accommodate up to twenty-six for overnight or longer charters. In Key West, *Appledore II* takes passengers on full-day trips to the only living coral reef in North America. During the winter season, our crew is given courses in celestial navigation and marlinespike seamanship, and of course twice a year we make the 2,000-mile offshore voyage between Key West and Camden.

Appledore II is owned and operated by Schooner Exploration Associates and its principal, John P. McKean.

Rig Gaff schooner, two-masted.
Contact John P. McKean, Schooner Exploration Associates, Ltd., "0" Lily Pond Drive, Camden, ME 04843; (207) 236-8353, (800) 233-PIER (sum-

mer); PO Box 4114, Key West, FL 33041-4114; (305) 296-9992 (winter).
Specs Sparred length: n/a. LOA: 86'. LOD: 65'. LWL: 57'. Draft: 10'6". Beam: 18'5". Rig height: 65'. Freeboard: 7'. Sail area: 2,700 sq. ft. Sail no.: n/a. Tons: 40 grt. Power: Cummins 210 diesel. Hull: wood. Built: 1978; Bristol, ME. Designer: D. C. McIntosh. Builder: Gamage Shipyard.
Coast Guard cert. Passenger Vessel (Subchapter T).
Crew 5-7. Trainees 20 (overnight); 49 (day). Age 21-40. Sex co-ed.
Program type Seamanship.
Affiliated institutions None.
Homeport/waters Camden, ME/ coastal Maine, Florida Keys.
Season June to October (Maine); November to May (Florida).
Cost Inquire.

ARGIA

Argia is a replica of a nineteenth-century schooner and was designed and built by her owner and captain, Frank Fulchiero. *Argia* is licensed to carry forty-nine passengers in inland waters. In addition to vacation day sails, she also offers educational and sail training programs. Cruises can be tailored to suit the passengers' needs.

Rig Gaff schooner, two-masted.
Contact Capt. Frank Fulchiero, Voyager Cruises, 73 Steamboat Wharf, Mystic, CT 06355; (203) 536-0416.
Specs Sparred length: 81'. LOA: 56'. LOD: n/a. LWL: 49'. Draft: 7'. Beam: 18'. Rig height: 72'. Freeboard: 4'. Sail area: 1,700 sq. ft. Sail no.: n/a. Tons: 20 grt. Power: diesel. Hull: wood. Built: 1986. Designer: Frank Fulchiero. Builder: Jennings Boat Yard, Reedville, VA.
Coast Guard cert. Passenger Vessel (Subchapter T).
Crew 3. Instructors 4. Trainees 49 (day). Age all. Sex co-ed.
Program type Marine biology, maritime history and environmental studies.
Affiliated institutions Mystic Seaport Museum and Mystic Marinelife Aquarium.
Homeport/waters Mystic, CT/ inland waters, southern New England.
Season April to October.
Cost Inquire.

B*EE*

H.M. Schooner *Bee* is a replica of the transport schooner-gunboat *Bee* that operated from the Royal Navy Establishment at Penetanguishene in the early 1800s. Discovery Harbour at Penetanguishene on Georgian Bay has been reconstructed and operates land and sailing programs for the public. Costumed interpreters bring the history and activities of the site to life with everything from musketry demonstrations to sailing programs. With an emphasis on living history, a sail on the *Bee* takes you back to the days of wooden ships and iron men.

Constructed at the Establishments and launched in 1984, the *Bee* is one of a growing fleet of vessels at this outpost of the Royal Navy. The *Bee* incorporates both traditional and modern technology in a faithful reproduction of a nineteenth-century vessel. The hull is a GRP-laminate structure on fir frames. Both her exterior and interior echo the old days of sail.

H.M. Schooner *Bee* is also fully equipped with a diesel engine, depth sounder, VHF radio and modern life-saving gear. She operates from June to September on the waters of Georgian Bay. Sail training adventures consist of three-hour trips where participants become part of the crew and learn to hoist sails, sweat halyards and take part in all operations of a Royal Navy vessel. Programs are open to anyone aged ten or older. The *Bee* takes a maximum of fourteen trainees per sail. No previous sailing experience is required.

Rig Gaff schooner, two-masted.
Contact Chris Bagley, Marine Coordinator, Discovery Harbour, PO Box 1800, Penetanguishene, Ontario L0K 1P0 Canada; (705) 549-8064.
Specs Sparred length: 78'. LOA: 48'6". LOD: n/a. LWL: 42'. Draft: 5'6". Beam: 14'6". Rig height: n/a. Freeboard: n/a. Sail area: 1,672 sq. ft. Sail no.: 6. Tons: 25. Power: 90 hp diesel. Hull: GRP and wood. Built: 1985; Penetanguishene, Ont. Designer: Steve Killing. Builder: Charlie Allen.
Coast Guard cert. n/a.
Crew n/a. Trainees 14. Age 10+. Sex n/a.
Program type Seamanship.
Affiliated institutions n/a.
Homeport/waters Penetanguishene, Ont./ Georgian Bay and Lake Huron.
Season June to September.
Cost Can$20 per person per three-hour sail.

BILL OF RIGHTS

The vision quest — a challenging wilderness experience — represented the Plains Indians youth's passage from adolescence to adulthood. For angry and troubled twentieth-century youths, there is often no clear-cut understanding of the responsibilities of adulthood, rather there is the confusion of adolescence. VisionQuest provides programs that stress challenge, honor, self-discipline, and the work ethic.

The VisionQuest sailing camps and OceanQuest have proven themselves to be extremely effective. The basic tenets of sail training, the development of a sense of responsibility, rigorous self-discipline and respect for authority are the basic treatment aims for a majority of troubled youth. Generally, twenty wilderness camp graduates are tapped to participate in OceanQuest. Their challenge is to complete a training course. This specialty training under the guidance of VisionQuest experts stresses theoretical and practical education. Focus is on the youngster's individual education plan, with additional emphasis on ocean-related subjects such as marine ecology, oceanography, map/compass orientation and astronomy. Training in water safety, swimming and boating for training staff and trainees is also included.

Rig Gaff topsail schooner, two-masted.
Contact VisionQuest National, Ltd., PO Box 447, Exton, PA 19341; (215) 458-0800.
Specs Sparred length: n/a. LOA: 136'. LOD: 94'10". LWL: 87'. Draft: 9'6". Beam: 23'10". Rig height: 115'. Freeboard: n/a. Sail area: 6,300 sq. ft. Sail no.: 3. Tons: 95. Power: diesel. Hull: wood. Built: 1971; South Bristol, ME. Designer: n/a. Builder: n/a.
Coast Guard cert. n/a.
Crew n/a. Trainees n/a. Age n/a. Sex n/a.
Program type n/a.
Affiliated institutions Participation is by reference from a cooperating agency.
Homeport/waters Philadelphia, PA/ northeastern U.S. and Canada (winter); Gulf Coast and Bahamas (summer).
Season Year-round.
Cost n/a.

*B*LACK PEARL

Built in 1951 by Lincoln Vaughan for his own use, *Black Pearl* was purchased by Barclay H. Warburton III in 1958. Long a believer in the sea as a teacher, Warburton selected the rig as a good one for sail training. In 1972, Warburton sailed the *Black Pearl* to England to participate in the Tall Ship Race in European waters, becoming the first American to do so. On his return to Newport, Warburton founded the American Sail Training Association.

Black Pearl is currently operated by the Aquaculture Foundation, a non-profit corporation formed to promote quality education in marine studies. Her programs take her throughout Long Island Sound, as well as into the North Atlantic, Gulf of Mexico and Caribbean.

Rig Hermaphrodite brig.
Contact Capt. Wendell Corey, Executive Director, The Aquaculture Foundation, Captain's Cove, One Bostwick Ave., Bridgeport, CT 06605; (203) 367-3327.
Specs Sparred length: 79'. LOA: 52'. LOD: n/a. LWL: 43'. Draft: 9'. Beam: 15'. Rig height: 62'. Freeboard: 4'6". Sail area: 1,990 sq. ft. Sail no.: TS US-33. Tons: 27 grt. Power: n/a. Hull: n/a. Built: 1951. Designer: n/a. Builder: Lincoln Vaughan.
Coast Guard cert. Uninspected yacht.
Crew 3-4. Trainees 6. Age 14-65. Sex co-ed.
Program type Maritime history, marine biology and environmental studies, and special education for middle school students through adults, and youth-at-risk.
Affiliated institutions University of Bridgeport, Housatonic Community College and seven Connecticut school districts.
Homeport/waters New York, NY/ North Atlantic, Gulf of Mexico, Caribbean Sea.
Season May to October.
Cost Inquire.

SAFETY...

One of ASTA's chief concerns is to ensure that the highest safety standards are met by all those who participate in sail training programs, whether as officers, crew, instructors or trainees.

BLUENOSE II

The original schooner *Bluenose*, built in 1921, was a typical Grand Banks fishing schooner, from Nova Scotia. In those days, a schooner's primary objectives were twofold: to get her cod to market quickly in order to realize a good price, and more importantly, to put in a good performance in the big International Fishermen's Races between Canada and the USA. *Bluenose* won the cup for Canada several times and became so famous that her likeness became a national emblem, depicted on stamps and coins in much the same way as the maple leaf. Eventually *Bluenose* had to be sold and continued to sail as a trader in the West Indies, where she ran onto a coral reef in 1946 and became a total loss.

Bluenose II was built in memory of the original schooner from the original plans and by the same yard. The only difference lies in the accommodation plan; this time the interior space is taken up by larger accommodations for the eighteen-member crew. The navigation instruments are of the most up-to-date type.

She serves as a goodwill ambassador for the Province of Nova Scotia, participating in tall ships events throughout the Western Hemisphere. *Bluenose's* contribution to sail training is mainly through the seamen apprentices who serve as part of the crew, learning as they work. Plans are now underway to build *Bluenose III* to carry on the *Bluenose* tradition.

Rig Gaff topsail schooner, two-masted.
Contact The Schooner *Bluenose* Foundation, Suite 303, Xerox Building, 1949 Upper Water St., P.O. Box 34009, Halifax, Nova Scotia B3J 3N3 Canada; (902) 429-8100, FAX (902) 429-8633.
Specs Sparred length: 161'. LOA: n/a. LOD: 143'. LWL: 112'. Draft: 16'. Beam: 27'. Rig height: 132'. Freeboard: 10'. Sail area: 12,550 sq. ft. Sail no.: n/a. Tons: 285. Power: twin diesels. Hull: wood. Built: 1963; Lunenburg, Nova Scotia. Designer: traditional. Builder: Smith & Rhuland, Ltd.
Coast Guard cert. Appropriate Coast Guard certification being pursued.
Crew 18 (inc. 5 Canadian Merchant Marine officers, 1 cook and 12 deckhands). Trainees 80 (day). Age n/a. Sex co-ed.
Program type Industrial promotion and government marketing.
Affiliated institutions n/a/.
Homeport/waters Lunenburg, Nova Scotia: Nova Scotia and beyond.
Season April to October.
Cost n/a.

H*MS BOUNTY*

The *Bounty* was built in 1960 by MGM Studios to be used in filming the movie *Mutiny on the Bounty*. To make the movie, she sailed 7,000 miles from her construction site in Nova Scotia to Tahiti. The *Bounty* anchored in Matavai Bay near the same location used in 1788 by its namesake, with Lieutenant Bligh as Captain. After going on tour to England and visiting the New York World's Fair, the *Bounty* was permanently moored in St. Petersburg, Florida in June 1965, and became a popular tourist attraction.

In 1986, as part of the MGM Studios library, the *Bounty* was purchased by Turner Broadcasting System, Inc. Shortly afterwards the *Bounty* was refitted, a new crew assembled, and once again went to sea. She participated in Liberty Weekend's Operation Sail '86 in Philadelphia with 200 other tall ships, toured the East and West coasts, the Great Lakes, and was used in several movies through the summer of 1991.

In 1993, following many months of planning and negotiations, Turner Broadcasting System, Inc. donated the *Bounty* to the Fall River Area Chamber Foundation, Inc. The ship was readied for the ocean voyage and sailed with an all volunteer crew from Miami to Fall River, visiting the ports of Norfolk, New York, Bridgeport, New London and Newport.

The *Bounty* is operated by the Tall Ship Bounty Foundation, Inc. with a mission to provide specialized support to the community, the state and the nation in the fields of education, environmental research, historic preservation and business development. During the first year at her new homeport *Bounty* became an integral part of the educational curricula of area-wide sixth grade students and began development of educational programs with local universities.

Bounty spends much of her time as a dockside attraction. While in Fall River and during port calls to other communities, period-costumed volunteers, including "Capt. Bligh, Fletcher Christian" and other members of the "original" crew, conduct 30 minute, hands-on, guided tours of the entire ship. Tour guides and sailing crew are selected from a list of dedicated volunteers that complete historical and sail training programs provided by the full-time crew

Rig Three-masted ship.
Contact Tom Brillat, Executive Director, Tall Ship Bounty Foundation, Inc., P.O. Box 990, Fall River, MA 02722; (508) 673-3886, Fax (508) 675- →

6592.
Specs Sparred length: 169'. LOA: n/a. LOD: 120'. LWL: n/a. Draft: 13'. Beam: 30'. Rig height: 115'. Freeboard: 12'. Sail area: 10,000 sq.ft. Sail no.: 18. Tons: 412 grt. Power: Twin 440 hp Caterpillar diesels. Hull: wood. Built: 1960. Designer: n/a. Builder: Smith & Rhuland, Lunenberg, Nova Scotia.
Coast Guard cer. Uninspected Yacht and Attraction Vessel.
Crew 20; trainees 20. Age 16 and over. Sex co-ed.
Program type Maritime history, youth-at-risk, volunteer sail training, adult, maritime literature.
Affiliated institutions n/a.
Homeport/ waters Fall River, MA/ New England, U.S., Canada. Documented for coastwise, fishery, registry and recreation.
Season April to October.
Cost Inquire.

Bowdoin

Rig Gaff schooner, two-masted
Contact Capt. Elliot D. Rappaport or Phil Harman, Director of Waterfront, Maine Maritime Academy, Castine, ME 04420; (207) 326-4311.
Specs Sparred length: 101'. LOA: 88'. LOD: n/a. LWL: 72. Draft: 10'. Beam: 21'. Rig height: 70'. Freeboard: 4'. Sail area: 3,000 sq. ft. Sail no. n/a. Tons: 66 grt. Power: 190 hp diesel. Hull: n/a. Built: 1921, Boothbay Harbor, ME. Designer: William Hand. Builder: Hodgdon Brothers Shipyard.
Coast Guard cert. Sailing School Vessel (Subchapter R) and Passenger Vessel (Subchapter T).
Crew 5; 1 instructor. Trainees 11 (overnight); 44 (day) . Age 16+. Sex co-educational.
Program type Marine biology, seamanship and nautical science, for college and high school students and educators.

The information here is provided as a service only and no warranty or endorsement of any individual programs or vessels by the American Sail Training Association is intended or implied. ASTA is not an agent for any vessels or programs and does not control, inspect or approve vessels or programs. All information in this directory is provided by the owners. Before booking or boarding, confirm important facts with the vessel's owner, including the status of safety certificates, equipment, and the suitability of the vessel or program to your abilities and needs.

BRILLIANT

The *Brilliant* program is a sea-going learning experience in which teenagers or adults can enjoy the adventure of saltwater cruising plus the practical applications of safety, seamanship and navigation. Aboard the *Brilliant*, the participants are the crew. Under the direction of the captain and the mate, the crew performs the ship's work, including steering, sail handling, cooking and cleaning.

The schooner *Brilliant* is one of the finest sailing yachts ever built. She was launched in 1932 from the yard of Henry B. Nevins in City Island, New York. She has participated in several Bermuda races and, in 1933, made a transatlantic crossing from Nantucket Lightship to Bishop's Rock in a record fifteen days, one hour, twenty-three minutes. In World War II, she served with the Coast Guard, and after the war she was refitted as a yacht by Briggs S. Cunningham, who gave her to the Mystic Seaport in 1953 to be used as a training vessel. She is equipped with a 97-hp diesel engine, ship-to-shore radio, radio direction finder, radar, and other up-to-date navigational aids. She carries 3,800 square feet of sail, and is inspected annually by the U.S. Coast Guard to ensure that she fully meets safety requirements.

The *Brilliant* program is open to individuals and organized groups of adults or teenagers, co-ed. Teens must have reached their fifteenth birthday by January 1 of the year for which they apply. Youth groups consist of one adult leader and nine teens. No previous experience is required for the coastwise cruises. Occasional ocean passages require some experience. All participants must be competent swimmers.

The *Brilliant* program offers spring and fall cruises for adults with cruises for teens during the summer months. A weekend cruise begins at 0900 Friday, and ends at 1600 Monday. A six-day cruise begins at 1600 Sunday, with the group coming aboard for an introduction before getting under way the next morning; they end at 1600 the following Friday. Longer cruises of up to fourteen days are also scheduled.

Rig Gaff schooner, two-masted.
Contact Capt. George H. Moffett, Jr., Mystic Seaport Museum, Box 6000, Mystic, CT 06355-0990; (203) 572-0711, ext. 5076.
Specs Sparred length: 74'. LOA: 61'6". LOD: n/a. LWL: 49'. Draft: 8'10". Beam: 14'8". Rig height: 80'. Freeboard: 4'. Sail area: 3,800 sq. ft. Sail no.: n/a. Tons: 30 grt; 42 disp. Power: 97 hp diesel. Hull: wood. Built: 1932; City Island, N.Y. Designer: Sparkman & Stephens. Builder: Henry B. Nevins.

Coast Guard cert. Sailing School Vessel (Subchapter R) and Passenger Vessel (Subchapter T).
Crew 2-4. Trainees 8 (overnight); 10 (day). Age 15-19 (teen program); 20+ (adult program). Sex n/a.
Program type General seamanship and navigation and environmental studies for high school students and adults.
Affiliated institutions n/a.
Homeport/waters Mystic, CT/ New England, Nova Scotia, Chesapeake Bay; occasionally Atlantic Ocean.
Season Spring to fall.
Cost $125 per person per day; $110 per person (group rate).

CALIFORNIAN

The *Californian* is a re-creation of the 1849 Campbell-class Revenue Marine Cutter, *C. W. Lawrence*. She was launched in time for the 1984 Olympic Parade of Traditional Ships in Long Beach, California. The founders of the Nautical Heritage Society have developed the *Californian's* programs out of a dedicated belief that traditional sail training is a unique and valuable form of education.

Time spent aboard the *Californian*, far from the distractions of modern life, is time that will be remembered the entire life of every cadet. In a small wooden world they find themselves totally immersed in their surroundings, yet open to experience the forces of nature and develop skills that directly relate to life ashore. Self-reliance, teamwork, American history and coastal ecology as well as sailing are the cornerstones of the *Californian* programs. Curriculum materials for in-school use, ship tours and day sails are available for elementary school students in the Sea Chest Program. High school students can receive academic credit for time spent aboard, and college-level programs are also available.

The Nautical Heritage Society is a non-profit organization that believes the youth of California should have the opportunity of experiencing the adventure of sailing aboard such a vessel. They have received state-wide support, and they have been designated as the Official tall ship Ambassador for the State, and flagship to the National Oceanic and Atmospheric Administration (NOAA). In addition to its ordinary coastwise sail training programs, during its first ten years of operation the *Californian* also made extended voyages to Hawaii and Canada, and it undertook an extraordinary relief mission to offer humanitarian aid to coastal Mexico villages devastated by the 1986 earthquake.

Rig Square topsail schooner, two-masted.
Contact Nautical Heritage Society, The Dana Lighthouse, 24532 Del Prado,

Dana Point, CA 92629; (714) 661-1001.
Specs Sparred length: 145'. LOA: 93'5". LOD: n/a. LWL: 84'. Draft: 9'5". Beam: 24'6". Rig height: 101'. Freeboard: 6'. Sail area: 7,000 sq. ft. Sail no.: n/a. Tons: 98 grt. Power: 100 hp diesel. Hull: wood. Built: 1984; San Diego, CA. Designer: Melbourne Smith. Builder: Nautical Heritage Society.
Coast Guard cert. Passenger Vessel (Subchapter T).
Crew 8; 2 instructors. Trainees 20 (overnight); 50 (day). Age 8+. Sex co-ed
Program type Marine biology, maritime history, full curriculum academics, special education and environmental studies for middle school through adult.
Affiliated institutions n/a.
Homeport/waters Sacramento, CA/ coastal California and Pacific Ocean.
Season Year-round.
Cost $750 per person for 11-day voyage. Sea Chest Program, $38 per student per program. Adult programs, $140 per person per day.

CANVASBACK

Rig Catamaran ketch.
Contact Canvasback Missions, Inc.,140 W. Industrial Way, Suite B, Benicia, CA 94510; (707) 746-7828; FAX (707) 747-1861.
Specs Sparred length: 71'. LOA: 71'. LOD: n/a. LWL: 65'. Draft: 4'3". Beam: 32'. Rig height: 83'. Freeboard: 7'. Sail area: 1,800 sq. ft. Sail no.: n/a. Tons: 69 grt. Power: diesel. Hull: aluminum. Built: 1986. Designer: Lock Crowther. Builder: Canvasback Missions.
Coast Guard cert. Attraction Vessel.
Crew 6. Trainees 6-9 (overnight); 53 (day) Age 15-19. Sex co-ed.
Program type Leadership training for youth-at-risk including deaf, blind and diabetics.

CHALLENGE

Challenge is a 96 ft. three-masted staysail schooner. She was built in Port Stanley, Ontario in 1980, then lengthened and rebuilt for charter in 1984. Her heavy steel construction and modern rig combine for safe and swift passages. *Challenge* is also powered by an auxiliary Volvo diesel, which enables her to maintain a planned itinerary. *Challenge* meets all Canadian Coast Guard requirements for safety equipment and is insured to the highest degree. She carries two life rafts for 20 people each, a life platform for 69 passengers, over 90 lifejackets, a lifeboat, and the most up-to-date fire detection, prevention, and extinguishing equipment. She is certified to carry 75 day passengers and 65 evening passengers. The ship is operated by a skilled crew of 6 professional sailors. *Challenge* is the perfect day sail training ship - large enough for comfort and safe-

Rig Three-masted topsail schooner
Contact Doug Prothero, Captain/Operations Manager, Great Lakes Schooner
   Company, Suite 111, Toronto, Ontario M5J 2N5; (416) 591-5355,
   (416) 591-5377.
Specs Sparred length: n/a. LOA: 96'. LOD: 86'. Draft: 8'. Beam: 16'6". Rig
   height: 96'. Freeboard: 5'. Sail Area: 3,500 sq. ft. Sail no.: 7. Tons:
   76. Power: single Volvo 160 hp. Hull: steel. Built: 1980-84; Port
   Stanley, Ontario, Canada. Designer: Bob Johnston. Builder: Kanter
   Yachts.
Coast Guard cert. Passenger Vessel, Minor Waters II, Canadian Coast Guard
   Certification.
Crew 6 (including 2 C.C.G. certified captains, 4 deckhands). Trainees 70 (day).
   Age open. Sex co-ed.
Program type Day sail training program, corporate charter & promotion.
Affiliated institutions CSTA, Harbourfront Centre, Marine Museum of Upper
   Canada.
Homeport/waters Toronto, Ontario/ Toronto and the lower Great Lakes
Season April to October.
Cost Training cruise: Canadian $10 per participant. 2 hour sail: Can $15.95
   per adult, Can $9.95 per child. 4 hour charter: Can $ 1750.

CHANCE

Rig Friendship sloop.
Contact Maine Maritime Museum
   Apprenticeshop, 243
   Washington St., Bath, ME
   04530; (207) 443-1316.
Specs Sparred length: 45'. LOA: 32'. LOD: n/a. LWL: 29'. Draft: 4'5".
   Beam: 10'. Rig height: 50'. Freeboard: 1'6". Sail area: 400 sq. ft.
   Sail no.: n/a. Tons: 5 grt. Power: n/a. Hull: wood. Built: 1916.
   Designer: n/a. Builder: Wilbur Morse.
Coast Guard cert. n/a.
Crew n/a. Trainees n/a. Age n/a. Sex n/a.
Program type n/a.
Affiliated institutions n/a.
Homeport/waters Bath, ME/ coastal Maine and southern New England.
Season n/a.
Cost Enrolled apprentices only.

See program description under Maine.

Running Free

Running Free is ASTA's bimonthly newsletter and is a benefit of membership for all levels of membership. Running Free is the most important forum for reporting on the work of ASTA and its members.

*C*LEARWATER

The *Clearwater* is the only full-sized replica of the eighteenth- and nineteenth-century cargo- and passenger-carrying vessels known as Hudson River sloops. Since 1969, *Clearwater* has served both as a platform for hands-on environmental education and as a symbol for grassroots action. The sloop is owned and operated by Hudson River Sloop *Clearwater*, Inc., a non-profit membership organization dedicated to defending and restoring the Hudson River and related waterways.

Between April and November, the sloop sails seven days a week, carrying groups of up to fifty passengers for three- to five-hour education programs. Passengers, whether children or adults, take part in a wide range of activities involving water life, water chemistry, sail-raising, steering, piloting and more. A U.S. Coast Guard licensed captain is in charge, and an education specialist directs the program. The permanent crew of first, second and third mates, bosun, engineer and cook are complemented by two apprentices, an education assistant and six volunteers.

Sail training opportunities aboard *Clearwater* include the apprentice and education assistant position as well as the berths devoted to volunteers. The apprenticeships are open to anyone age sixteen and over, regardless of experience. Two apprentices are selected each month throughout the year. During their month on board, apprentices are given in-depth training in many aspects of sailing and maintaining a wooden ship and in the education program. The education assistant serves two months; the first concentrates on sail training, and the second is dedicated to education.

Each week, six new volunteers join the sloop. Because many have never sailed before, they are all given a six-hour introduction to the sloop soon after boarding. *Clearwater's* volunteers play a vital role in the operation of the vessel and in the education program. Many of the sloop's crew first came aboard as volunteers. *Clearwater* carries more than two hundred volunteer crew each year.

Rig Gaff topsail sloop.
Contact Capt. Betsy Garthwaite, Hudson River Sloop Clearwater, Inc., 112 Market St., Poughkeepsie, NY 12601-4095; (914) 454-7673, fax: (914) 454-7953.
Specs Sparred length: 106'. LOA: 76'6". LOD: n/a. LWL: 64'7". Draft: 6'6" (max.); 13'6" (min) Beam: 24'7". Rig height: 108'. Freeboard: n/a. Sail area: 4,305 sq. ft. Sail no.: n/a. Tons: 69 grt. Power: diesel.

Hull: wood. Built: 1969; South Bristol, ME. Designer: Cy Hamlin. Builder: Harvey Gamage Shipyard.
Coast Guard cert. Passenger Vessel (Subchapter T).
Crew 7-9. Trainees 9 (overnight); 50 (day). Age no limit. Sex co-ed.
Program type Environmental studies for elementary, middle and high school students and adults.
Affiliated institutions n/a.
Homeport/waters Poughkeepsie, NY/ Hudson River, New York Harbor and Long Island Sound.
Season April 15 to November 15 (daily education program); winter maintenance program.
Cost $30 per week for crew-trainee berth; $700-$1,250 per group for three-hour education sails; $25 per year membership; $7.50 for low income.

COMPASS ROSE

The *Compass Rose* is modeled on an eighteenth-century coastal schooner and has the appearance of a pirate ship. She participates in historical reenactments and is active in environmental projects involving endangered marine species.

Rig Gaff topsail schooner, two-masted.
Contact Robert Entin, *Compass Rose*, Bowen's Wharf, PO Box 1339, Newport, RI 02840; (401) 849-7988 (summer); Robert Entin, *Compass Rose*, PO Box 22598, Fort Lauderdale, FL 33335; (305) 524-0096 (winter).
Specs Sparred length: 57'. LOA: 47'. LOD: n/a. LWL: 40'. Draft: 6'. Beam: 14'. Rig height: 55'. Freeboard: n/a. Sail area: 2200 sq. ft. Sail no.: n/a. Tons: 25 grt. Power: 85 hp diesel. Hull: mahogany. Built: 1969; Nova Scotia. Designer: n/a. Builder: n/a.
Coast Guard cert. Uninspected Yacht.
Crew n/a. Trainees n/a. Age n/a. Sex n/a.
Program type Environmental studies for college students.
Affiliated institutions n/a.
Homeport/waters Ft. Lauderdale, FL/ New England (summer), Florida coast and Bahamas (winter).
Season Year-round.
Cost n/a.

CONCORDIA

Class Afloat is an exciting sail-training adventure for senior high school students that combines a challenging accredited academic program with international travel aboard a majestic tall ship. Class Afloat brings the classroom to the world.

Students learn the skills and traditions of crewing a tall ship, explore a wide variety of foreign countries and cultures and pursue a curriculum that addresses their intellectual, physical and social growth. Class Afloat is the trip of a lifetime for any young student with a keen sense of adventure, a thirst for challenge and a desire to learn.

There are forty-eight students of both sexes, in grades eleven and twelve, for each five-month semester. Crew members are selected on the basis of strong academic profiles, demonstrated strength of character and social suitability, health and fitness, and on their degree of commitment and dedication.

At sea, daily academic classes are held in the ship's modern classroom. Under the supervision of a fully certified faculty, students are instructed in a full curriculum including social studies and global issues, anthropology, marine biology and physical education. Optional, non-credit enrichment courses are also offered in seamanship, celestial navigation and the history and traditions of the sea.

Concordia sails to twenty ports of call during her five-month semester afloat. Visits are made to remote and primitive countries, as well as those rich in recorded history. Students explore fascinating cities and countryside, share experiences with foreign students, participate in a wide variety of exciting adventure-based activities, and, in doing so develop an international awareness and sensitivity to foreign cultures.

Rig Barkentine, three-masted.
Contact Marie-Josee Valiquette, Director of Admissions, Class Afloat Ecole-en-Mer, 1812 Maritime Mews, Vancouver, British Columbia V6H 3X2 Canada; (604) 682-4353; FAX (604) 682-5399.
Specs Sparred length: 188'. LOA: 154'. LOD: n/a. LWL: 142'. Draft: 13'. Beam: 31'. Rig height: 120'. Freeboard: 8'. Sail area: 10,000 sq. ft. Sail no.: square sails emblazoned with Canadian maple leaf. Tons: 495 grt. Power: 560 hp diesel. Hull: n/a. Built: 1992. Designer: n/a. Builder: n/a.
Coast Guard cert. n/a.

Crew 8; 8 instructors. Trainees 48 (overnight); 120 (day). Age 16-19. Sex co-ed.
Program type Full-curriculum academics and marine biology for high school students.
Affiliated institutions West Island College (high school); College Marie-Victoria; I.S.A.M.; and A.I.E.S.
Homeport/waters Nassau, Bahamas/ world wide, unrestricted.
Season n/a.
Cost $13,500 USD per student per semester; $23,500 USD per student per year.

CONSTITUTION, USS

USS Constitution is open year-round, rain or shine, for free public tours led by active-duty U.S. Navy sailors in 1812 uniforms at the Boston National Historical Park, Charlestown Navy Yard. "Old Ironsides" is the oldest commissioned warship afloat in the world. The Constitution is one of six ships ordered by President George Washington for construction to protect America's growing maritime interests in the 1790s. *Constitution* soon earned widespread renown for her ability to punish French privateers in the Caribbean and thwart Barbary pirates of the Mediterranean. The ship's greatest glory came during the War of 1812 when she defeated four British frigates. During the battle against *HMS Guerrière* in 1812, seamen watched British cannon balls glance off her 21"-thick oak hull, and gave her the famous nickname, "Old Ironsides."

In the 1830s, the ship was slated to be broken up, but a public outcry sparked by a poem by Oliver Wendell Holmes saved her. Over the following century, the ship undertook many military assignments, including circumnavigating the world and acting as both a barracks and training ship. She was restored in 1927 with contributions from the nation's school children. After a final tour during which she was towed coast-to-coast, in 1934 she was moored in her homeport, the Charlestown Navy Yard.

In order to ensure even weathering at the pier, every Fourth of July she is maneuvered into Boston Harbor for the Turnaround Cruise and 21-gun salute in honor of the nation's birthday. Although she has been repaired several times, her basic lines have not been altered nor the ship's symbolic value reduced, and the ship accurately depicts a U.S. Navy ship of the War of 1812, the period of greatest reknown for *Constitution*. Nearby, the Constitution Museum and the World War II destroyer *Cassin Young*, operated by the National Park Service, are also open to the public.

CONSTITUTION, USS continued

Rig Ship, three-masted; 44-gun frigate.
Contact LT. B.D. Bena, Executive Officer, USS Constitution, Charlestown Navy Yard, Charlestown, MA 02129-1797; (617) 242-5670.
Specs Sparred length: 308'. LOA: 204'. LOD: n/a. LWL: 175'. Draft: 22'6". Beam: 43'6". Rig height: 185'. Freeboard: 19'. Sail area: originally 42,710 sq. ft. (no longer carries sails). Sail no.: n/a. Tons: 2,200 disp. Power: n/a. Hull: wood. Built: Oct. 21, 1797(launch); Boston, MA. Designer: Joshua Humphreys and Josia Fox. Builder: Colonel George Claghorn at Edmond Harrt Shipyard.
Coast Guard cert. Commissioned U.S. Navy; National Landmark.
Crew 50. Trainees n/a. Age n/a. Sex co-ed.
Program type US Naval history.
Affiliated institutions USS Constitution Museum.
Homeport/waters Charlestown, MA/ Boston Harbor.
Season Year-round.
Cost n/a.

CORWITH CRAMER (see also Westward)

SEA's educational programs include SEA Semester (college level, 12 weeks long), SEA Summer Session (college level, 8 week long) and SEA Seminars for high school students, teachers and adults. Nearly all of these programs include a seagoing component on board the sailing school vessels *Westward* and *Corwith Cramer*. SEA programs attract outstanding educators and a variety of motivated and adventuresome students who are admitted by competitive selection.

SEA Semester (six sessions each year) offers college students a comprehensive undergraduate marine education and combines classroom study ashore in Woods Hole with an offshore voyage aboard a sailing vessel fully equipped for oceanographic research. Students spend the first half of SEA Semester (and SEA Summer Session) at SEA's Woods Hole campus receiving classroom and laboratory instruction in three 3-credit ocean-related courses: Oceanography, (scientific processes in the oceans); Nautical Science (navigation, ship operations, meteorology); and Maritime Studies (maritime history, literature, art and contemporary maritime affairs). During the second half of the program, students sail aboard the *Westward* and the *Corwith Cramer*, where theories and problems raised ashore are tested in the practice of oceanography and ship operations at sea. Students are enrolled in two sequential 4-credit courses: Practical Oceanography I

→

and Practical Oceanography II. (During SEA Summer Session, students are enrolled in one 3-credit, Practical Oceanographic Research.) Aboard ship, students stand eight hours of watch in the lab and on deck and attend two hours of lectures each day. Research projects in oceanography, designed ashore, are carried out at sea while the vessel is underway. Students earn a full term's academic credit (17 semester hours) for their participation in SEA Semester.

SEA Seminars: SEA offers a variety of shorter programs for high school students (three-week summer seminars: Science at SEA and The Oceanography of the Gulf of Maine), teachers (SEA Experience: an intensive five-week summer seminar for teachers of grades k through 12) and lifelong learners (Elderhostel). Seminars are offered primarily in summer months.

In addition to the SEA Semester's described under *Westward*, SEA has developed new programs called SEA Seminars, which are geared to participants other than college undergraduates, primarily teachers and high school students.

Rig Brigantine.
Contact Sea Education Association (SEA), Inc., PO Box 6, Woods Hole, MA 02543; (508) 540-3954, (800) 552-3633; FAX (508) 457-4673.
Specs Sparred length: n/a. LOA: 134'. LOD: 100'. LWL: 87'6". Draft: 13'. Beam: 26'. Rig height: 110'. Freeboard: n/a. Sail area: 7,830 sq. ft. Sail no.: n/a. Tons: 158. Power: 500 hp diesel. Hull: steel. Built: 1987; Bilbao, Spain. Designer: Woodin & Marean. Builder: ASTACE.
Coast Guard cert. Sailing School Vessel.
Crew 10 instructors (6 professional mariners and 4 scientists). Students 24 college students in SEA Semesters. SEA Seminars include high school students and teachers. Sex co-ed.
Program type Ocean studies including oceanography, nautical science and maritime history and literature.
Affiliated institutions Boston University, Colgate University, College of Charleston, Cornell University, Drexel University, Eckerd College, Franklin & Marshall College, Rice University, University of Pennsylvania. More than 150 additional colleges and universities award credit for SEA programs.
Homeport/waters Woods Hole, MA/ waters worldwide.
Season Year-round.
Cost Inquire.

Conferences...

From the first, ASTA's annual conferences have gathered a broad spectrum of educators, ships' masters, port representatives, public officials, marine suppliers, naval architects, program administrators, festival managers, preservationists, environmentalists and crew.

DISCOVERY

The 215' *Discovery* will be the first full-rigged ship built in this country during the twentieth century. Scheduled to begin construction within the coming year, *Discovery* is a project of Sail Adventures In Learning, Inc. (SAIL, Inc.). Her program is educational in the broadest sense. She will serve as flagship of the maritime heritage movement with an active program of day sails, deep water cruises, as well as outreach programs which go into the school systems at a variety of levels. Built of steel to stringent safety standards by Washburn & Doughty in East Boothbay, Maine, and finished off at the SAIL, Inc., site in Bath, *Discovery* will be certified under the Sailing School Vessels Act of 1982, and will be built to American Bureau of Shipping standards. Her programs will be available to people of all ages and occupations, will have scholarships available, and will have many programs accessible to those with physical challenges.

Rig Ship, three-masted.
Contact David or Arden Brink, Sail Adventures In Learning, Inc., 99 Commercial St., Bath, ME 04530; (207) 443-6222.
Specs Sparred length: 215'. LOA: 170'. LOD: 162'6". LWL: 152'. Draft: 15'6". Beam: 33'. Rig height: 118'9". Freeboard: 10'6". Sail area: 14,000 sq. ft. Sail no.: n/a. Tons: 497. Power: 1,200 hp diesel. Hull: steel. Built: n/a. Designer: Roger Long. Builder: Washburn & Doughty.
Coast Guard cert. Sailing School Vessel (Subchapter R) and Attraction Vessel.
Crew 20; 2 instructors. Trainees 48 (overnight); 75 (day). Age 16+ (overnight); 7+ (day). Sex co-ed and single-sex crews.
Program type Maritime history, special education, marine biology and environmental studies for high school and college students, youth-at-risk, and youth of all ages.
Affiliated institutions n/a.
Homeport/waters Bath, ME/ Eastern seaboard, Great Lakes, Gulf of Mexico and West Coast; occasional trips to Europe and elsewhere.
Season Year-round.
Cost n/a.

THE ENVIRONMENT...

Environmental stewardship is a natural response to sailing the waters of the world. Sail training and adventure cruises are the primary means of achieving these ends.

*E*AGLE, USCG

It is on the decks and in the rigging of the USCG Bark *Eagle* that the young men and women of the Coast Guard Academy get a first taste of salt air and a life at sea. From this experience, they develop a respect for wind and water that they carry throughout their lifetime. In the *Eagle*, cadets have a chance to apply the navigation, engineering and other training they receive at the Coast Guard Academy. As underclassmen, they fill positions normally taken by the enlisted crew of a ship, including watches at the helm. They handle the more than 20,000 square feet of sail and more than 20 miles of rigging. Over 200 lines must be coordinated during a major ship maneuver, and the cadets must learn the name and function of each line. As upperclassmen, they perform functions normally handled by officers guiding the ship and serving as the leaders they will one day become in the Coast Guard.

Eagle is one of five sister ships built by the Blohm & Voss Shipyard to the same design. (The others are *Gorch Foch*, Germany; *Mircea*, Romania; *Sagres II*, Portugal; and *Tovarisch*, Russia.) Built as the *Horst Wessel*, she was intended to serve as the German Navy's second training ship. She had been on only a few training voyages when World War II broke out. During the war's early years, the ship was used extensively for transporting men and supplies in the Baltic. At the war's conclusion, she was included in reparations paid to the U.S.

Former name ex-*Horst Wessel*.
Rig Bark, three-masted.
Contact U.S. Coast Guard Academy, Commanding Officer, USCG Cutter Eagle (WIX 327), New London, CT 06320; (203) 444-8595; when away from port: Lt. Cdr. Graham, Eagle Support Branch, (203) 444-8279.
Specs Sparred length: 295'. LOA: 266'8". LOD: n/a. LWL: 231'. Draft: 17'. Beam: 39'. Rig height: 147'4". Freeboard: n/a. Sail area: 22,245 sq. ft. (23 sails). Sail no.: n/a. Tons: 2,186. Power: 1,000 hp diesel. Hull: steel. Built: 1936; Hamburg, Germany. Designer: n/a. Builder: Blohm & Voss.
Coast Guard cert. n/a.
Crew 50. Trainees 120. Age 18-22. Sex co-ed.
Program type Seamanship.
Affiliated institutions U.S. Coast Guard Academy.
Homeport/waters New London, CT/ Atlantic Ocean, Caribbean and Pacific Ocean.
Season Year-round.
Cost Included in school tuition.

ELISSA

The bark *Elissa* was built by Alexander Hall and Sons in Aberdeen, Scotland, in 1877. Her riveted iron hull has put to sea under five flags during her ninety-year commercial career: English, Norwegian, Swedish, Finnish and Greek. She has traveled the world many times over.

Discovered in the Mediterranean by archaeologist Peter Throckmorton, the ship lay in a Greek scrapper's yard when the Galveston Historical Foundation purchased her in 1975. The Foundation is a broad-based community organization which exists to preserve and promote the material history and culture of Texas's oldest port city. The ship was acquired to focus attention on the link between the city and the sea, and to enhance the experience of the visitor to the historic port city.

Over a period of seven years, the ship was completely restored to her original configuration and rig. The Foundation committed early in the project to maintaining the ship as an active sailing vessel, and in 1982 she put to sea under sail for the first time in many decades. Continuing improvements to the ship have included the installation of auxiliary power and watertight bulkheads, enabling her to come under U.S. Coast Guard inspection as a yacht.

Elissa spends most of her time as a dockside attraction at the new Texas Seaport Museum. A large, active corps of volunteers work to maintain the vessel and interpret her to the museum's tens of thousands of visitors. Dockside demonstrations, overnight youth programs, and special events and festivals are major components of the interpretive calendar. The ship puts to sea every year for a series of "sea trials": day sails in the Gulf of Mexico. Except for professional officers, her crew is composed entirely of volunteers who have completed an extensive training program at the dock. Each year a pool of fifty to seventy five people learn the ropes and are put to the test of handling the ship under sail during her trials.

Elissa has made longer voyages: tours of Gulf Coast ports several times, and her very special voyage to New York for Operation Sail 1986/Salute to Liberty for the centennial of the Statue of Liberty. These voyages occur on an irregular basis as the mission of the Foundation and funding permit.

Former name ex-*Pioneer*, ex-*Achaios*, ex-*Christophoros*, ex-*Gustaf*, ex-*Fjeld*, ex-*Elissa*.
Rig Bark, three-masted.
Contact Texas Seaport Museum, 2016 Strand, Galveston, TX 77550; (409) 763-1877.
Specs Sparred length: 202'. LOA: 160'. LOD: 151'. LWL: 141'. Draft: 10'. Beam: 28'. Rig height: 102'. Freeboard: n/a. Sail area: 12,000 sq. ft. Sail no.: 19. Tons: 411. Power: 450 hp diesel. Hull: iron. Built:

1877; Aberdeen, Scotland. Designer: n/a. Builder: Alexander Hall and Sons Yard.
Coast Guard cert. Inspected Yacht.
Crew 40. Age 16-80. Sex co-ed.
Program type Sail training for adults.
Affiliated institutions Galveston Historical Foundation.
Homeport/waters Galveston, TX/ Gulf of Mexico, Atlantic Ocean.
Season Year-round.
Cost Volunteers and guests only.

ELIZABETH II

Elizabeth II is a public vessel, owned and operated by the state of North Carolina, and maintained at the *Elizabeth II* State Historic Site. Built with private funds to commemorate America's 400th anniversary, *Elizabeth II* is representative of those vessels that brought the first English colonists to settle on these shores during the Roanoke voyages. Between 1584 and 1587, Sir Walter Raleigh sponsored several voyages to the New World. The first was to reconnoiter the area, while the second was to establish a military colony. Founding a permanent settlement was the objective of a later voyage.

Elizabeth II is named for a vessel which sailed from Plymouth, England, to Roanoke Island in the second expedition in 1585. She probably carried marines, colonists and supplies to be used in establishing a military garrison to support England's claim to the New World.

The sail training program at the *Elizabeth II* is designed to give volunteer crew applicants and members the opportunity to learn as well as preserve our sixteenth-century maritime heritage. In addition to classroom instruction and dockside training, volunteer crew members also learn and participate in the care and maintenance of wooden vessels. The ship's boat, *Silver Chalice*, is utilized for underway training; it also travels with *Elizabeth II* when she sails. Voyages are scheduled during the spring and fall seasons.

Sponsorship for the volunteer crew program is provided by the Friends of *Elizabeth II*, Inc., a non-profit organization dedicated to supporting the *Elizabeth II* State Historic Site. Membership in the friends is a requirement for all crew. Benefits include free admission, guest passes, ship's store discounts and the newsletter, "Bos'n's Call."

Rig Bark, three-masted (lateen mizzen).
Contact *Elizabeth II* State Historic Site, PO Box 155, Manteo, NC 27954; (919) 473-1144.

ELIZABETH II continued

Specs Sparred length: 78'. LOA: 68'6". LOD: n/a. LWL: 58'6". Draft: 8'. Beam: 16'6". Rig height: 65'. Freeboard: n/a. Sail area: 1,920 sq. ft. Sail no.: n/a. Tons: 97. Power: Twin 115 hp diesel engines. Hull: wood. Built: 1983; Manteo, NC. Designer: W. A. Baker and Stanley Potter. Builder: O. Lie-Nielsen.
Coast Guard cert. None.
Crew n/a. Trainees n/a. Age 16+. Sex co-educational
Program type Educational.
Affiliated institutions None.
Homeport/waters Manteo, NC/ North Carolina sounds.
Season Spring and fall.
Cost Volunteers with organization.

ERNESTINA

The *Ernestina* was built as the *Effie M. Morrissey*, a Grand Banks fishing schooner, in 1894, an era of extreme pride in craftsmanship. She fished the Grand Banks both winter and summer for more than twenty-five years. Captain Bob Bartlett, shipmaster for Admiral Peary in his quest for the North Pole, acquired her for Arctic exploration in 1925. Under Bartlett, the *Effie M. Morrissey* went north for the next twenty years, including a stint in the U.S. Navy during World War II.

After the war, she was purchased by Captain Henrique Mendes to bring immigrants to the United States from the Cape Verde Islands off West Africa. She became the last regular Atlantic sailing packet, making twelve 8,000-mile round trips from the Cape Verde Islands to southern New England carrying goods and passengers back and forth up until 1965. In 1982 she was given by the Republic of Cape Verde to the people of the United States as a symbol of the close ties between the lands, and the Commonwealth of Massachusetts was selected to hold the ship's title.

Ernestina's seasons of training and sea experience involve people of all ages and walks of life. Education programs and voyages include coastwise programs for inner city youth, organizational leadership seminars, public and private school trips, dockside programs, and community-based education and sesrvices. Both dockside and under way, the vessel's educational programs and seminars are tailored to meet the specific needs of schools, colleges and other educational and cultural organizations. Staff educators coordinate and complement programs and activities, some of which take place under sail and others at *Ernestina's* many ports of call. The ship continues to make history as a cultural

→

resource rich in tradition and diversity, often serving as memorable setting for civic, social and corporate events.

Schooner *Ernestina* is owned by the Commonwealth of Massachusetts and is aNational Historic Landmark.

Former name *Effie M. Morrissey*.
Rig Gaff topsail schooner, two-masted.
Contact Gregg Swanzey, Schooner *Ernestina* Commission, State Pier, P.O. Box 2010, New Bedford, MA 02741-2010; (508) 992-4900, FAX (508)-984-7719.
Specs Sparred length: 156'. LOA: 112'. LOD: n/a. LWL: 94'. Draft: 13'. Beam: 24'5". Rig height: 115'. Freeboard: 3'6". Sail area: 8,323 sq. ft. Sail no.: n/a. Tons: 98 gross tons. Power: 259 hp diesel. Hull: wood. Built: 1894; Essex, MA.. Designer: George M. McClain. Builder: Tarr and James Shipyard.
Coast Guard cert. Sailing School Vessel (Subchapter R) and Passenger Vessel (Subchapter T).
Crew 11. Passengers (day sails): 80. Trainees(overnight): 24. Age n/a. Sex n/a.
Program type Educational programming.
Affiliated institutions n/a.
Homeport/waters New Bedford, MA/ East Coast, Canada (summer).
Season Year-round.
Cost $125 per person per day (approx.)

FEDERALIST

Federalist is a full-size replica of a miniature ship built in Baltimore in 1788 to celebrate the state of Maryland's ratification of the United States Constitution. Under the command of Captain Joshua Barney, the original *Federalist* sailed from Baltimore to Mount Vernon where she was presented to General George Washington as a gift from the merchants of Baltimore. She sank in a hurricane a short time later.

The replica *Federalist* was built by members of the Potomac Maritime Historical Society, and was christened at the Alexandria Red Cross Waterfront Festival in June of 1987. Since then, she has participated in many nautical events in Alexandria and elsewhere. In April 1988, *Federalist* became the first square-rigger in history to sail in Washington's Tidal Basin. She was also present at the launching of the *Pride of Baltimore II*. In May and June of 1988, she recreated the voyage of her 1788 namesake from Baltimore to Mount Vernon.

Federalist was present at the parade of sail in New York harbor on July 4, 1992, and also participated with her fel-

FEDERALIST continued

low tall ships in the summer's events in Baltimore, Philadelphia and Boston. In addition to her sailing role in these ports, she was also part of ASTA's dockside demo program, which offers the public hands-on appreciation of what it's like to sail a tall ship.

Despite her small size, the replica *Federalist* is a fully operational square-rigged sailing vessel. She is equipped with a 3.5 hp engine which allows her to maintain station with other vessels in nautical parades and pageants. Unlike her larger sisters, however, *Federalist* is also at home on land. She frequently participates in street parades, riding on a decorated trailer and pulled by her crew using special traces. For period events such as the George Washington birthday parade, the crew marches in eighteenth-century sailors' uniforms.

Federalist flies the flags of Virginia, Maryland and the District of Columbia, the three jurisdictions adjoining the upper Potomac. The District flag, normally flown on the mizzen mast, also honors George Washington, whose coat-of-arms inspired the flag's design.

Rig Bark, three-masted.
Contact Peter Ansoff, *Federalist* Coordinator, Alexandria Seaport Foundation, 1000 South Lee Street, Alexandria, VA 22314; (703) 549-7078.
Specs Sparred length: 25'. LOA: 15'. LOD: 15'. LWL: 13'. Draft: 2'. Beam: 5'. Rig height: 19'. Freeboard: 1'6". Sail area: 90 sq. ft. Sail no.: n/a. Tons: 0.3 grt. Power: 3.5 hp engine. Hull: wood. Built: 1987. Designer: n/a. Builder: The Potomac Maritime Historical Society, Inc.
Coast Guard cert. None required.
Crew 4-6. Trainees 2-3. Age 4+ (on-land instruction); 12+ (on-water instruction). Sex co-ed.
Program type Maritime history.
Affiliated institutions None.
Homeport/waters Alexandria, VA/ inlands bays and rivers; and on-land exhibit.
Season Year-round.
Cost Inquire.

FRANCIS TODD

This vessel was built in 1947 in Thomaston by Newbert and Wallace for the Stinson Canning Company and named for Mr. Stinson's daughter — Lou Ann. It was originally used as a sardine carrier with a pilot house aft and single mast with a steadying sail. The *Lou Ann* always fished for Stinson Canning Company and was later converted to a herring seiner and carrier with a pilot house forward. The hull was constructed from double sawn oak frames and long leaf yellow pine planking. The *Lou Ann* was always well maintained by her owners. She worked well and hard in her years in the sardine (herring) fishing business.

The career of the *Lou Ann* as a fishing vessel ended tragically in July, 1991, when in coming back with a full load of herring in a heavy fog, she struck a ledge off of Prospect Harbor and sank in seventy feet of water. Although the vessel was raised the next day and the herring salvaged, the canning company decided not to rebuild the seriously damaged hull. Captain Pagels saw the possibilities in the shapely hull with schooner like lines and purchased the *Lou Ann* in August of 1991. After putting new plywood patches over the holes in the hull, the vessel was floated off from where she had been grounded out.

Initially, the renamed schooner *Francis Todd* was towed to Bar Harbor where the pilot house and engine were removed. (The pilot house is at the Captain's home in Cherryfield.) In October, 1991, the *Francis Todd* was towed to Southwest Harbor and the hull stripped of all its gear. In November, the vessel was hauled out at the Hinckley Yard. From November, 1991, to May, 1992, the hull was completely rebuilt. In the interest of seeing a local wooden vessel restored, the Hinckley Yard allowed Captain Pagels' carpentry crew to do the rebuilding of the schooner at their yard and they were exceptionally supportive during the project.

Because of damage from grounding out on the ledge, the outer oak keel had been torn off and had to be entirely replaced, as well as many planks and frames. Due to the age and service of the vessel, major rebuilding was done to the deck frames, sheer clamp and shelf as well as repairing and adding new watertight bulkheads.

Captain Pagels designed a new two-masted gaff schooner rig with topsails for the former sardine carrier. With the restoration now fully complete, the *Francis Todd* is running three trips daily sailing from the Bar Harbor Inn Pier.

Rig Two-masted topsail schooner.
Contact Capt. Steven F. Pagels, P.O. Box 8, Cherryfield, ME 04622; (207) 288-4585, (207) 546-2927.
Specs Sparred length: n/a LOA: 101'. LOD: 78'. LWL: n/a. Draft: 7.5' Beam: 17.5'. Rig height: 80'. Freeboard: n/a. Sail area: 2,800 sq. ft. Sail no.: n/a. Tons: 55 grt. Power: GM 671. Hull: Wood. Built: 1947. Designer: Newbert and Wallace. Builder: Newbert & Wallace.
Coast Guard cert. 81 day passengers.
Crew Trainees (overnight); (day). Age 13-25. Sex co-ed.
Program type Two-hour sails and sail training.
Affiliated institutions American Schooner Association, Maine Working Sail Association.
Homeport/waters Bar Harbor, ME/Frenchman's Bay, Coastal Maine.
Season May to October.
Cost Inquire.

FYRDRACA

Fyrdraca is a 32'-long, single-masted vessel based on the design of a small ninth-century warship excavated on the German island of Rugen in the Baltic. It is one of a number of historic replicas owned and operated by the Longship Company, Ltd., a member-supported, non-profit educational institution.

Rig Viking longship.
Contact Bruce Blackistone, Longship Co., Ltd., Oakley Farm, Avenue, MD 20609; (301) 769-2627.
Specs Sparred length: 34'. LOA: 32'2". LOD: n/a. LWL: 29'. Draft: 2'. Beam: 9'2". Rig height: 24'. Freeboard: 2'6". Sail area: 240 sq. ft. Sail no.: n/a. Tons: 6 grt. Power: n/a. Hull: wood. Built: 1979; Keyport, NJ. Designer: traditional Norse. Builder: Hans Pederson & Sons.
Coast Guard cert. Uninspected yacht.
Crew 6. Trainees 12 (overnight); 18 (day). Age 14+. Sex co-ed.
Program type Maritime history.
Affiliated institutions None.
Homeport/waters Oakley, MD/ Potomac River and Chesapeake Bay.
Season March to November.
Cost $30 annual dues.

Photo by Albert C. Cizaukas, Jr.

GAZELA OF PHILADELPHIA

The *Gazela of Philadelphia* is the oldest wooden square-rigged sailing vessel still in operation. *Gazela of Philadelphia* was built as a Grand Banks fishing vessel, one of a large number of Portuguese ships which fished for cod in that area for hundreds of years. She is currently owned and operated by the Philadelphia Ship Preservation Guild, a private, non-profit organization. She sails as a goodwill ambassador for the Commonwealth of Pennsylvania and the Port of Philadelphia at significant events worldwide. *Gazela of Philadelphia* is open to the public on weekends when at

→

Penn's Landing, from May 15 to September 15.

She is maintained and sailed by a very active and knowledgeable volunteer group who participate in sail training activities throughout the year. After twenty-five hours of work on the vessel, they are eligible for a crew position on the next available cruise. An educational grant permits the teaching of young people sixteen years and older, many of whom go on to become volunteer crew.

Former name ex-*Gazela Primeiro*.
Rig Barkentine, three-masted
Contact Karen H. Love, Executive Vice President, Philadelphia Ship Preservation Guild, Penn's Landing, Chestnut St. and Delaware Ave., Philadelphia, PA 19106; (215) 923-9030; (215) 928-1819; FAX (215) 923-2801.
Specs Sparred length: 178'. LOA: 150'. LOD: 140'. LWL: 133'. Draft: 16'. Beam: 27'9". Rig height: 100'. Freeboard: n/a. Sail area: 8,910 sq. ft. Sail no.: n/a. Tons: 299. Power: diesel. Hull: wood. Built: 1883. Designer: n/a. Builder: master shipwrights in Cacilhas, Portugal.
Coast Guard cert. Attraction Vessel and Uninspected Yacht.
Crew 35. Trainees n/a. Age 18-72. Sex co-ed.
Program type n/a.
Affiliated institutions n/a.
Homeport/waters Penn's Landing, PA/ Delaware River and Atlantic Coast.
Season n/a.
Cost n/a.

GERONIMO

Students who sail aboard *Geronimo* receive an introduction to marine science and the discipline and rewards of life at sea. The course in marine science concentrates on the life histories of sharks and sea turtles, but often is also directed toward preparation for specific research projects.

Geronimo's primary research has always included tagging sharks and collecting biological samples for the Apex Predator Investigation of the National Marine Fisheries Service. *Geronimo* also tags sea turtles in cooperation with the Archie Carr Center for Sea Turtle Research of the University of Florida.

Geronimo makes three six-to-eight week trips during the school year, carrying students from St. George's School. Marine science and English are taught on board, and the students continue their other courses by correspondence with

GERONIMO

the faculty at St. George's. Students receive full academic credit for their time on board. The winter cruises usually include operations along the eastern seaboard and in the waters of the Bahamas and the northern Caribbean.

In the summer, *Geronimo* makes two four-week cruises. These cruises usually sail out of Newport to fish the waters south of New England and the territorial waters of Bermuda. Each summer cruise includes a series of lectures on marine biology and fisheries management. In 1987, *Geronimo* made a transatlantic research cruise to study sea turtles and sharks in the eastern Atlantic. Tagging projects were conducted in the Azores, Spain and Portugal in cooperation with fisheries biologists from these areas.

Rig Yawl.
Contact St. George's School, Newport, RI 02840; (401) 847-7565.
Specs Sparred length: 61'. LOA: 54'. LOD: n/a. LWL: 36'. Draft: 8'11". Beam: 13'. Rig height: 63'6". Freeboard: n/a. Sail area: 1,433 sq. ft. Sail no.: 1277. Tons: 22. Power: diesel. Hull: aluminum. Built: 1965; West Germany. Designer: William Tripp. Builder: Abeking & Rasmussen.
Coast Guard cert. Sailing School Vessel (Subchapter R).
Crew 2-3. **Trainees** 6-7. **Age** 10th-12th grade students. **Sex** co-ed.
Program type Full curriculum academics, marine science, environmental studies for high school students.
Affiliated institutions St. George's School.
Homeport/waters Newport, RI/ North Atlantic and Caribbean.
Season Year-round.
Cost Regular school tuition (winter); inquire for summer 1995 cruise.

GLENN L. SWETMAN

The *Glenn L. Swetman* is the first of two replica Biloxi oyster schooners built as part of the Biloxi Schooner Project under the auspices of the Maritime and Seafood Industry Museum. She was launched in 1989 as part of the effort to preserve the maritime and seafood industry history of the Mississippi Gulf Coast. Money for construction and equipping the *Glenn L. Swetman* and her sister ship, *Mike Sekul*, has come from donations by interested individuals, businesses, civic groups and a variety of museum-sponsored fund-raising events.

The *Glenn L. Swetman* is available for charter for 2-1/2 hour, half-day and full-day trips in the Mississippi Sound and to the barrier islands: Cat Island, Horn Island and Ship Island. Walk-up "day sailing" trips are made when she is not

→

under charter. Groups of up to 49 passengers can learn about the maritime and seafood heritage of the Gulf Coast and about the vessels that got Biloxi's seafood industry started.

Sailing classes are offered through local college physical education departments. In addition, *Glenn L. Swetman* accommodates weddings, parties, and Elderhostel and school groups. She is also an integral part of the museum's Sea and Sail Adventure Summer Camp.

Rig Gaff topsail schooner, two-masted.
Contact Robin Krohn, Manager, Maritime and Seafood Industry Museum, PO Box 1907, Biloxi, MS 39533; (601) 435-6320.
Specs Sparred length: 76'. LOA: 65'. LOD: 50'. LWL: 47'. Draft: 4'7". Beam: 17'. Rig height: 68'. Freeboard: 4'6". Sail area: 2,400 sq. ft. Sail no.: n/a. Tons: 21 grt. Power: 4-71 Detroit Diesel. Hull: n/a. Built: 1989; Biloxi, MS. Designer: n/a. Builder: William T. Holland.
Coast Guard cert. Passenger Vessel (Subchapter T).
Crew 3. Trainees 25 (day). Age 15+. Sex co-ed.
Program type Maritime history for college students and adults; children's summer camp and private charter.
Affiliated institutions William Carey College.
Homeport/waters Biloxi, MS/ coastwise Gulf of Mexico.

*G*ODSPEED

"On Saturday, the twentieth of December in the year 1606, the fleet fell from London," wrote George Percy, who kept an account of the voyage to Virginia. Three small ships – Susan Constant of 120 tons, *Godspeed* of 40 tons and Discovery of 20 tons – were underway on a voyage of colonization to the new world. On May 13, 1607, the colonists chose a site on the banks of the James River, naming it for their king. Jamestown was the first successful English colony in North America.

Today at Jamestown Settlement, a living history museum which recreates America's first permanent English colony, the three ships have been accurately recreated and serve as working exhibits. To further the educational mission of the museum, a volunteer sail-training program is offered to people of all ages. *Susan Constant* and *Godspeed* embark on several sail training and educational outreach voyages each year. Participants

→

*G*ODSPEED continued

are trained in sailing a seventeenth-century merchant vessel including handling square sails, marlinespike seamanship, navigation, safety procedures, watch standing and maritime history.

Rig Bark, three-masted (lateen mizzen).
Contact Capt. Eric Speth, Maritime Program Manager, Jamestown-Yorktown Foundation, PO Drawer JF, Williamsburg, VAa. 23187; (804) 229-1607; FAX (804) 253-7350.
Specs Sparred length: n/a. LOA: 69'. LOD: 52'. LWL: 46'. Draft: 6'10". Beam: 14'8". Rig height: 55'. Freeboard: n/a. Sail area: 1,128 sq. ft. Sail no.: n/a. Tons: 40. Power: 135 hp diesel. Hull: wood. Built: 1984; Williamsburg, Va. Designer: Duncan Stewart. Builder: Carl Peterson.
Coast Guard cert. n/a.
Crew n/a. Trainees n/a. Age n/a. Sex n/a.
Program type Seamanship; maritime history.
Affiliated institutions Jamestown Settlement, Williamsburg, VA.
Homeport/waters Jamestown, VA/ James River and Chesapeake Bay.
Season March to November.
Cost n/a.

*G*OVERNOR STONE

Built for Charles Greiner in Pascagoula, Mississippi, in 1877 for use as a cargo freighter, the *Governor Stone* is named for the first man elected governor of Mississippi after the War between the States. The last known of a class of shallow-draft schooners unique to the Gulf Coast, she was declared a National Historic Landmark by the National Park Service on December 4, 1991. The *Governor Stone* has seen service as an oyster buy boat, rum runner, sponge freighter, U.S. Merchant Marine training vessel, yacht club committee boat and pleasure yacht. This fine old vessel, now fully restored, is leading a new life in sail training teaching the values of yesterday to the young people of today. She is U.S.C.G. for 23 passengers, plus two crew. At present, we are sailing her as a hands-on museum. She offers a unique opportunity to sail an authentic vessel that is over 100 years old in the waters for which she was designed.

The coastal areas around the warm, bright, shallow waters of Apalachicola Bay, Florida, are the last frontier of relatively undeveloped land on the Gulf Coast. The river, estuary, bay, barrier islands, marshes and beaches are home to many endangered species of birds, animals and plants. This bay and river system is one of the most unspoiled in the country, with old ports, steamboat land-

→

ings, miles of varied backlands and clear open bay sailing between undeveloped barrier islands. The city of Apalachicola was once one of the three major ports on the Gulf Coast, along with New Orleans and Mobile. A major portion of the present city is on the National Historic Register, and includes over 200 buildings of historical interest.

Rig Gaff-rigged schooner, two-masted.
Contact Pam Vest, Executive Director, Apalachicola Maritime Museum, Inc., PO Box 625, Apalachicola, FL 32329-0625; (904) 653-8708.
Specs Sparred length: 66'. LOA: n/a. LOD: 43'. LWL: 38'. Draft: 3'. Beam: 13'. Rig height: 55' (35' with lowered topmast). Freeboard: 5'. Sail area: 1,400 sq. ft. Sail no.: n/a. Tons: 12 grt. Power: 80 hp diesel. Hull: wood. Built: 1877; Pascagoula, MS. Designer: n/a. Builder: n/a.
Coast Guard cert. Passenger Vessel (Subchapter T) and documented commercial vessel in coastwise fishery.
Crew 2; 1 instructor. Trainees 6-15. Age 10+. Sex co-ed.
Program type Sail training for youth, including those at risk, business team building, maritime history groups, wildlife and marine biology studies and environmental education.
Affiliated institutions Gulf Coast Community College, Panama City, FL, Florida Department of Health and Rehabilitative Service, Florida Association of Museums.
Homeport/waters Apalachicola, FL/ Gulf of Mexico, upper coast.
Season Year-round.
Cost Inquire.

GRACE BAILEY

Former name ex-*Mattie*.
Rig Gaff schooner, two-masted.
Contact Ray Williamson, Maine Windjammer Cruises, PO Box 617, Camden, ME 04843; (207) 236-2938.
Specs Sparred length: 123'. LOA: 101'. LOD: 81'. LWL: 70'. Draft: 6' (centerboard up); 16' (max). Beam: 23'5". Rig height: 72'. Freeboard: 4'6". Sail area: n/a sq. ft. Sail no.: n/a. Tons: 59 grt. Power: n/a. Hull: wood. Built: 1882. Designer: n/a. Builder: Oliver Perry Smith.
Coast Guard cert. Passenger Vessel (Subchapter T).
Crew 5. Trainees 29. Age 16+. Sex co-ed.
Program type By charter; windjammer vacations.

GRAY

Rig Bark, three-masted.
Contact M. Friedman Corp./The *Gray*, Suite 101, 21 Montauk Ave., New London, CT 06320-4913; (203) 447-0706.
Specs Sparred length: n/a. LOA: 137'. LOD: 98'. LWL: 87'. Draft: 9'. Beam:

GRAY continued

24'. Rig height: 72'. Freeboard: 1 meter. Sail area: 4,000 sq. ft. Sail no.: n/a. Tons: 98.55 grt. Power: 134 hp B&W alpha diesel. Hull: wood. Built: 1920; Denmark. Designer: unknown. Builder: Morse Skiboraerft, Denmark.
Coast Guard cert. Uninspected yacht.
Crew 5. Trainees 6. Age n/a. Sex co-ed.
Program type Marine biology, maritime history, special education and drug rehabilitation for adjudicated youth, youth-at-risk, middle- and high-school students, and adults.

GYRFALCON

Rig Faering boat.
Contact Bruce Blackistone, The Longship Co., Ltd., Oakley Farm, Avenue, MD 20609; (301) 769-2627.
Specs Sparred length: n/a. LOA: 20'. LOD: n/a. LWL: n/a. Draft: 2'. Beam: 5'. Rig height: 10'. Freeboard: 1'. Sail area: 80 sq. ft. Sail no.: n/a. Tons: 200 lb. Power: n/a. Hull: n/a. Built: n/a. Designer: Traditional norse. Builder: Geofferey Scoffield.
Coast Guard cert. Uninspected yacht.
Crew 3-5. Trainees 1-3. Age 14+. Sex co-ed.
Program type Serves as afterboat for *Fyrdraca* but is often used independently for school and other demonstrations.
Affiliated institutions None.
Homeport/waters Oakley, MD/ Potomac River and Chesapeake Bay.
Season March to November.
Cost $30 annual dues.

For program information, see Fyrdraca.

The information here is provided as a service only and no warranty or endorsement of any individual programs or vessels by the American Sail Training Association is intended or implied. ASTA is not an agent for any vessels or programs and does not control, inspect or approve vessels or programs. All information in this directory is provided by the owners. Before booking or boarding, confirm important facts with the vessel's owner, including the status of safety certificates, equipment, and the suitability of the vessel or program to your abilities and needs.

HALF MOON (HALVE MAEN)

The original *Half Moon* (or *Halve Maen*) was built in 1608 by the Dutch East India Company, which chose her for Henry Hudson's third exploring voyage. Her voyages of exploration made her one of the most traveled ships of her day and one of the best-known ships in the world today. Her 1609 voyage led to the Dutch founding of "Nieu Nederlandt" in 1614, comprising the present states of Connecticut, Delaware, New Jersey, New York and Pennsylvania.

The *Half Moon* replica was launched on June 10, 1989 to draw attention to the Dutch role in exploring and colonizing America. She is based on careful historical research of hundreds of documents of the Dutch East India Company, including the Resolution of 1608 ordering her construction and the detailed log of her 1609 voyage of exploration, kept by crew member Robert Juet. Henry Hudson's *Half Moon* takes you back to the "Age of Exploration," and her crew strives to expand people's knowledge of maritime history and the sea. Sailing waters include the Atlantic Ocean, the Great Lakes, and various rivers.

Rig Dutch Jagøt.
Contact Nicholas Burlakoff, Museum Director, Half Moon Visitor Center and New Netherland Museum, Liberty State Park, Jersey City, NJ 07305; (201) 433-5900.
Specs Sparred length: 95'. LOA: 84'. LOD: 64.3'. LWL: 84'. Draft: 8.5'. Beam: 17.6'. Rig height: 78'. Freeboard: 10'5". Sail area: 2,757 sq. ft. Sail no.: 6. Tons: 112 grt. Power: 250 hp diesel. Hull: wood. Built: Keel 1988, launched 1989. Designer: Nicholas Benton. Builder: Nicholas Benton.
Coast Guard cert. Uninspected yacht.
Crew 12. Trainees n/a. Age 19 +. Sex co-ed.
Program type Maritime history.
Affiliated institutions New Netherland Museum.
Homeport/waters Liberty State Park, Jersey City, NJ/ Atlantic Ocean, Great Lakes, and various rivers.
Season n/a.
Cost n/a.

*H*AROLD K. ACKER

The *Harold K. Acker* operates as a day and weekend charter vessel in the lower Potomac River and Chesapeake Bay. Her program specializes in small group youth training with emphasis on teamwork, responsibility and respecting the needs of others. Groups are responsible for the daily operation and maintenance of the vessel under the supervision of her master and mate. This includes sailing and piloting as well as meal planning and preparation. One-and two-week winter season charters can also be arranged. The *Harold K. Acker* is a participant in most of the Potomac River and Chesapeake Bay area waterfront festivals.

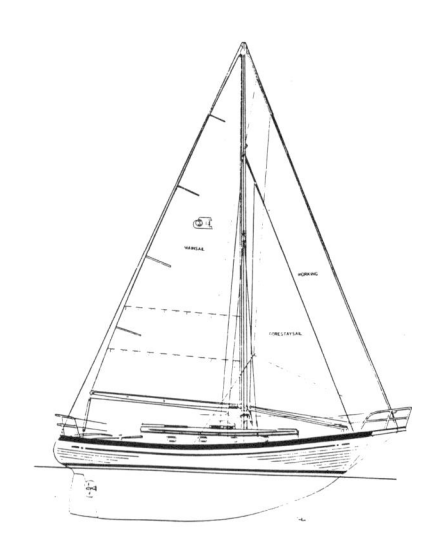

Rig Cutter.
Contact Capt. John Wesley Gardner, SV *Harold K. Acker*, 3105 Weller Rd., Silver Spring, MD 20906; (301) 946-0621.
Specs Sparred length: 39'6". LOA: 34'. LOD: n/a. LWL: 29'6". Draft: 5'2". Beam: 10'3". Rig height: 47'6". Freeboard: n/a. Sail area: 741 sq. ft. Sail no.: n/a. Tons: net 7. Power: 34 hp diesel. Hull: GRP and wood. Built: 1978; Taiwan. Designer: n/a. Builder: Ta Chou Shipyards.
Coast Guard cert. Uninspected yacht.
Crew 2. Trainees 2-4. Age all ages. Sex co-ed.
Program type Marine biology for high school students and adults.
Affiliated institutions None.
Homeport/waters Cobb Island, MD/ Lower Potomac River, Chesapeake Bay (summer); Caribbean (winter)
Season April to October
Cost Inquire.

*H*ARVEY GAMAGE

Harvey Gamage Sea Education Voyages serve a wide range of student groups. We offer a semester-at-sea for high school students, as well as accredited college semesters and interim terms. We work with youth agencies and school systems to produce programs for youth-at-risk, specially designed to increase student motivation and self-esteem. Each year we sail with Sea Explorer expeditions, and hold a summer Seafaring Camp for teens. For adults, we sail on teacher recertificaton programs, and continuing education and adventure trips. In *Harvey Gamage* programs, students participate fully in the life of the ship and receive continual training in traditional seamanship.

Rig Gaff topsail schooner, two-masted.
Contact Bert Rogers, Program Director, or Arden Brink, Executive Director, Challenge, Inc., 99 Commercial St., Bath, ME 04530-2564; (207) 443-6222, fax (207) 443-6260.
Specs Sparred length: 131'. LOA: 95'. LOD: 95'. LWL: 85'. Draft: 9'7". Beam: 23'7". Rig height: 91'. Freeboard: n/a. Sail area: 4,200 sq. ft. Sail no.: n/a. Tons: 129. Power: 220 hp diesel. Hull: wood. Built: 1973; Maine. Designer: McMurdy & Rhodes. Builder: Harvey Gamage Shipyard.
Coast Guard cert. Passenger Vessel (Subchapter T).
Crew 8. Trainees 27 (overnight); 65 (day). Age all. Sex co-ed.
Program type Seamanship, marine biology and maritime history for middle school through adults.
Affiliated institutions n/a.
Homeport/waters Bath, ME/ New England in the summer, Caribbean in the winter.
Season Year-round.
Cost Varies with program.

HAWAIIAN CHIEFTAIN

The *Hawaiian Chieftain* is a 103 foot square-topsail ketch based in Sausalito, California. A replica of a type of Northern European coastal trading vessel from the 1790's, with a rig typical of the 1840's, she is an excellent classroom for the teaching and learning of traditional sailing skills and techniques. Through a variety of on-the-water day programs, the professional crew works closely with the cadets and passengers to teach hands-on sailing experience. The *Hawaiian Chieftain* coordinates with other organizations such as the Orange County Marine Institute and the Sea Training Institute to extend the opportunity for Bay Area schoolchildren to participate in a unique experience not only promotes the learning of skills normally unavailable to them

*H*AWAIIAN CHIEFTAIN continued

through the school system, but also develops their self-esteem in a challenging environment. An experiential program of awareness and conservation of San Francisco Bay's delicate ecosystem is an integral part of these programs. The *Hawaiian Chieftain* also offers sail training for adults, private charters (both day and overnight), and Natural History Cruises. Her distinctive presence has become a familiar sight on the windy waters of the Bay.

Rig Square-topsail ketch.
Contact Capt. Ian McIntyre, Hawaiian Chieftain, Suite 266, 3020 Bridgeway, Sausalito, CA 94965; (415) 331-3214.
Specs Sparred length: n/a. LOA: 103'9". LOD: 65'. LWL: 62'. Draft: 5'6". Beam: 21'9". Rig height: 75'. Freeboard: 4'. Sail area: 4,200 sq. ft. Sail no.: 10. Tons: 64. Power: Twin Volvo TAMD 61A Diesels. Hull: Steel. Built: 1985-88; Lahaina, Maui, Hawaii. Designer: Raymond R. Richards. Builder: Lahaina Welding Co.
Coast Guard cert. Passenger Vessel (Subchapter T).
Crew 8. Trainees 45. Age all. Sex co-ed.
Program type Sail training for adults and children; marine environmental education; private charter.
Affiliated institutions Orange County Marine Institute: Sea Training Institute
Homeport/waters Sausalito, CA/ San Francisco Bay (summer); Southern California coast (winter).
Season Year-round.
Cost Daysails: $25-$59. Overnight: $100-$200.

*H*ERITAGE

Rig Gaff topsail schooner, two-masted.
Contact Capts. Douglas K. and Linda J. Lee, Schooner *Heritage*, Box 482, Rockland, ME 04841; (800) 648-4544, (800) 542-5030, fax (207) 594-8015.
Specs Sparred length: n/a. LOA: 140'. LOD: 94'. LWL: 75'. Draft: 8'. Beam: 24'. Rig height: 102'. Freeboard: n/a. Sail area: 5,000 sq. ft. Sail no.: n/a. Tons: 89. Power: yawl boat. Hull: wood. Built: 1983; Rockland, ME. Designer: n/a. Builder: North End Shipyard.
Coast Guard cert. n/a.
Crew n/a. Trainees n/a. Age n/a. Sex n/a.
Program type Windjammer cruises.

Conferences... *From the first, ASTA's annual conferences have gathered a broad spectrum of educators, ships' masters, port representatives, public officials, marine suppliers, naval architects, program administrators, festival managers, preservationists, environmentalists and crew.*

HERITAGE OF MIAMI II, Topsail Schooner

The *Heritage of Miami II* is an 83' square topsail schooner that is modern in its materials and construction but traditional in its style. She has been built specifically for crossing wide expanses of open water; her deck is wide and spacious, which allows a tremendous amount of room for working the sails, lounging in the sun and sleeping in the evening. Her shoal draft makes even small islands accessible while her long bowsprit, topmasts and yards allow extra sails for speed in between.

The *Heritage of Miami II's* travels take her through the Florida Keys and out to Fort Jefferson in the Dry Tortugas in the Gulf of Mexico. She operates from the Boy Scouts of America's High Adventure Seabase in Islamorda (75 miles east of Key West). Passages are one week. The program offers a unique opportunity to explore a part of the Florida Keys, while enjoying the challenge of a hands on sail training adventure.

Sea Exploring cruises last for six days and five nights. Her professional captain and crew help the Explorers experience the life of the sea: setting and furling sails, manning the helm, standing watch, navigation, even catching, cleaning and cooking fish. The program offers a unique opportunity to explore a part of the Florida Keys while enjoying the hands-on nature of this sailing experience.

Rig Two master topsail schooner.
Contact Capt. Joseph A. Maggio, Schooner Heritage of Miami, Inc., 3145 Virginia St., Coconut Grove, FL. 33133; 305 442-9697.
Specs Sparred length: n/a. LOA: 85'. LOD: 65'. LWL: 65'. Draft: 6'. Beam: 17' 9". Rig height: 53'. Freeboard: n/a. Sail area: 2,300 sq. ft. Sail no.: n/a. Tons: 47. Power: 130 hp, 6 cyl, Ford Lehman. Hull: Steel Built: 1988. Designer: Merritt Walters. Builder: Howdy Bailey.
Coast Guard cert. 49 day pass, 18 overnight pass, licensed for exposed waters.
Crew Master, mate, two deck hands. Trainees: 18. Age: 16 to 73. Sex: both.
Program type High Adventure Sea exploring. Trainees crew and operate vessel under Captain and ship's crew.
Affiliated institutions Dade County Public Schools, Barry University, Boy Scouts of America, and various prep schools throughout the country.
Homeport/waters Miami, FL.: Biscayne Bay, Florida Keys, Gulf of Mexico (Dry Tortugas).
Season Year-round.
Cost 1994: $450 per person.

INLAND SEAS

Launched May 1994, the Inland Seas Education Association's new schooner *Inland Seas* was built as a "science ship," a hands-on laboratory for students to learn about themselves and the Great Lakes. *Inland Seas* is a steel-hulled schooner with detailing similar to vessels constructed during the tall ship era. In addition, the vessel is equipped with scientific gear for studying the Great Lakes ecosystem. *Inland Seas* will inspire an appreciation for and a commitment to the Great Lakes natural and cultural heritage.

The Inland Seas Education Association also operates the Schoolship Program aboard the schooners *Malabar* and *Manitou*.

Rig Gaff schooner, two-masted.
Contact Inland Seas Education Association, 101 Dame St., Millside Building, Suttons Bay, MI 49682-0218; (616) 271-3077.
Specs Sparred length: 78'. LOA: 61'6". LOD: n/a. LWL: 53'. Draft: 6'6". Beam: 17'. Rig height: 64'. Freeboard: 3'6". Sail area: 1,800 sq. ft. Sail no.: n/a. Tons: 43 disp. Power: 135 hp diesel. Hull: steel. Built: construction begun 1993, completed 1994. Designer: Charles W. Wittholz, consulting architects: Woodin & Marean. Builder: Treworgy Yachts, Palm Coast, FL.
Coast Guard cert. Passenger Vessel (Subchapter T).
Crew 5. **Trainees** 12 (overnight); 32 (day). **Age** 11+. **Sex** co-ed.
Program type Marine biology, maritime history and environmental studies for middle school, high school and college students, adults and youth-at-risk.
Affiliated institutions Great Lakes Maritime Academy and Eastern Michigan University.
Homeport/waters Suttons Bay, MI/Grand Traverse Bay, MI/Great Lakes.
Season Spring, summer, and early fall.
Cost n/a.

Sailing School Vessels (SSV)... are certified as Subchapter R–Nautical Schools–under Title 46 of the Code of Federal Regulations. An SSV is a vessel of less than 500 gross tons carrying six or more sailing school students or instructors, principally propelled by sail, and operated by a non-profit educational organization exclusively for the purpose of sailing education.

ISAAC H. EVANS

Rig Gaff schooner, two-masted.
Contact Capt. Edward B. Glaser, Schooner *Isaac H. Evans*, PO Box 482, Rockland, ME 04843; (207) 594-8007, (800) 648-4544.
Specs Sparred length: 98'. LOA: n/a. LOD: 65'. LWL: 60'. Draft: 6'. Beam: 19'. Rig height: 82'. Freeboard: n/a. Sail area: n/a sq. ft. Sail no.: n/a. Tons: 52 grt. Power: yawl boat. Hull: wood. Built: 1886. Designer: n/a. Builder: George Vannaman.
Coast Guard cert. Passenger Vessel (Subchapter T).
Crew 4. Trainees 22. Age n/a. Sex n/a.
Program type Windjammer cruises.

J. & E. RIGGIN

Rig Gaff schooner, two-masted.
Contact Capt. David Allen, Schooner *J. & E. Riggin*, PO Box 571, Rockland, ME 04841; (207) 594-2923; (800) 869-0604.
Specs Sparred length: n/a. LOA: 120'. LOD: 90'. LWL: 76'. Draft: 6'6". Beam: 23'. Rig height: 75'. Freeboard: n/a. Sail area: n/a sq. ft. Sail no.: n/a. Tons: 61. Power: n/a. Hull: n/a. Built: 1927; Dorchester, NJ. Designer: n/a. Builder: n/a.
Coast Guard cert. Passenger Vessel (Subchapter T).
Crew 5. Trainees 26. Age n/a. Sex n/a.
Program type n/a.

JOHN E. PFRIEM

The *John E. Pfriem* is a classic design Chesapeake Bay bugeye ketch built in Gloucester, Massachusetts, in 1964. She operates as a marine environmental education vessel sailing the waters of Long Island Sound from April through November.

Former names ex-*J. N. Carter*.
Rig Chesapeake Bay bugeye ketch.
Contact Capt. Wendell Corey, Executive Director, The Aquaculture Foundation, Captain's Cove, One Bostwick Ave., Bridgeport, CT 06605; (203) 367-3327.
Specs Sparred length: 65'. LOA: 55'. LOD: n/a. LWL: 47'. Draft: 3'. Beam: 14'6". Rig height: 49'. Freeboard: 2'6". Sail area: 1,200 sq. ft. Sail no.: n/a. Tons: 14 grt. Power: n/a. Hull: wood. Built: 1964;

JOHN E. PFRIEM continued

Gloucester, MA. Designer: Russell Grinnell. Builder: Russell Grinnell.
Coast Guard cert. Research Vessel (Subchapter U).
Crew 3. Trainees 22. Age 5+. Sex co-ed.
Program type Maritime history, marine biology and environmental studies, and special education for middle school students through adults, and youth-at-risk.
Affiliated institutions University of Bridgeport, Housatonic Community College, seven Connecticut school districts, and community organizations.
Homeport/waters Bridgeport, CT/ Long Island Sound.
Season April to November.
Cost Inquire.

JOSEPH CONRAD

Mystic Seaport's Sail Education Program offers young people the rare experience of living aboard the square-rigged ship *Joseph Conrad* as they learn sailing, seamanship, rowing, navigation and the arts of the sailor. The emphasis is on learning by doing and working together as a crew, while living aboard this famous ship which is permanently berthed at Mystic Seaport Museum.

Built in Copenhagen as the *Georg Stage*, this illustrious vessel served as a school ship for the Danish merchant service until 1934, when she was purchased by the well-known Australian sea captain and author, Alan Villiers, who renamed her *Joseph Conrad* and sailed her around the world. During World War II, she was given to the U.S. Maritime Commission as a training ship. In 1947 she was deeded by Congress to Mystic Seaport Museum. She has now been extensively refitted to serve as a permanently moored ship accommodating 50 in Navy-type bunks, with ample toilet and shower facilities and electricity. The iron-hulled ship is also equipped with fire detection and heating systems. There are separate quarters for group leaders and staff.

The *Joseph Conrad* program is open to individual boys and girls and organized groups, ages ten through fifteen. Applicants must have reached their tenth birthday by January 1 of the year for which they are applying. Organized

→

groups must have one adult leader per ten participants. No prior experience is required for beginner sessions, only a desire to participate and learn. Intermediate sessions are for those who have attended a previous beginner session or have had sailing experience. All must hold current Red Cross swimmers certification or its equivalent.

The *Joseph Conrad* program offers six-day sessions from July until the end of August. A typical day begins at 6:30a.m. with all hands rising and attending to clean-up detail. After breakfast, there is time for learning about the wind and currents in the Mystic River, sailing, rowing, marlinespike seamanship, exploring the museum and perhaps training aloft. Evenings are filled with activities including chantey singing, a planetarium show, role-players, and cookouts.

Former name *Georg Stage*.
Rig Ship, three-masted.
Contact Mystic Seaport Museum, P.O. Box 6000, Mystic, CT 06355-0990; (203) 572-5323.
Specs Sparred length: 153'7". LOA: 118'6"'. LOD: n/a. LWL: 100'8". Draft: 12'. Beam: 25'3". Rig height: 98'6". Freeboard: n/a. Sail area: n/a sq. ft. Sail no.: n/a. Tons: 212.16 grt. Power: n/a. Hull: iron. Built: 1882; Copenhagen, Denmark. Designer: Burmeister & Wain. Builder: Burmeister & Wain.
Coast Guard cert. n/a.
Crew 4. **Trainees** 50. **Age** n/a. **Sex** co-ed.
Program type Shore-based maritime history and small boat handling program.
Affiliated institutions n/a.
Homeport/waters Mystic, CT/ dockside.
Season July through August.
Cost $450 per person per week.

LADY MARYLAND

Lady Maryland is a full-size replica of a pungy schooner, an elegant work boat of a kind that used to haul perishable cargo and luxury items quickly from port to port around Chesapeake Bay during the nineteenth century. Instead of carrying watermelon and oysters, her mission today is to provide students with the opportunity to experience sailing a schooner while studying American history, sailing, seamanship, economics and the ecology of the waters of the Chesapeake and Delaware Bays and the coastal

*L*ADY MARYLAND continued

waters of the north coast.

The Living Classrooms Foundation has developed a flexible educational program which can fit the needs of a variety of school groups. More than 25,000 students participate in Foundation programs each year. Lady Maryland carries up to thirty-two passengers for educational day trips and extended live-aboard sail training programs for up to fourteen students are also available.

Rig Pungy schooner (gaff rigged), two-masted.
Contact James Bond, Executive Director, Living Classrooms Foundation, The Lighthouse at Pier 5, 717 Eastern Ave., Baltimore, MD 21202; (410) 685-0295; FAX (410) 752-8433.
Specs Sparred length: 103'. LOA: 72'. LOD: 55'. LWL: 64'3". Draft: 7'. Beam: 22'. Rig height: 85'. Freeboard: 3'. Sail area: 2,994 sq. ft. Sail no.: none. Tons: 60 grt. Power: Twin Cummins diesel. Hull: Douglas fir over white oak. Built: 1986; Baltimore, MD. Designer: Thomas Gillmer, N.A. Builder: Lady Maryland Foundation.
Coast Guard cert. Passenger Vessel (Subchapter T).
Crew 6-8. Trainees 12-14 (overnight); 32 (day). Age 13+. Sex co-ed and single sex cruises available.
Program type Sailing and seamanship, marine biology, environmental studies and maritime history for middle and high school students, youth-at-risk and adults.
Affiliated institutions n/a.
Homeport/waters Baltimore, MD/ Chesapeake and Delaware Bays, East Coast between Maryland and Maine.
Season March through November.
Cost $110 per person per day; $7,200 for 14 people for 5 days; $1,250 for day sail for 32 people.

*L*ADY WASHINGTON

The brig *Lady Washington* was a ranging tender and consort to the *Columbia Rediviva*, the first American ship to circumnavigate the globe. The two ships left Boston for the lucrative fur trade of the uncharted Pacific Northwest on October 1, 1787. While in command of the *Columbia Rediviva*, Captain Robert Gray later discovered the Columbia River and Gray's Harbor.

During the stormy passage around Cape Horn, Gray in the *Lady Washing-*

ton and Captain John Kendrick in the *Columbia Rediviva* became separated. Gray, clearly more decisive, arrived first at Nootka Sound on Vancouver Island, and after Kendrick arrived, they swapped ships. Kendrick engaged the *Lady Washington* in the fur trade with China. At Macao he had her re-rigged from a single-masted sloop to a two-masted brig, with both masts square rigged. Under Kendrick's command, the *Lady Washington* was the first flag flying the Stars and Stripes to visit Japan, and logged eight years of trading between Macao and Canton and the Pacific Northwest.

Built primarily of old-growth Douglas fir, the recreation of *Lady Washington* is the largest sailing replica built on the West Coast. The new vessel is as close to the original *Lady Washington* as historical records and U.S. Coast Guard regulations will allow. Launched in March 1989, she was licensed by the U.S. Coast Guard as a passenger vessel. She is also used for educational purposes.

Rig Brig.
Contact Les Bolton, Gray's Harbor Historical Seaport, P.O. Box 2019, Aberdeen, WA 98520; (206) 532-8611.
Specs Sparred length: 105'. LOA: n/a. LOD: 72'. LWL: n/a. Draft: 9'6". Beam: 22'. Rig height: 89'. Freeboard: n/a. Sail area: 4,443 sq. ft. Sail no.: n/a. Tons: 170. Power: diesel. Hull: wood. Built: 1989. Designer: Ray Wallace. Builder: G.H. Historical Seaport.
Coast Guard cert. Passenger Vessel (Subchapter T).
Crew 5. Trainees 12. Age 14+. Sex co-ed.
Program type Maritime history and environmental studies.
Affiliated institutions Public Development Authority (Aberdeen, WA) and Aberdeen School District, Aberdeen, WA.
Homeport/waters Gray's Harbor, WA/ Gray's Harbor, Puget Sound, southern British Columbia and West Coast.
Season March to January.
Cost $1500 charter for 45 people for 3-hour sail.

*L*AND'S END

Square Sails School offers two distinct programs. The sail outreach program provides an on-water platform for non-profit youth groups. Introduction to sail is a series of adult education classes in marlinespike seamanship, navigation, piloting, dinghy building, and safe-boating and emergency procedures. The Boy Scout Camp Aboard Programs offer two-week liveaboards with sailing, oceanography, and weather Merit Badges.

*L*AND'S END continued

Rig Ketch.
Contact Bob Booth, Square Sails School, P.O. Box 3216, Newport, RI 02840; (401) 842-0647.
Specs Sparred length: 48'. LOA: 39'3". LOD: n/a. LWL: 35'1". Draft: 6'. Beam: 10'10". Rig height: 54'. Freeboard: 4'. Sail area: 868 sq. ft. Sail no.: n/a. Tons: 12.5 grt. Power: n/a. Hull: n/a. Built: n/a. Designer: S. Crocker. Builder: Britt Brothers, West Lynn, MA.
Coast Guard cert. Uninspected yacht.
Crew 2. **Trainees** 4 (overnight); 6 (day). Age 10+. Sex co-ed.
Program type At-risk teenagers, high school students, Boy Scout Merit Badge Programs: Sailing, oceanography, and weather camp aboards.
Affiliated institutions Area high schools, and Boy Scouts of America.
Homeport/waters Newport, RI/Long Island Sound to Cape Cod Bay.
Season March 15 to November 15.
Cost Boy Scout Camp Aboard (Two Weeks) $300.00, Sail Outreach Youth Program Day Sails ($10 per student).

*L*ARK

Rig Gaff rigged sloop.
Contact Capt. Eric Little, *Lark*, 2 Huettner Rd., Woods Hole, MA 02543 (508) 458-9207, or (508) 540-7897.
Specs Sparred length: 50'. LOA: 52'. LOD: 44'10". LWL: 29'6". Draft: 5'5". Beam: 10'9". Rig height: 55'. Freeboard: 4'. Sail area: 900 sq. ft. Sail no.: none. Tons: 20 grt. Power: 44 hp Universal diesel. Hull: mahogany over oak. Built: 1932. Designer: John Alden. Builder: F. D. Lawley, Quincy, MA.
Coast Guard cert. Uninspected yacht.
Crew 7. **Trainees** 2 (overnight); 4 (day). Age 12+. Sex co-ed.
Program type Sail training.

The information here is provided as a service only and no warranty or endorsement of any individual programs or vessels by the American Sail Training Association is intended or implied. ASTA is not an agent for any vessels or programs and does not control, inspect or approve vessels or programs. All information in this directory is provided by the owners. Before booking or boarding, confirm important facts with the vessel's owner, including the status of safety certificates, equipment, and the suitability of the vessel or program to your abilities and needs.

*L*ETTIE G. HOWARD

The schooner *Lettie G. Howard* was launched at the famed shipyard of A.D. Story in Essex, Massachusetts in 1893 as a smaller example of that graceful seaworthy class of vessels known as the "Fredonia" model fishing schooner. The *Lettie* was built for Captain Fred Howard of Beverly, Massachusetts, who fished her on the notorious Georges Banks.

In 1901, she was sold to Pensacola, Florida snapper fishing interests. She fished in the Gulf of Mexico until 1960s. She was acquired by the newly formed South Street Seaport Museum in 1968 as an example of the typical type of fishing schooner that landed their catch at the adjacent Fulton Fish Market.

Now fully restored and recently U.S. Coast Guard certified as a Sailing School Vessel, the *Lettie G. Howard* is carrying out sea education and sail training voyages and day trips. Curricula employ the unique nature of this fast and able type of fishing schooner to enhance the students' awareness of marine and littoral environments and the cultural heritage of the sea that Americans share. The principle thrust however is sailing the vessel and the independence, interdependence, and confidence that the process both begins and builds. The programs are available to established institutions, with some available to the general public.

Former name ex-*Caviare*, ex-*Mystic C.*, ex-*Lettie G. Howard*.
Rig Gaff schooner.
Contact Don Birkholz, Jr., Director, Maritime Operations, South Street Seaport Museum, 207 Front St., New York, NY 10038; (212) 748-8600.
Specs Sparred length: 125'4". LOA: 84'2". LOD: 78'7". LWL: 70'4". Draft: 10'6". Beam: 21'1". Rig height: 90'6". Freeboard: 3'5". Sail area: 5,072 sq. ft. Sail no.: n/a. Tons: 54 gross, 16 net. Power: twin diesel, twin screw. Hull: wood. Built: 1893 (rebuilt 1993); Essex, CT. Designer: George "Mel" McClain. Builder: A.D. Story, Essex, MA (rebuilt by South Street Seaport, David Short, shipwright).
Coast Guard cert. Sailing School Vessel (Subchapter R).
Crew 5; 1 instructor. Trainees 14 (overnight); 24 (day). Age 14-18. Sex co-ed.
Program type Environmental studies, maritime history, seamanship.
Affiliated institutions n/a.
Homeport/waters New York City, NY/ New York Harbor and coastal waters of New England.

*L*EWIS R. FRENCH

Rig Gaff schooner, two-masted.
Contact Capt. Dan and Kathy Pease, Schooner *Lewis R. French*, P.O. Box 992, Camden, ME 04843; (800) 469-4635.
Specs Sparred length: 95'. LOA: n/a. LOD: 65'. LWL: 58'. Draft: 7'6". Beam: 18'6". Rig height: 82'. Freeboard: n/a. Sail area: n/a sq. ft. Sail no.: n/a. Tons: 50. Power: yawl boat. Hull: n/a. Built: 1871; Maine. Designer: n/a. Builder: n/a.
Coast Guard cert. n/a.
Crew n/a. **Trainees** 22. **Age** n/a. **Sex** n/a.
Program type n/a.

*L*ISA

The brig *Lisa* offers teenagers the opportunity to sail before the mast in a new brig. Students can spend an academic year learning geography, history and math by direct experience, all while experiencing the disciplines of life at sea and the thrill of manning a traditional vessel.

Rig Brig.
Contact Capt. John Leibolt, P.O. Box 16-1510, Altamonte Springs, FL 32716; (407) 884-8333.
Specs Sparred length: 72'. LOA: 55'. LOD: 50'. LWL: 45'. Draft: 6'3". Beam: 18'. Rig height: 55'. Freeboard: 5'. Sail area: 3,000 sq. ft. Sail no.: n/a. Tons: 40 grt. Power: 100 hp diesel. Hull: steel. Built: 1985. Designer: Thomas Colvin. Builder: Bolot Shipbuilding Ltd..
Coast Guard cert. Uninspected yacht.
Crew 4. **Trainees** 6. **Age** 13-19. **Sex** co-ed.
Program type Full curriculum academic and special education programs for high school students and youth-at-risk.
Affiliated institutions n/a.
Homeport/waters Wilmington, DE/ world wide.
Season Year-round.
Cost Inquire.

L OTUS

Ship 303 was established in 1965, dedicated to nautical experience and training for boys and girls ages fourteen to twenty in boating and marine skills with special emphasis on sailing. The traditional BSA Sea Explorer training and advancement program is followed, leading to the prestigious Quartermaster award. Ship members sail and help maintain the seventy six year-old schooner *Lotus* and two nine foot Dyer sailing dinghies. Cruises vary from one day to several weeks and visit ports around Lake Ontario from Toronto to the Thousand Islands. The ship is on the National Register of historic vessels, a member of ASTA and is operated by US Coast Guard licensed masters. A major renovation of *Lotus* was completed in 1993 with the help of private and public funds. Public tours are conducted by its members at scheduled times throughout the sailing season. As a tall ship, *Lotus* participates in historic reenactments, ASTA rallies and OpSail organized activities.

Former names ex-*Dickens*, ex-*Lotus*, ex-*Miss Glouster*.
Rig Gaff schooner, two-masted.
Contact Lenny Damaso, 4185 County Line Road, Fairport, NY 14450; (716) 377-5683.
Specs Sparred length: 57'. LOA: 54'. LOD: 48'. LWL: 37'. Draft: 4'9". Beam: 13'. Rig height: 55'. Freeboard: 2'6". Sail area: 1,000 sq. ft. Sail no.: 4. Tons: 16 grt. Power: diesel. Hull: wood. Built: 1918. Designer: William H. Hand, Jr., N.A. Builder: Thomas B. Van Dorn.
Coast Guard cert. uninspected yacht.
Crew 5. Trainees 6. Age 14-20. Sex co-ed.
Program type Maritime history and career awareness.
Affiliated institutions Otetiana Council, Inc., Boy Scouts of America, (716) 244-4210, Sea Exploring.
Homeport/waters Sodus Bay, NY/ Lake Ontario and St. Lawrence River.
Season May-October.
Cost Inquire.

Passenger vessels... are certified according to size and the number of passengers carried. Subchapter C—Uninspected Vessels may operate with no more than six passengers for hire. Subchapter T—Small Passenger Vessels are vessels of under 100 gross tons that carry passengers for hire. Most sail training vessels listed in this directory are certified as Subchapter T vessels. Subchapter H—Passenger Vessels are vessels of more than 100 tons. Because passenger vessels are technically engaged in trade or commerce, they cannot operate under a certificate of inspection as SSVs.

*M*ABEL STEVENS

The ketch *Mabel Stevens* offers a wide range of charter services in the Washington, D.C., and Chesapeake Bay areas. Sail training cruises, group and individual charters and other tailored sailing/maritime education programs are offered by Captain Chalker aboard the *Mabel Stevens*.

Built of wood in 1935 by Captain "Dick" Hartge of Galesville, Maryland, the *Mabel Stevens* holds a special place in the Washington metropolitan area. During the 1980s, the *Mabel Stevens* officially represented the District of Columbia at the tall ships events in Boston (350th anniversary) and New York (Statue of Liberty centennial) and in 1992 in New York at the Christopher Columbus Quincentennial Celebrations. Besides being the District of Columbia's good-will ambassador vessel at major historic events, the *Mabel Stevens* competes in ASTA rallies and has in the past raced with the best of the Class C tall ships.

Captain Chalker is a member of the ASTA board of directors and is firmly committed to sail training. The *Mabel Stevens* sails from May to October in and around the lower Potomac River and the Chesapeake Bay.

Rig Ketch.
Contact Capt. Ned Chalker, Ketch *Mabel Stevens*, 119 Fifth St., N.E., Washington, DC 20002; (202) 543-0110, (301) 259-4458.
Specs Sparred length: 47'6". LOA: 35'. LOD: n/a. LWL: 31'9". Draft: 4'6". Beam: 11'6". Rig height: 45'. Freeboard: 3'. Sail area: 1,200 sq. ft. Sail no.: TS-US 159. Tons: 17 grt. Power: 52 hp diesel. Hull: wood. Built: 1935; Galesville, MD. Designer: n/a. Builder: Ernest H. Hartge.
Coast Guard cert. Uninspected yacht.
Crew 1. Trainees 4. Age all. Sex co-ed and single-sex cruises.
Program type Maritime history and environmental studies.
Affiliated institutions n/a.
Homeport/waters Cobb Island, MD/ Potomac River, Chesapeake Bay.
Season April to October.
Cost $70 per day; inquire for group rates.

MADELINE

Madeline is a replica 1800s merchant schooner operated by the Maritime Heritage Alliance. She conducts regular sail training for Maritime Heritage Alliance members, and voyages to Great Lakes ports each summer.

Rig Gaff topsail schooner, two-masted.
Contact Linda Strauss, Director of Operations, Maritime Heritage Alliance, P.O. Box 1108, Traverse City, MI 49685-1108; (616) 946-2647.
Specs Sparred length: 92'. LOA: 55'6". LOD: n/a. LWL: 52'. Draft: 7'7". Beam: 16'2". Rig height: 65'. Freeboard: 2'2". Sail area: 2,200 sq. ft. Sail no.: 5. Tons: 34 grt. Power: 4-71 Detroit Diesel. Hull: wood. Built: 1985-1990. Designer: MHA Design Committee. Builder: Bob Corr.
Coast Guard cert. Dockside attraction.
Crew 4; 9 instructors. Trainees 7 (overnight); 21 (day). Age 12+. Sex co-ed.
Program type Sail training and maritime history for middle school and high school students and adults.
Affiliated institutions The Association for Great Lakes History, ASTA.
Homeport/waters Traverse City, MI/ Northern Great Lakes.
Season May through September.
Cost Maritime Heritage Alliance members only.

The information here is provided as a service only and no warranty or endorsement of any individual programs or vessels by the American Sail Training Association is intended or implied. ASTA is not an agent for any vessels or programs and does not control, inspect or approve vessels or programs. All information in this directory is provided by the owners. Before booking or boarding, confirm important facts with the vessel's owner, including the status of safety certificates, equipment, and the suitability of the vessel or program to your abilities and needs.

*M*AHINA TIRE

Complete vessel information on the *Mahina Tire* was not available at press time.

Please see the Mahina Productions, Inc. listing under the Directory of Programs.

*M*AINE

Maine was built by student apprentices at the Maine Maritime Academy between 1981 and 1985. She serves as a sail training ship for enrolled students and as a roving ambassador for the Museum at special events.

Rig Pinky schooner (two-masted, gaff-rigged).
Contact Maine Maritime Museum Apprenticeshop, 963 Washington St., Bath, ME 04530; (207) 443-1316, fax (207) 443-1665.
Specs Sparred length: 53'. LOA: n/a. LOD: 40'. LWL: 36'. Draft: 6'. Beam: 12'. Rig height: 54'. Freeboard: n/a. Sail area: 1,500 sq. ft. Sail no.: n/a. Tons: 24. Power: 60 hp diesel. Hull: wood. Built: 1985; Bath, ME. Designer: n/a. Builder: Maine Maritime Museum.
Coast Guard cert. n/a.
Crew n/a. Trainees n/a. Age n/a. Sex n/a.
Program type n/a.
Affiliated institutions n/a.
Homeport/waters Bath, ME/ coastal Maine and southern New England.
Season n/a.
Cost Enrolled apprentices only.

MALABAR

Owned and operated by the Traverse Tall Ship Co., the schooner *Malabar* is one of the largest sailing vessels on the Great Lakes. She can accommodate twenty-one overnight guests and forty-seven passengers for day excursions. *Malabar* is fully certified by the U.S. Coast Guard. In conjunction with the Inland Seas Education Association, *Malabar* offers the Schoolship Program (Spring), an environmental, historical and sail training educational experience for junior high school students. The schooner also offers day sails, group charters and a popular floating bed and breakfast package.

Rig Gaff topsail schooner, two-masted.
Contact Traverse Tall Ship Co., 13390 S. West Bay Shore Dr., Traverse City, MI 49684; (616) 941-2000.
Specs Sparred length: 105'. LOA: n/a. LOD: 65'. LWL: 60'. Draft: 8'6". Beam: 21'. Rig height: 75'. Freeboard: 6'. Sail area: 3,000 sq. ft. Sail no.: n/a. Tons: 73 grt. Power: 136 hp diesel. Hull: ferro/steel. Built: 1975; Bath, ME. Designer: M. D. Lee. Builder: Long Reach Shipyard.
Coast Guard cert. Passenger Vessel (Subchapter T).
Crew 7; 6 instructors. Trainees 21 (overnight); 40 (day). Age 11-18. Sex co-ed.
Program type Marine biology, environmental studies and maritime history for middle school students.
Affiliated institutions Inland Seas Education Association.
Homeport/waters Traverse City, MI/ Great Lakes.
Season May to October.
Cost Inquire.

Sailing School Vessels (SSV)... are certified as Subchapter R–Nautical Schools– under Title 46 of the Code of Federal Regulations. An SSV is a vessel of less than 500 gross tons carrying six or more sailing school students or instructors, principally propelled by sail, and operated by a non-profit educational organization exclusively for the purpose of sailing education.

MANITOU

Owned and operated by the Traverse Tall Ship Co., the schooner *Manitou* is one of the largest sailing vessels on the Great Lakes. She can accommodate twenty-four overnight guests and sixty passengers for day excursions. *Manitou* is fully certified by the U.S. Coast Guard. In conjunction with the Inland Seas Education Association, *Manitou* offers the Schoolship Program (Spring), an environmental, historical and sail training educational experience for junior high school students. In addition to other special programs, the schooner *Manitou* offers three- and six-day windjammer cruises in northern Lakes Michigan and Huron.

Rig Gaff topsail schooner, two-masted.
Contact Traverse Tall Ship Co., 13390 S. West Bay Shore Drive, Traverse City, MI 49684; 616 941-2000.
Specs Sparred length: 114'. LOA: n/a. LOD: 77'. LWL: 65'. Draft: 7' (centerboard up); 11' (max.). Beam: 22'. Rig height: 80'. Freeboard: 6'. Sail area: 3,000 sq. ft. Sail no.: n/a. Tons: 82 grt. Power: 150 hp diesel. Hull: steel. Built: 1982; Portsmouth, NH. Designer: Woodin & Marean. Builder: Roger Gagnon Steel Ship Corp.
Coast Guard cert. Passenger Vessel (Subchapter T).
Crew 6; 6 instructors. Trainees 24 (overnight); 56 (day). Age 12-60. Sex co-ed.
Program type Marine biology, environmental studies and maritime history for middle-school through college-level students and adults.
Affiliated institutions Inland Seas Education Association.
Homeport/waters Northport, MI/ Great Lakes.
Season May to October.
Cost Inquire.

BILLET BANK...

As a service to members, ASTA maintains a Billet Bank through which experienced sailors (licensed or not) can be put in touch with ships in need of crew. ASTA members who pay a nominal fee of $5 per year are sent crew requests received from ships. In addition, those enrolled in the Billet Bank are listed as available crew so that ships can reach them.

MARY DAY

Built in 1962 by Harvey Gamage, *Mary Day* combines the best aspects of the New England centerboard coaster with modern design thinking. *Mary Day* operates out of Camden, Maine, in the traditional windjammer trade from late May to early October. She carries thirty passengers on week-long vacation cruises in mid-coast Maine. *Mary Day* is a pure sailing vessel; she has no engine aboard, depending on a small yawl boat when winds fail. She has a large and powerful rig and exhibits outstanding sailing abilities.

Mary Day carries a professional crew of six, including captain, mate, cook, two deck hands and one galley hand. The galley and one deck hand positions are considered entry-level positions, and a great many sailing professionals have started out or gained valuable experience on board the schooner *Mary Day*.

Rig Gaff topsail schooner, two-masted.
Contact Capt. Steve Cobb, Schooner *Mary Day*, P.O. Box 798, Camden, ME 04843; (207) 236-8489, (800) 992-2218.
Specs Sparred length: 125'. LOA: 90'. LOD: n/a. LWL: 80'. Draft: 7' (min.), 15' (max.). Beam: 22'. Rig height: 100'. Freeboard: 5'. Sail area: 5,000 sq. ft. Sail no.: n/a. Tons: 86 grt. Power: none. Hull: n/a. Built: 1962. Designer: Havilah Hawkins. Builder: Harvey Gamage.
Coast Guard cert. Passenger Vessel (Subchapter T).
Crew 6. Trainees 30 (day); 45 (overnight). Age n/a. Sex n/a.
Program type Environmental studies.
Affiliated institutions n/a.
Homeport/waters Camden, ME/ Penobscot Bay, coastal Maine.
Season May to October.
Cost $100 per person per day.

Oceanographic Research Vessels (ORV)... are certified as Subchapter U under the Coast Guard Regulations. An ORV is a vessel employed exclusively in either oceanographic (salt-water) or limnologic (fresh-water) instruction and/or research. ORVs generally will not hire any instructors without proper scientific credentials.

MARYLAND DOVE

Rig Bark, three-masted (lateen mizzen).
Contact Capt. Will Gates, Historic St. Mary's City Commission, P.O. Box 39, St. Mary's City, MD 20686; (301) 862-0982.
Specs Sparred length: 76'. LOA: 76'. LOD: 56'. LWL: 51'. Draft: 6'6". Beam: 16'. Rig height: 59'. Freeboard: n/a. Sail area: 1,965 sq. ft. Sail no.: n/a. Tons: 42 grt. Power: twin 90 hp diesel. Hull: wood. Built: 1977-78; Cambridge, MA. Designer: William Avery Baker. Builder: James B. Richardson.
Coast Guard cert. Uninspected yacht (historic replica ship).
Crew 10. Trainees 7 (overnight); 22 (day). Age 13-70. Sex co-ed.

MAYFLOWER II

Rig Ship, three-masted (lateen mizzen).
Contact John Reed, Plimouth Plantation, Inc., P.O. Box 1620, Plymouth, MA 02360-1620; (508) 746-1622, x250; fax (508) 746-4978.
Specs Sparred length: 136'. LOA: 106'. LOD: n/a. LWL: 85'. Draft: 13'. Beam: 25'. Rig height: 100'. Freeboard: 7'5". Sail area: 5,000 sq. ft. Sail no.: n/a. Tons: 194 grt. Power: n/a. Hull: wood. Built: n/a. Designer: n/a. Builder: n/a.
Coast Guard cert. Passenger Vessel (Subchapter T).
Crew 26. Trainees 49 (day). Age n/a. Sex co-ed.
Program type Maritime history and special education for adults.

MERCANTILE

Rig Gaff schooner, two-masted.
Contact Ray Williamson, Maine Windjammer Cruises, Inc., P.O. Box 617, Camden, ME 04843; (207) 236-2938.
Specs Sparred length: 115'. LOA: 80'. LOD: n/a. LWL: 70'. Draft: 5' (centerboard up); 12' (max.). Beam: 22'6". Rig height: 62'. Freeboard: 4'. Sail area: n/a sq. ft. Sail no.: n/a. Tons: 47 grt. Power: n/a. Hull: wood. Built: 1916. Designer: n/a. Builder: Billings.
Coast Guard cert. Passenger Vessel (Subchapter T).
Crew 5. Trainees 29. Age 16+. Sex co-ed.
Program type Windjammer vacations; informal sail training.

MIKE SEKUL

The *Mike Sekul* is the second and newest of two Biloxi oyster schooner replicas built as part of the Biloxi Schooner Project under the auspices of the Maritime and Seafood Industry Museum. She was launched in April 1994 as part of the effort to preserve the maritime and seafood industry history of the Mississippi Gulf Coast. Money for construction of and fitting out of the *Mike Sekul* and her sister ship Glenn L. Swetman has come from donations by interested individuals, businesses, civic groups and a variety of museum-sponsored fund-raising events.

The *Mike Sekul* is available for charter for 2-1/2 hour, half-day and full-day trips in the Mississippi Sound and to the barrier islands Cat Island, Horn Island and Ship Island. Walk-up day sailing trips are made when she is not under charter. Groups of up to forty-nine passengers can learn about the maritime and seafood industry heritage of the Gulf Coast and about the vessels that got Biloxi's seafood industry started.

Sailing classes are offered through local college physical education departments. In addition, she accommodates weddings, parties, and Elderhostel and school groups. She is also an integral part of the museum's Sea and Sail Adventure Summer Camp.

Rig Gaff topsail schooner, two-masted.
Contact Robin Krohn, Manager, Maritime and Seafood Industry Museum, P.O. Box 1907, Biloxi, MS 39533; (601) 435-6320.
Specs Sparred length: n/a. LOA: 82'9'". LOD: 50'. LWL: n/a. Draft: 4'10". Beam: 17'. Rig height: n/a. Freeboard: n/a. Sail area: 2,499 sq. ft. Sail no.: n/a. Tons: 24. Power: 4-71 Detroit Diesel. Hull: n/a. Built: 1994; Biloxi, MS. Designer: n/a. Builder: Neil Covacevich.
Coast Guard cert. Passenger Vessel (Subchapter T).
Crew 3. Trainees 25 (day). Age 15+. Sex co-ed.
Program type Maritime history for college students and adults; children's summer camp and private charters.
Affiliated institutions William Carey College.
Homeport/waters Biloxi, MS/ coastwise Gulf of Mexico.
Season Year-round.
Cost $15 per person (2-1/2 hours); $13 per person for groups of 20 or more; $400 for 1/2 day charter; $600 for day charter.

MILWAUKEE LAKE SCHOONER

For three centuries the primary method of travel throughout the Great Lakes region was by water. The Lake Schooner Project is committed to re-establishing historical, cultural and recreational bonds between the community and its finest natural resource, Lake Michigan.

Milwaukee Lake Schooner, Ltd. is specifically committed to using the Maritime Center on Milwaukee' lakefront, its' adjacent berth, and the full sized *Lake Schooner*, as an educational tool. The schooner not only will provide a catalyst for renewed interest in maritime education, it will enhance academic study and develop a deeper sense of stewardship for the precious resource that is the Great Lakes. In addition, the schooner will be a promotional tool for the city and state.

During Milwaukee's past, these vessels were built by the thousands along the shore of Lake Michigan; with as many as 30 vessels per day arriving at our port. These schooners established the trading outposts that have become today's cities.

The schooners were based loosely on Baltimore clippers, but differed in many important respects. Great Lakes schooners tended to be longer, somewhat narrower, and utilized a centerboard instead of a keel.

At the Milwaukee Maritime Center, a full-sized reproduction of a Great Lakes schooner is being constructed. The design is based loosely on four Great Lakes schooners built between 1852 and 1868: *The Challenge* (1852), *Clipper City* (1854), *Lucia A. Simpson* (1857), and the *Rouse Simmons* (1868). The ship will be lofted during the winters of 1994 and 1995. The keel will be laid in the spring of 1995. Work is progressing steadily, with completion scheduled for the summer of 1998.

Rig Three masted schooner.
Contact David Falzetti, Milwaukee Maritime Center, 500 N. Harbor Drive, Milwaukee, WI 53202; (414) 276-5664, info. (414) 276-7700, FAX (414)-276-8838.
Specs Sparred length: 125'. LOA: 97'. LOD: 92'. LWL: 86'. Draft: 8'6". Beam: 23'6". Rig height: 95'. Freeboard: 6'8". Sail area: n/a sq. ft. Sail no.: 10. Tons: 97. Power: twin diesel. Hull: wood. Built: not completed. Design: Timothy Graul. Builder: n/a.
Coast Guard cert. Passenger vessel (Subchapter T). Sailing School Vessel (SSV), pending.
Crew 5-7. Trainees 25 (overnight) 40 (day). Age youth and adult. Sex both.
Program type Environmental, youth-at-risk, marine science, public.
Affiliated institutions Milwaukee Public Schools, University of Wisconsin, Wisconsin Department of Natural Resources.
Homeport/waters Milwaukee, WI/ Great Lakes and Eastern United States.

MINNIE V.

Minnie V. is part of America's last fleet of working sail, dredging oysters from Chesapeake Bay in the winter and providing harbor tours and educational programs in the summer. She is owned by the City of Baltimore and managed by the Radcliffe Maritime Museum of the Maryland Historical Society. The summer programs are operated by the Ocean World Institute, Inc., a private, non-profit organization.

Groups of young people participate in the Water's Edge program, hoisting the sails and steering this classic vessel through the Old Port section of Baltimore for an unforgettable experience in social studies and ecology. History, economics and geography come to life as they observe the flow of national and world commerce through one of America's busiest seaports and discover landmarks that played key roles in American history. Teachers or group leaders are supplied with packets of teaching exercises about maritime Baltimore in advance of the visit so that the group can make the most of this unique program.

Activities include visits to the Museum of Industry and a fish trawl. The ship passes historic Fort McHenry, containership terminals, grain and coal docks, shipyards and manufacturing plants important to Baltimore's industrial life. Along the way, they learn something of the life of a sailor, the importance of the maritime world to their own lives, and the importance of keeping the waters clean.

Rig Skipjack sloop.
Contact Robert Keith, Ocean World Institute, Inc., 831 South Bond St., Baltimore, MD 21231; (410) 522-4214.
Specs Sparred length: 69'. LOA: 45'. LOD: n/a. LWL: n/a. Draft: 3'. Beam: 16'. Rig height: 58'. Freeboard: 2'. Sail area: 1,500 sq. ft. Sail no.: n/a. Tons: 12 grt. Power: yawl boat; gas. Hull: wood. Built: 1906; Wenona, Md. Designer: n/a. Builder: n/a.
Coast Guard cert. Passenger Vessel (Subchapter T).
Crew 2. Trainees 24. Age all. Sex co-ed.
Program type Maritime history and environmental studies for children and adults.
Affiliated institutions Maryland Historical Society.
Homeport/waters Baltimore, MD/ Patapsco River.
Season May through September.
Cost $200 per group for 1 1/2 hours; $350 half day; $600 per day.

MISTRESS

Rig Gaff topsail schooner, two-masted.
Contact Ray Williamson, Maine Windjammer Cruises, Inc., P.O. Box 617, Camden, ME 04843; (207) 236-2938.
Specs Sparred length: 60'. LOA: 46'. LOD: n/a. LWL: 40'. Draft: 6'. Beam: 13'. Rig height: 40'. Freeboard: 4'. Sail area: n/a sq. ft. Sail no.: n/a. Tons: 15 grt. Power: diesel. Hull: wood. Built: 1962. Designer: n/a. Builder: n/a.
Coast Guard cert. Uninspected passenger vessel (Subchapter C).
Crew 2. **Trainees** 6. **Age** 16+. **Sex** co-ed.
Program type Windjammer vacations and chartering.

MISTY ISLES

In July 1990, her current owner bought Misty Isles, a 1915 ocean cruiser, and began restoration immediately. In 1992, she returned to duty in Learn-to-Sail day trips with Pacific Currents Sailing Club of Oxnard, California. In 1993, with a new mizzen mast, *Misty Isles* was a Born Again Gaff-Rigged Ketch. Her motto is "Serving Fishers of Men," and current programs are an outgrowth of years of experience with hands-on environmental education and Outward Bound programs.

Misty Isles' sailing Season will be from Thanksgiving through Labor Day, conducting day and weekend sails in California waters. Her 1995 mission is with three primary groups: Promise Keepers, Mt. Zion Missionary Baptist Church in Los Angeles, and Pacific Currents Sailing Club. She will be an outreach vessel working to bring those served by the three groups into the sail training environment.

Promise Keepers, a national Christian men's ministry, will sail with the children of single parent families. The youth ministries of Mt. Zion will develop leadership training programs. The Pacific Currents Sailing Club will provide experienced crew members who will help the programs grow.

From our core program, "Training Leaders Through Seamanship", comes character building experiences: teamwork, discipline, obedience, flexibility, self-reliance, and judgment, both moral and technical. Academic content will be integrated into *Misty Isles'* programs gradually. Marine and environmental studies will focus on the Channel Islands and coastal California and Mexico. A key long range plan is to develop a shipboard program to help adults in preparation for the GED test, the high school equivalency examination. The only cost for sailing adventures on the *Misty Isles* is supplying your own food. The preparation and serving of food underway is part of the teamwork, as is sail handling, navigating, anchoring, and standing watches.

→

Rig Gaff-rigged ketch.
Contact Ray Pike, 3844 W. Channel I. Blvd., Suite 117, Oxnard, CA 93035; (805) 984-2166, (818) 706-6819, or Box 123, Newburyport, MA 01950 (permanent address).
Specs Sparred length: 60'. LOA: 50'. LOD: 50'. LWL: 44". Draft: 9'. Beam: 12'. Rig height: 65'. Freeboard: 3'. Sail area: 1500 ft. Sail no.: n/a. Tons: 30. Power: 80 hp Ford Lehman diesel. Hull: wood. Built: 1915. Designer: n/a. Builder: n/a.
Coast Guard cert. Uninspected yacht.
Crew 3. Trainees 9 (overnight); 21 (day). Age 6 - adult. Sex co-ed.
Program type Special education, environmental, youth-at-risk, seamanship, leadership training.
Homeport/waters 1995: Channel Islands, CA/California and Mexico.
Season Thanksgiving through Labor Day.
Cost None. Guests provide their own food.

MYSTIC CLIPPER

Mystic Clipper is based on the design of a traditional nineteenth-century Baltimore clipper. Together with her near sister ship *Mystic Whaler* (laid up for repairs this season), *Mystic Clipper* takes passengers on cruises of various lengths in the southern New England waters. Following the winds, they are likely to be seen in Newport, Rhode Island, Martha's Vineyard, Nantucket or among the Elizabeth Islands south of Cape Cod.

Rig Gaff schooner, two-masted.
Contact Rita M. Schmidt, Out o' Mystic Schooner Cruises, Inc., 88B Howard Street, New London, CT 06320; (203) 437-0385
Specs Sparred length: n/a. LOA: 125'. LOD: n/a. LWL: 86'. Draft: 7'6". Beam: 26'. Rig height: 78'. Freeboard: n/a. Sail area: n/a sq. ft. Sail no.: n/a. Tons: 100. Power: diesel. Hull: wood. Built: 1983. Designer: Charles Wittholz. Builder: Blount Shipyard.
Coast Guard cert. Passenger for hire.
Crew Captain + 4. Trainees n/a. Age n/a. Sex n/a.
Program type n/a.
Affiliated institutions n/a.
Homeport/waters New London, CT/ Long Island Sound, southern New England.
Season May to November.
Cost $89-$619 per person for one-five days.

NATALIE TODD

The *Natalie Todd* was originally built in 1941 as a two-masted schooner-dragger for commercial offshore fishing on the Grand Banks and Georges Banks off the coast of New England. Former skippers and crew always praised her as a fine and able deepwater vessel. She was a working fishing boat until 1986. She caught cod, haddock, hake, flounder, ocean perch and pollack on one- and two-week trips at sea. In 1987, the *Natalie Todd* was completely rebuilt by Captain Pagels and a crew of Maine shipwrights using Maine oak and pine timbers, and re-rigged as a three-masted schooner.

Rig gaff schooner, three-masted.
Contact Capt. Steven F. Pagels, Schooner Natalie Todd, P.O. Box 8, Cherryfield, ME 04622; (207) 288-4585; (207) 546-2927, fax (207) 546-2023.
Specs Sparred length: n/a. LOA: 129'. LOD: 101'. LWL: 89'. Draft: 10'. Beam: 21'. Rig height: 88'. Freeboard: n/a. Sail area: 3,900 sq. ft. Sail no.: n/a. Tons: 197 grt. Power: diesel. Hull: wood. Built: 1941; Brooklyn, N.Y. Designer: Alan Woods. Builder: Muller Boatworks.
Coast Guard cert. 100 day passengers.
Crew 4. Trainees 34. Age n/a. Sex co-ed.
Program type Two-hour sails, and sail training.
Affiliated institutions American Schooner Association, Maine Working Sail Association.
Homeport/waters Bar Harbor, ME/ Frenchman's Bay, coastal Maine.
Season May through mid-October.
Cost Inquire.

The information here is provided as a service only and no warranty or endorsement of any individual programs or vessels by the American Sail Training Association is intended or implied. ASTA is not an agent for any vessels or programs and does not control, inspect or approve vessels or programs. All information in this directory is provided by the owners. Before booking or boarding, confirm important facts with the vessel's owner, including the status of safety certificates, equipment, and the suitability of the vessel or program to your abilities and needs.

NEHEMIAH

The *Nehemiah* was built in 1971 in Santa Barbara by two brothers. Woodworkers by profession, the brothers spent two years using traditional ship building techniques to transform line-drawing plans into a fifty-seven foot sailing ketch. Built of Port Orford cedar planking on steam-bent oak frames, the boat is primarily as it was when constructed. It remains a fine example of expert craftsmanship, and has proven its seaworthiness by twice circumnavigating the world and cruising the Pacific Ocean.

Crosscurrent is a California non-profit public benefit corporation. Sailing trips can last from a few hours to a few days. Most are within the San Francisco Bay and Delta. Occasional trips run along the coast.

On-board programs are directed towards group involvement with their leaders and are intended to complement their goals. types of groups include church youth, police activity leagues, youth-at-risk, and sea scouts. The experiences can be transferred to every-day situations.

Seamanship, maritime experience, oceanography and ecology serve as a backdrop for the program structure while emphasis is placed on personal growth and responsibility in the group living situation. On-board education is further enriched by special opportunities such as harbor festivals, races, companionship, and semi-predictable happenings - such as sighting a sea lion, maneuvering in a crowded channel, being seasick, and taking part in search and rescue.

Rig Ketch.
Contact Crosscurrent Voyages, Capt. Rod Phillips, 92 Seabreeze Drive, Richmond, CA 94804; (510) 234-8202.
Specs Sparred length 57'. LOA: 50'. LOD: 50'. LWL: n/a. Draft: 6'6". Beam: 13'6". Rig height: 58'. Freeboard: 4'6". Sail area: n/a. Sail No.: n/a. Tons: 27 grt. Power: 85 hp Perkins. Hull: wood. Built 1971; Santa Barbara, CA. Designer: modified William Garden. Builder: J. Meyr.
Coast Guard cert. Passenger Vessel, (Subchapter T).
Crew 2 Trainees 15 (overnight; 25 (daysails). Age: n/a. Sex: Co-ed.
Program type Marine biology, environmental, youth-at-risk, adjunct character-building for other youth programs.
Affiliated institutions None.
Homeport/waters Richmond, CA/ coastwise, 20 miles from safe harbor, San Francisco area.
Cost Inquire.

NEW WAY

The vision quest – a challenging wilderness experience – represented the Plains Indians youth's passage from adolescence to adulthood. For angry and troubled twentieth-century youths, there is often no clear-cut understanding of the responsibilities of adulthood; rather there is the confusion of adolescence. VisionQuest provides programs that stress challenge, honor, self-discipline and the work ethic.

The VisionQuest sailing camps and OceanQuest have proven themselves to be extremely effective. The basic tenets of sail training, the development of a sense of responsibility, rigorous self-discipline and respect for authority are the basic treatment aims for a majority of troubled youth. Generally, twenty wilderness camp graduates are tapped to participate in OceanQuest. Their challenge is to complete a training course.

The *New Way* was originally put into service in 1939 as the Western Union to lay and repair underwater telephone and telegraph cables in the seas near Key West, Florida. She was acquired by VisionQuest in 1984.

Former name ex-*Western Union*.
Rig Gaff topsail schooner, two-masted.
Contact VisionQuest National, Ltd., P.O. Box 447, Exton, PA 19341; (215) 458-0800.
Specs Sparred length: n/a. LOA: 130'. LOD: n/a. LWL: 96'. Draft: 7'6". Beam: 23'6". Rig height: 96'. Freeboard: n/a. Sail area: 5,000 sq. ft. Sail no.: n/a. Tons: 91. Power: twin diesels. Hull: wood. Built: 1939; Key West, Fla. Designer: n/a. Builder: n/a.
Coast Guard cert. n/a.
Crew n/a. Trainees 20. Age n/a. Sex n/a.
Program type n/a.
Affiliated institutions n/a.
Homeport/waters Philadelphia, PA/ northeast U.S. and Canada (summer); southeast U.S., Gulf Coast and Bahamas (winter).
Season Year-round.
Cost Participation by reference through a cooperating agency.

Attraction vessels.. Generally speaking, attraction vessels are museum ships tied up to a dock, usually but not always on a permanent basis. Although an attraction vessel's operators are entitled to charge admission to visitors or fees for programs conducted while the ship is at the dock, attraction vessels cannot charge trainees, passengers or guests for any use of the vessel under way.

NIAGARA, U.S. Brig

The *Niagara* is a working vessel operated by the Pennsylvania Historical and Museum Commission to educate the public about the ships and sailors of the War of 1812. She has been officially designated as The Flagship of the Commonwealth of Pennsylvania.

On September 10, 1813, a small squadron of nine warships under the command of Commodore Oliver Hazard Perry defeated a British squadron of ships near Put-In Bay. This naval engagement gave control of Lake Erie to the United States. Perry's report of the victory — "We have met the enemy and they are ours..." and his battle flag emblazoned with the legend "Don't give up the ship" are the best known remembrances of this battle. The present Niagara is a reconstruction built in 1988-90, and has auxiliary power and modern navigational equipment.

Niagara is inspected as an attraction vessel in port, and sails as an uninspected yacht. Her mission is to present living history, which in turn requires training of volunteer crew to sail the ship. *Niagara's* typical schedule is two day sails per week and several weeks of voyaging to other ports for public visitation, usually a four-day passage and three days in port.

Rig Brig.
Contact Capt. Walter Rybka, U.S. Brig Niagara, Pennsylvania Historical and Museum Commission, 164 East Front St., Erie, PA 16502; (814) 871-4596.
Specs Sparred length: 198'. LOA: 123'. LOD: 116'. LWL: 110'. Draft: 11'. Beam: 32'6". Rig height: 120'. Freeboard: 4'. Sail area: 12,665 sq. ft. Sail no.: n/a. Tons: 162 grt. Power: twin 180 hp diesel. Hull: wood. Built: 1988. Designer: Melbourne Smith. Builder: Melbourne Smith.
Coast Guard cert. Uninspected yacht and Attraction Vessel.
Crew 44. Trainees 20 professionals, 20 volunteers. Age 16-80. Sex co-ed.
Program type Maritime history for adults.
Affiliated institutions n/a.
Homeport/waters Erie, PA/ coastwise and Great Lakes.
Season June to September.
Cost $15 for membership in the Flagship Niagara League.

NIGHTHAWK

Rig Gaff schooner, two-masted.
Contact Capt. Martin D. Weiss, Schooner Nighthawk Cruises, 1715 Thames St., Box 38153, Baltimore, MD 21231; (410) 276-SHIP.
Specs Sparred length: 82'. LOA: 82'. LOD: 65'. LWL: 60'. Draft: 5' Centerboard: 11'. Beam: 20'. Rig height: 107'. Freeboard: 5'. Sail area: 2,000 sq. ft. Sail no.: n/a. Tons: 45 grt. Power: twin 120 hp diesels. Hull: steel. Built: 1980. Designer: Harold Haglund, Florida. Builder: Harold Haglund, Florida.
Coast Guard cert. Passenger Vessel (Subchapter T).
Crew 3. Trainees 10 (overnight); 49 (day). Age n/a. Sex n/a.
Program type Passenger vessel.

NINA

These replicas of the *Nina*, the *Pinta*, and the *Santa Maria* are the ships that toured the gulf and East coasts of the U.S. in the spring and summer of 1992, for the Quincentenary of Christopher Colombus' first voyage west. The ships were built by the Spanish government to retrace his voyage to the New World to create a greater awareness and understanding of the links that unite Spain and America.

The Corpus Christi Museum of Science and History houses artifacts from one of the oldest known Spanish shipwrecks in the western hemisphere. Ships of Discovery, Inc., marine archaeologists who excavate age of discovery wrecks, are housed there. The main exhibit of the is from the several ships wrecked on Padre Island in April 1554. The impact of the "discovery" on the indigenous peoples of the Americas, and their impact on European cultures will be grandly displayed in the Smithsonian Institution's "Seeds of Change" exhibit, scheduled to open at the Corpus Christi Museum in October of 1995. This 10,000 square foot exhibit traces the exchange of diseases, corn, potatoes, horses, and sugar, between Spain and the United States.

The fleet is berthed in Corpus Christi under a lease agreement between the Columbus Fleet Association, a nonprofit organization in Corpus Christi, and the Spanish government through the Spain '92 Foundation, a non-profit organization in Washington, DC, set up to promote a better understanding and closer relationship between Spain and the United States. The Columbus Fleet Association sail the *Nina* in Corpus Christi Bay on training cruises. The Association has applied to the USCG for Sailing School Vessel Certification.

Rig Caravel.
Contact Capt. David Hiott, Fleet Captain, Las Carabelas Columbus Fleet Association, Corpus Christi Museum of Science and History, Corpus Christi, TX 78401; (512) 882-1260.
Specs Sparred length: 85'. LOA: 70'. LOD: 64'. LWL: 60'. Draft: 6'6". Beam: 21'. Rig height: 57'. Freeboard: 3'. Sail area: 1,507 sq. ft. Sail no.: n/a. Tons: 57 grt. Power: 120 hp, 3209 Cat. Hull: pine and oak. Built: 1989. Designer: José Maria Martinez Hidalgo, Barcelona Maritime Museum. Builder: Naval Shipyard, Cartagena, Spain.
Coast Guard cert. Attraction Vessel, application in process for Sailing School Vessel.
Crew 3. Trainees 15-20 volunteers per trip. Age 14-70+. Sex co-ed.
Program type Maritime history.
Affiliated institutions Corpus Christi Museum of Science and History.
Homeport/waters Corpus Christi, TX/ Corpus Christi Bay.
Season Year-round.
Cost $5 dockside visit.

NORFOLK

The skipjack *Norfolk* was built at Deal Island, Maryland, in 1900 and christened the *George W. Collier*. She plied her trade, dredging oysters, for many years. Under Maryland law, then and now, oysters could be harvested from the Chesapeake Bay only under sail. Thus, an active fleet of skipjacks still survives on the upper Bay. Skipjacks were introduced on the Bay in about 1860. They are identified by their hard chines, large centerboard, sloop rig, and a foresail set on a bowsprit.

In the 1960's, the Allegheny Beverage Company purchased the skipjack, repaired her, and rechristened her the *Allegheny*. She sailed the Chesapeake Bay under that name as an ambassador for ecology until, in 1978, she was donated to the City of Norfolk and rechristened the *Norfolk*. The *Norfolk* was rebuilt and refitted as a result of a city grant from the Dalis Foundation in 1990. She is now operated by the City of Norfolk Parks and Recreation Department in cooperation with qualified volunteers, Sea Scouts, and Nautical Adventures, Inc.

The skipjack is used for sail training cruises, ambassador trips to other ports, activities with other Sea Explorer ships, youth-at-risk programs, and work parties for the ship's care and maintenance under the guidance and instruction of a licensed skipper and several adult advisors. The Explorers also help raise funds for her upkeep and operation by holding events such as the annual Downtown Dock Party.

The *Norfolk* is U.S. Coast Guard inspected and fully equipped for the safety and comfort of her crew.

NORFOLK continued

Former name Ex-*Allegheny*, ex-*Norfolk*, ex-*George W. Collier*.
Rig Chesapeake Bay Skipjack.
Contact Betty Webb, City of Norfolk Parks and Recreation, 501 Boush Street, Norfolk, VA 23510; (804) 441-2400.
Specs Sparred length: 71'. LOA: 58'. LOD: n/a. LWL: 51'. Draft: 3'-7'. Beam: 15'7". Rig height: 61'. Freeboard: 2'6". Sail area: 1,800 sq. ft. Sail no.: n/a. Tons: 10. Power: diesel. Hull: wood. Built: 1900; Deal Island, MD. Designer: n/a. Builder: n/a.
Coast Guard cert. Passenger vessel (Subchapter T).
Crew 2. Trainees 6 (overnight); 18 (day). Age 14-21. Sex co-ed.
Program type Youth emphasis, youth-at-risk related programs, maritime history, ambassador for the city of Norfolk, and environmental studies.
Affiliated institutions Sea Scout Ship No. 6.
Homeport/waters Norfolk, VA/Chesapeake Bay.
Season n/a.
Cost Scout training: no cost.

NORFOLK REBEL

Captain Lane Briggs's "Tugantine" is a favorite flagship for sail assisted working vessels and is credited with a "circumnavigation of Virginia," with sail training and Tall Ships events along the way in 1984 and 1994.

Rig Gaff schooner, two-masted.
Contact Rebel Marine Service, Inc., 1553 Bayville St., Norfolk, VA., 23503; (804) 588-6022.
Specs Sparred length: 62'. LOA: 54'. LOD: 51'. LWL: 50'. Draft: 6'. Beam: 12'. Rig height: 65'. Freeboard: n/a. Sail area: 1,300 sq. ft. Sail no.: n/a. Tons: 38. Power: diesel. Hull: steel. Built: 1981. Designer: Merritt Walter. Builder: Howdy Bailey.
Coast Guard cert. Commercial towing and salvage.
Crew n/a. Trainees, volunteer crew upon occasion. Age n/a. Sex n/a.
Program type n/a.
Affiliated institutions n/a.
Homeport/waters Norfolk, VA/ Atlantic coast, Chesapeake Bay, and Great Lakes.
Season Year-round.
Cost Inquire.

NORSEMAN

Built in 1992, the Leif Ericson Viking Ship *Norseman* offers people a glimpse of Viking culture. With its crew dressed in full Viking regalia, the *Norseman* makes appearances at events that commemorate Leif Ericson Day as well as events that celebrate Scandinavian culture.

The *Norseman* has participated in many sailing events, including the 1994 Kalmar Nyckel Tall Ships Festival and OPSAIL '92. With floodlights illuminating her dragon head, and strings of lights outlining her hull, rigging, and tail, the *Norseman* has also made impressive appearances at several after-dark parades. Members and Friends of the *Norseman* often join together for picnics and dinners to share their interests in the Viking culture and Scandinavian heritage.

Rig Single square sail.
Contact Dennis Johnson, President, 511 E. Mt. Pleasant Avenue, Philadelphia, PA 19119, (215) 242-3063; Captain David Segermark, 144 Ridgefield Road, Newtown Square, PA 19073, (610) 356-3723.
Specs Sparred length: 40'. LOA: 40'. LOD: 36'. LWL: 30'. Draft: 3'. Beam: 9'. Rig height: 25'. Freeboard: 4'. Sail area: 297 sq. ft. Sail no.: 1. Tons: 2 grt. Power: Outboard, 35 hp. Hull: fiberglass. Built: 1992. Designer and Builder: Applecraft, Inc., Isle of Man, United Kingdom.
Coast Guard cert. Uninspected yacht, documented.
Crew 7-12. **Trainees** 2-4 (day sails). Age 18-80. Sex co-ed.
Program type Ethnic education.
Affiliated institutions Leif Ericson Viking Ship, Inc.
Homeport/waters Delaware River (Philadelphia, Wilmington, Newcastle), Hudson River and New York Harbor; Chesapeake Bay; New Jersey shore. Ship is trailerable.
Season Late spring, summer, fall.
Cost Not established.

ASTA's Mission

"To encourage character building through sail training, promote sail training to the American public, and support education under sail."

OMF ONTARIO

An 85' steel schooner is under construction at the Oswego Maritime Foundation's Boating Education Center, the site of a ship-building center on Lake Ontario in the 1800s. Traditional in appearance, the schooner will be the focal point of the Education Through Involvement program and serve as a floating classroom for public service awareness about the Great Lakes. Each three-hour on-board experience will include activities about the history, heritage, resources and ecology of the Great Lakes for school children, community groups and senior citizens. The hull was launched July 2, 1994. Fitting out is expected to take another two years, with the ship being placed into service in 1996.

Rig Gaff topsail schooner, two-masted.
Contact Henry Spang, Vice President and Education Through Involvement (ETI) Director, Oswego Maritime Foundation, McCrobie Building, 41 Lake St., Oswego, NY 13126; (315) 342-5753.
Specs Sparred length: 85'. LOA: 65'. LOD: 60'. LWL: 50'. Draft: 8'. Beam: 16'. Rig height: 70'. Freeboard: 5'. Sail area: 2,000 sq. ft. Sail no.: n/a. Tons: 42 grt. Power: 100 hp diesel. Hull: steel. Built: 1994. Designer: Francis MacLaclan, N.A. Builder: Volunteers.
Coast Guard cert. Passenger Vessel (Subchapter T).
Crew 6. Trainees 25. Age 10+. Sex co-ed.
Program type Great Lakes history, heritage and environmental studies.
Affiliated institutions n/a.
Homeport/waters Oswego, NY.
Season Spring, summer, fall.
Cost Public service program.

The information here is provided as a service only and no warranty or endorsement of any individual programs or vessels by the American Sail Training Association is intended or implied. ASTA is not an agent for any vessels or programs and does not control, inspect or approve vessels or programs. All information in this directory is provided by the owners. Before booking or boarding, confirm important facts with the vessel's owner, including the status of safety certificates, equipment, and the suitability of the vessel or program to your abilities and needs.

PACIFIC SWIFT

Pacific Swift, a 111' topsail schooner modelled on the brig *Swift of 1778*, was built at EXPO '86 in Vancouver, British Columbia, as a working exhibit at the World's Fair. Since her completion in 1988, she has sailed over 68,000 deep-sea miles, crossing both the Pacific and Atlantic twice in the course of her offshore sail training programs.

During the summer months she usually returns to the Pacific Northwest, where she is engaged in ten-day trips with SALTS' other training ship, the Grand Banks schooner *Robertson II*.

Both vessels take over a thousand young people to sea each year. These teenagers participate in all facets of shipboard life from bosun's chores to helmsmanship, with formal instruction in navigation, pilotage, seamanship and small boat handling.

Rooted in Christian values, SALTS believes that training under sail provides the human spirit a real chance to develop and mature.

Rig Square topsail schooner, two-masted.
Contact Capt. Martyn J. Clark, Executive Director, Sail and Life Training Society (SALTS), P.O. Box 5014, Station B, Victoria, British Columbia V8R 6N3 Canada; (604) 383-6811; fax (604) 383-7781.
Specs Sparred length: 111'. LOA: 78'. LOD: n/a. LWL: 65'. Draft: 10'. Beam: 20'6". Rig height: 90'. Freeboard: n/a. Sail area: 4,111 sq. ft. Sail no.: n/a. Tons: 98. Power: diesel. Hull: wood. Built: 1986; Vancouver, British Columbia. Designer: traditional. Builder: SALTS.
Coast Guard cert. Canadian Passenger Vessel; Sail Training Vessel.
Crew 5. Trainees 30. Age 13-25. Sex co-ed.
Program type Maritime history and nautical instruction.
Affiliated institutions Sail and Life Training Society.
Homeport/waters Victoria, B.C./ Pacific Northwest, North and South Pacific, Caribbean and Atlantic.
Season Year-round.
Cost Can$55 per day per trainee.

*P*ATHFINDER

The STV *Pathfinder* is a purpose built sail training vessel operating primarily on the Great Lakes. She has a complement of twenty-six comprised of fifteen new trainees, three petty officers, bosun's mate, bosun, three watch officers and an executive officer, all between the ages of fourteen and eighteen. The captain is the only adult on board.

In a hands-on program aboard *Pathfinder* and her sister ship *Playfair*, trainees are encouraged to learn by doing, and progress is monitored by the TBI five-level grade standards in use since 1978. Officers are graduates of the Seaman Program and the Winter Training Program where they attend lectures on seamanship, navigation and safety, and ship's systems while doing the bulk of the maintenance on the ship. Every year each ship sails over 4,000 miles, spends in excess of forty full nights at sea and introduces one hundred fifty trainees to the rigors of life aboard ship while visiting numerous ports all over the Great Lakes.

Toronto Brigantine also has a lead-up program for twelve to thirteen year olds aboard two 30' sloops sailing on Lake Ontario and the St. Lawrence River. Under the motto "Building character through adventure," Toronto Brigantine has been taking youth to sea since 1963, in the belief that hard work and responsibility at a young age create better citizens for the future.

Rig Brigantine.
Contact Gordon Laco, Toronto Brigantine, Inc. (TBI), 283 Queens Quay West, Toronto, Ontario M5V 1A2 Canada; (416) 203-9949.
Specs Sparred length: 72'. LOA: 60'. LOD: n/a. LWL: 45'. Draft: 8'. Beam: 15'3". Rig height: 54'. Freeboard: 4'. Sail area: 2,400 sq. ft. Sail no.: n/a. Tons: 32 grt. Power: 100 bhp diesel. Hull: steel. Built: 1962; Kingston, Ontario. Designer: Francis A. Maclachlan. Builder: Kingston Shipyards.
Coast Guard cert. Sail Training Vessel (Canadian).
Crew 10. Trainees 18 (overnight); 25 (day). Age 14-18. Sex co-ed.
Program type Seamanship, leadership training.
Affiliated institutions Canadian Sail Training Association, ASTA.
Homeport/waters Toronto, Ont./ Great Lakes.
Season April to November (sailing); shoreside winter program.
Cost Can$60 per person per day; inquire for group rates.

PATRICIA DIVINE

Patricia Divine is a square topsail schooner combining traditional lines with luxurious interior and state-of-the-art technology. She provides sail training and charter opportunities for groups of twenty-four or less in the Chesapeake Bay.

Rig Gaff topsail schooner, two-masted.
Contact Capt. Helmut Hawkins, Box 25, 1000 Water St., SW, Washington, DC, 20024; (202) 488-7353.
Specs Sparred length: 69'5". LOA: n/a. LOD: n/a. LWL: 40'5". Draft: 6'9". Beam: 14'8". Rig height: 58'6". Freeboard: n/a. Sail area: 1,800 sq. ft. Sail no.: n/a. Tons: n/a. Power: 85 hp diesel. Hull: steel. Built: 1987; Norfolk, VA. Designer: Merrit Walter. Builder: Marine Metals.
Coast Guard cert. n/a.
Crew n/a. Trainees 24. Age n/a. Sex n/a.
Program type n/a.
Affiliated institutions n/a.
Homeport/waters Washington, DC/ Chesapeake Bay.
Season n/a.
Cost n/a.

PICARA

The Nauset Sea Explorer group celebrates more than forty years of sail training. This program teaches seamanship and sailing to young people between the ages of fourteen and twenty through education and annual cruises along the New England Coast. While on extended cruises, each scout takes part in every aspect of the voyage, from cooking and planning meals to navigation and sail repair, to actually sailing the boat. The group has chartered for a week-long cruise in the Virgin Islands each winter, and undertakes summer cruises along the New England Coast. They also operate two 17' sailboats and a 21' Boston Whaler. They

PICARA continued

have participated in such tall ships gatherings as the New York World's Fair 1964, Montreal's Expo '67, OpSail '76 for the nation's bicentennial, Boston's 350th anniversary in 1980, and the culminating events of the Grand Regatta 1992 Columbus Quincentenary in both New York and Boston.

Rig Sloop
Contact Capt. Michael F. Allard, Nauset Sea Explorers, Boy Scouts of America, Allard Construction, Inc., P.O. Box 1236, Orleans, MA 02653; (508) 255-5260.
Specs Sparred length: 36'. LOA: 36'. LOD: n/a. LWL: 28'. Draft: 5'5". Beam: 12'. Rig height: 49'. Freeboard: 4'. Sail area: 750 sq. ft. Sail no.: n/a. Tons: 15 grt. Power: n/a. Hull: n/a. Built: n/a. Designer: n/a. Builder: n/a.
Coast Guard cert. Uninspected yacht.
Crew 2. **Trainees** 9 (overnight); 18 (day). **Age** 14-20. **Sex** co-ed.
Program type Maritime history and environmental studies for high school students and Sea Explorer groups.
Affiliated institutions Sea Explorers, BSA.
Homeport/waters Orleans, MA/ Massachusetts Bay and southern New England.
Season n/a.
Cost $100-$200 per trainee per week depending on trip.

PICTON CASTLE

This ship, the Barque *Picton Castle*, will be devoted to making long voyages with expense sharing amateur crew under the direction of experiences professionals. The first voyage planned is an eighteen-month around the world voyage, followed by shorter voyages to the South Pacific, the Canadian Maritimes, Europe, the West Indies, and around the world again. The ship, to be rigged as a three-masted Barque, was built in England in 1928 of riveted steel, employing the finest in old world design and craftsmanship. She will be a safe and comfortable home afloat for a few lucky adventurers under the experienced sailing ship master Captain Daniel Moreland.

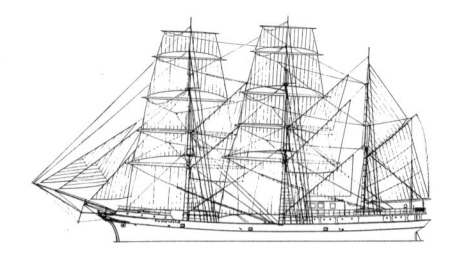

The mission of the *Picton Castle* is to take folks deep sea as crew in a strong, well found square-rigged ship to learn the arts of the seafarer and see the world. The vessel also has a 200 ton cargo hold for trading goods and supplies throughout the islands of the tropics.

The *Picton Castle* was recently delivered to the States on a 6,000 mile "shake down" cruise on her way to refitting as a world voyaging Barque in Lunenburg, Nova Scotia.

Rig Barque.
Contact Daniel D. Moreland, Master, Box 18, Rowayton, CT 06853; tel (203) 838-7894, fax (203) 866-0182.
Specs Sparred length: 178'. LOA: 146'. LOD: 140. LWL: 130'. Draft: 14' loaded. Beam: 24'. Rig height: 100'. Freeboard: 5'. Sail area: 11,000 sq. ft. Sail no.: 5. Tons: 299 grt. Power: 700 hp Burmeister & Wain Alpha diesel. Hull: riveted steel, hard pine decks. Built: 1828. Designer: n/a. Builder: Cochranes; Selby, England.
Coast Guard cert. Bureau Vevitas.
Crew 10. Trainees none (day sails); 35 (overnight). Age 17-65. Sex co-ed.
Program type Deep water square rig sail training.
Affiliated institutions n/a.
Homeport/waters New York/ ocean waters, cruising areas are the tropics and Northern Europe.
Season Year-round.
Cost $50 to $100.

PILGRIM

The *Pilgrim* is a full-scale replica of the ship immortalized by Richard Henry Dana in his American seafaring classic, *Two Years Before the Mast*. The ship has been fully restored by the Orange County Marine Institute and is kept in sailing condition by her all-volunteer crew of 23.

During the months of September to June, the Institute offers a unique living history program for elementary and junior high school students. The life aboard ship as seen by Dana is dramatically recreated by a crew in costume and in character for the young "green hands." They perform the everyday tasks of a common seaman under the guidance of a stern and sometimes demanding captain. The program is fully subscribed and operates more than 250 nights of the year. In the summer, the *Pilgrim's* decks come alive with the sights and sounds of the sea, as audiences seated as "sailors of old" are entertained by highly acclaimed theatrical or musical performances.

In September, the *Pilgrim* leads the Southern California Tallship Festival, an annual gathering of large sailing vessels operating in local waters. Participating vessels sail along the coast and into Dana Point Harbor in a spectacular tall ship parade amid a flotilla of spectator boats. The festival is carried live on local television to increase awareness and support

→

PILGRIM continued

for California's nautical heritage. The *Pilgrim* is dedicated to a unique brand of experience under sail. Those who work with her believe that, "Sometimes the best way to see the future is to glimpse the past."

Rig Brig.
Contact Daniel T. Stetson, Director of Maritime Affairs, Orange County Marine Institute, 24200 Dana Point Harbor Drive, Dana Point, CA 92629; (714) 496-2274; fax (714) 496-4296.
Specs Sparred length: n/a. LOA: 121'. LOD: n/a. LWL: 98'. Draft: 8'6". Beam: 23'. Rig height: 96'. Freeboard: n/a. Sail area: 7,600 sq. ft. Sail no.: n/a. Tons: 99. Power: diesel. Hull: wood. Built: 1945, Denmark. Designer: Raymond Wallace. Builder: A. Nielsen.
Coast Guard cert. Uninspected yacht.
Crew 23. Trainees 26. Age n/a. Sex n/a.
Program type Maritime living history and environmental studies.
Affiliated institutions n/a.
Homeport/waters Dana Point, CA/ Pacific coast.
Season Year-round.
Cost Inquire.

PILOT

Pilot is one of the last of the great American Gloucester Fishing Schooners. She was designed originally to race the Nova Scotian schooner *Bluenose*, but was purchased by the Boston Harbor Pilots Association while still under construction in 1924. *Pilot* was never to race *Bluenose*, but if she had been a contender, her speed and stability might well have returned the Cup to the United States and the Gloucester fleet. *Pilot* is a historic vessel that carried the Boston Lights Pilots for 52 years. *Pilot* was the only schooner launched by a child with a bouquet of flowers. She is now on her second voyage from New England to California to work with people of all ages who want to learn to sail and appreciate such a magnificent vessel. *Pilot* will offer sail training and educational classes to help people and our planet. *Pilot* arrived in San Diego April, 1993. She is currently being certified for school ship US Coast Guard certification, and it is estimated that she will be ready for service in the Winter and Spring of 1995.

Rig Gaff topsail schooner, two-masted.
Contact Mr. E. N. Paulsen, Schooner Pilot Trust, 1220 Rosecrans Street, Suite 308, San Diego, CA 92106; (805) 686-4484 (phone/FAX); (619) 226-2100.
Specs Sparred length: 154'. LOA: 154'. LOD: 126'. LWL: 120'. Draft: 14'. Beam: 25'6". Rig height: 120'. Freeboard: 5'. Sail area: 10,800 sq. ft. Sail no.: n/a. Tons: 140 grt; 65 net. Power: Twin diesels. Hull: wood. Built: 1924; Essex, CT. Designer: W. Starling Burgess. Builder: James Tarr Yard, Essex, MA.
Coast Guard cert. n/a.
Crew n/a. Trainees n/a. Age n/a. Sex n/a.
Program type n/a.
Affiliated institutions n/a.
Homeport/waters San Diego, CA/ coastal California.
Season n/a.

PIONEER

The *Pioneer* was built as an iron sloop in 1885 by the Pioneer Iron Company of Marcus Hook, Pennsylvania. She was the first iron sloop built in the United States, and is the only surviving American iron-hulled sailing vessel.

Pioneer spent her first ten years bringing sand from various points on the Delaware River to a large iron foundry in Chester, Pennsylvania. Converted to a schooner in 1895, she continued to haul sand on the Delaware for a plaster company until 1900. She was operated by stone merchants for three more years before receiving an engine. She continued to haul raw materials: coal, lumber, brick, and eventually oil. She was towed to Massachusetts in 1930, and worked as a small tanker in Boston and New Bedford until 1956, when the old iron-riveted hull became so porous that tanker certification was no longer possible. She then went to work for a marine contracting company in Woods Hole, Massachusetts.

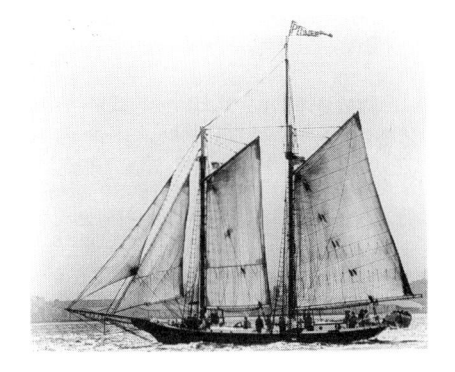

After several more years, her hull had deteriorated to the point where she was unserviceable. In 1966 her owner, Dan Clark, realizing her history, sold the hull to his friend Russell Grinnell, Jr., a dockbuilder from Gloucester, Massachusetts. Grinnell saw her through a complete restoration to a functional schooner based on traditional usage, but taking advantage of more modern materials. He used *Pioneer* in his dock building business until his death in 1970; shortly thereafter, she was donated to the South Street Seaport Museum. For her first years there, she carried New York City

PIONEER continued

residents of drug rehabilitation centers up the New England coast for two weeks at a time.

The *Pioneer* is now dedicated to recreating nineteenth-century sailing for the public. She offers public sails, private charters, programs for the handicapped and school programs, carrying a crew of professionals and volunteers. She operates in the waters of New York Harbor during the summer months, and she generally heads south in the fall to tour some of her old home waters: the Delaware and Chesapeake Bays.

Rig Gaff schooner, two-masted.
Contact Eric Rice, South Street Seaport Museum, 207 Front St., New York, NY 10038; (212) 748-8600.
Specs Sparred length: 102'. LOA: 64'5". LOD: n/a. LWL: 58'11". Draft: 4'8". Beam: 21'6". Rig height: 56'6"; 76' with topmast. Freeboard: 3'. Sail area: 2,700 sq. ft. Sail no.: 4. Tons: 43 grt; 77 dwt; 37 net. Power: 135 hp diesel. Hull: originally iron, replated in steel. Built: 1885; Marcus Hook, NJ (rebuilt 1968; Somerset, MA). Designer: n/a. Builder: Pioneer Iron Company.
Coast Guard cert. Passenger Vessel (Subchapter T).
Crew 4-12; 2 instructors. Trainees 40 (day). Age 2nd to 12th grade (7-18). Sex co-ed.
Program type Maritime history and special education programs for middle- and high-school students.
Affiliated institutions New York City public school system and various private schools.
Homeport/waters New York, NY/ New York Harbor, Hudson River and Atlantic coast.
Season Spring, summer and fall.
Cost $200 per 90-minute group program.

PLAYFAIR

Rig Brigantine.
Contact Gordon Laco, Toronto Brigantine, Inc. (TBI), 283 Queens Quay West, Toronto, Ontario M5V 1A2 Canada; (416) 203-9949.
Specs Sparred length: 72'. LOA: 60'. LOD: n/a. LWL: 45'. Draft: 8'. Beam: 15'3". Rig height: 54'. Freeboard: 4'. Sail area: 2,400 sq. ft. Sail no.: n/a. Tons: 32 grt. Power: 100 bhp diesel. Hull: steel. Built: 1972; Kingston, Ontario. Designer: Francis A. Maclachlan. Builder: Canada Dredge and Dock Co.

Coast Guard cert. Training ship (Canadian).
Crew 10. **Trainees** 18 (overnight); 26 (day). **Age** 14-18. **Sex** co-ed.
Program type Seamanship, leadership training.
Affiliated institutions Canadian Sail Training Association, ASTA.
Homeport/waters Toronto, Ont./ Great Lakes.
Season April to November (sailing); shoreside winter program.
Cost Can$60 per person per day; inquire for group rates.

See program description under Pathfinder.

*P*RIDE

Southern Windjammer, Ltd., offers a wide range of both recreational and sail training programs aboard the southern built schooner *Pride*. Sail training programs are individually designed for groups of up to forty-nine for day cruises and twenty overnight. Nautical and marine science programs have been designed for scouts, church groups, school classes, corporate employees, teachers, college credit courses and the like. Full participation in all functions of the vessel are encouraged. Cruises range from two-hour introduction-to-sail cruises to five-day cruises. The *Pride* also offers regular cruises and private charters. While capable of long-range cruising, the Pride typically sails the coastal waters of South Carolina and Georgia anchoring each night in quiet inland waters. Southern Windjammer, Ltd., is constructing a 135', 100 ton, four masted schooner which will be sailing out of Chicago, Illinois in the summers and Charleston, South Carolina in the winters.

Rig Gaff topsail schooner, three-masted.
Contact Capt. Robert Marthai, Ph.D., Southern Windjammer, Ltd., 2044 Wappoo Hall Road, Charleston, SC 29412-2057; (803) 795-1180.
Specs Sparred length: 84'. LOA: 65'. LOD: n/a. LWL: 60'. Draft: 6'. Beam: 18'. Rig height: 61'. Freeboard: n/a. Sail area: 2,200 sq. ft. Sail no.: 9. Tons: 57 grt. Power: 80 hp diesel. Hull: steel. Built: 1988; Charleston, SC. Designer: n/a. Builder: MTI/SW.
Coast Guard cert. Passenger Vessel (Subchapter T).
Crew 2-6. **Trainees** 20 (overnight); 49 day. **Age** 10+. **Sex** co-ed.
Program type Nautical Science for middle and highschool students and adults.
Affiliated institutions n/a.
Homeport/waters Charleston, SC/ n/a.
Season March to January.
Cost $10-$75 per person depending on cruise.

PRIDE OF BALTIMORE II

The *Pride of Baltimore II* is a topsail schooner built to the lines of an 1812-era Baltimore Clipper. She is owned by the State of Maryland and operated by Pride of Baltimore, Inc. *Pride of Baltimore II* sails as a goodwill ambassador of the State of Maryland, City of Baltimore, and the Port of Baltimore, and her primary mission is to promote tourism and economic development.

Pride of Baltimore II is licensed by the U.S. Coast Guard as a Subchapter T passenger vessel. She is available for charter, for dockside and sailing receptions anywhere on her schedule, and she can accommodate up to six passengers for hire between ports of call. Passengers are encouraged to fully participate in the operation of the vessel alongside the professional crew.

The *Pride of Baltimore II* sails year-round with two full-time rotating captains and a crew of eleven. Positions include first mate (license required), second mate, bosun, cook, engineer/deckhand and six deckhands. Preference in hiring is given to Maryland residents. The *Pride of Baltimore II* maintains an international sailing schedule, and most recently has visited Europe, South America, Hawaii and Alaska. In 1995, she will sail mostly in the Chesapeake Bay and New England waters.

Rig Square topsail schooner, two-masted.
Contact W. Bruce Quackenbush, Jr., Executive Director, Pride of Baltimore, Inc., World Trade Center, Suite 222, 401 East Pratt St., Baltimore, MD 21202-3045; (410) 539-1151; fax (410) 539-1190.
Specs Sparred length: 170'. LOA: 108'. LOD: 96'6". LWL: 91'. Draft: 12'4". Beam: 26'. Rig height: 107'. Freeboard: 6'. Sail area: 10,442 sq. ft. Sail no.: n/a. Tons: 97 grt. Power: twin 165 hp Caterpillar diesels. Hull: wood. Built: 1988. Designer: Thomas C. Gillmer. Builder: G. Peter Boudreau.
Coast Guard cert. Passenger Vessel (Subchapter T), S.O.L.A.S., A.B.S.
Crew 12. Trainees 6 (overnight); 35 (day). Age 18+. Sex co-ed.
Program type Goodwill Ambassador Vessel.
Affiliated institutions State of Maryland, City of Baltimore, Maryland Port Administration.
Homeport/waters Baltimore, MD/ world wide.
Season Year-round.
Cost $100 per person per day.

PROVIDENCE

Providence is a full-sized replica of John Paul Jones's first command, the ex-merchant vessel *Katy*, and the first ship selected by the Colonial Navy. The original *Providence* carried twelve guns and was so successful in her campaign against the British that she became known as the "Lucky Sloop." All told she sank or captured forty fighting ships, most of which greatly exceeded her in fire power as well as crew and tonnage. John Paul Jones made his first command famous and said of her, "She was the first, and she was the best." Under the command of subsequent captains, she became the first ship to land U.S. Marines and to fly the American flag on foreign soil.

Seaport '76, a non-profit foundation governed by an elected board of directors, built the replica of the famous Continental Navy sloop in celebration of the U.S. Bicentennial and to stimulate interest in early maritime heritage. The modern *Providence* has logged more than 100,000 nautical miles and inspired more than one million visitors in carrying out her educational mission, and has been featured in many 18th century documentary films.

Individuals interested in joining the crew aboard her as apprentices are welcome year-round for periods of one week or more. She is available for underway as well as dockside education and events, corporate and group charters, public day sails, documentary and film use and historic reenactments. Fully inspected and certified, she may carry up to forty passengers, providing a unique opportunity to experience history under sail.

Rig square topsail sloop.
Contact Marvin Ronning, Executive Director, Continental Sloop *Providence*, P.O. Box 76, Newport R.I. 02840; (401) 846-1776, FAX (401) 848-0360.
Specs Sparred length: 110'. LOA: 66'7". LOD: n/a. LWL: 59'. Draft: 10'. Beam: 20'. Rig height: 94'. Freeboard: 8'. Sail area: 3,470 sq. ft. Sail no.: n/a. Tons: 68 grt. Power: 170 hp diesel. Hull: fiberglass and wood. Built: 1976; Melville, RI. Designer: Charles W. Wittholz. Builder: Seaport '76 Foundation.
Coast Guard cert. Passenger Vessel (Subchapter T).
Crew 7-10. Trainees 7 (overnight); 24-40 (day). Age all. Sex co-ed.
Program type Maritime history for youth-at-risk, middle-and high school students and adults; chartering.
Affiliated institutions n/a.
Homeport/waters Newport, RI/Atlantic Ocean.
Season Year-round.

*Q*UINNIPIACK

Founded in 1975, Schooner, Inc., provides educational opportunities in environmental marine sciences and owns and operates the *Quinnipiack*, a 91' wooden schooner. Students of all ages and abilities participate in science studies under sail exploring the biology and ecology of Long Island Sound while experiencing a taste of our maritime heritage.

Shipboard programs with Schooner's marine biologist complement traditional classroom studies in many subject areas. While the emphasis of the program is on biology and ecology, aspects of geography, history, chemistry and navigation are covered. At the interactive learning stations aboard the *Quinnipiack*, students look at plankton through microscopes, trawl for marine life, perform water chemistry tests and conduct land-use surveys. Subject matter and level of instruction are tailored to the needs of the group.

Former name ex-*Janet May*.
Rig Gaff schooner, two-masted.
Contact Karl Rosenbaum, Executive Director, Schooner, Inc., 60 South Water St., New Haven, CT 06519; (203) 865-1737.
Specs Sparred length: 91'. LOA: 91'. LOD: 58'. LWL: 52'. Draft: 4'6". Beam: 20'. Rig height: 62'. Freeboard: n/a. Sail area: 2,500 sq. ft. Sail no.: n/a. Tons: 41. Power: 135 hp. Hull: wood. Built: 1984. Designer: Howard Chappelle. Builder: Phil Sheldon.
Coast Guard cert. Passenger Vessel (Subchapter T).
Crew 4. **Trainees** 12. **Age** 12-18. **Sex** co-ed.
Program type Marine studies.
Affiliated institutions Various public and private elementary and high schools.
Homeport/waters New Haven, CT/ Long Island Sound.
Season April to November.
Cost Call for program rates.

*R*ACHEL B. JACKSON

Rig Gaff topsail schooner, two-masted.
Contact Capt. Jeff Crafts, Sailing Crafts, Inc., P.O. Box 131, Southwest Harbor, ME 04679; (716) 244-7813.
Specs Sparred length: n/a. LOA: 67'. LOD: 55'. LWL: 42'. Draft: 7'6". Beam: 16'. Rig height: 81'. Freeboard: 2'. Sail area: 2,500 sq. ft. Sail no.: n/a. Tons: 52. Power: 115 hp diesel. Hull: wood. Built: 1982; Freeport, ME. Designer: Bert Frost. Builder: George Emery.
Coast Guard cert. Passenger Vessel (Subchapter T).
Crew 2 inland; 4 offshore. **Trainees** 30 (day). **Age** n/a. **Sex** co-ed.
Program type n/a.

RICHARD ROBBINS

Rig Gaff schooner, two-masted.
Contact Classic Sail Windjammer Co., Inc., P.O. Box 459, Madison, NJ 07940; (201) 966-1684.
Specs Sparred length: 80'. LOA: 80'. LOD: 60'. LWL: 50'. Draft: 5'. Beam: 19'. Rig height: 50'. Freeboard: n/a. Sail area: 2,500 sq. ft. Sail no.: 4. Tons: 54. Power: 120 hp diesel. Hull: wood. Built: 1902; Greenwich, NJ. Designer: n/a. Builder: William Parsons.
Coast Guard cert. Passenger Vessel (Subchapter T).
Crew 4. Trainees 20 (overnight); 49 (day). Age 12+. Sex co-ed.
Program type Maritime history.

RENDEZVOUS

Under the command of our U.S. Coast Guard licensed captain and highly qualified staff, the Brigantine *Rendezvous* embarks on a voyage of learning and confidence building. Your students get to be the ship's crew! *Rendezvous'* Maritime Education Program offers a unique educational experience. It's the opportunity to participate in sailing a piece of California's maritime heritage, while learning the colorful history of San Francisco's waterfront, marine environment and ecosystem.

Rendezvous' program embraces the integrated thematic approach to the curriculum. A comprehensive package is provided with information regarding related topics that can be presented in the classroom. This package will serve as a basis for understanding the "hands on" instruction aboard the Brigantine *Rendezvous*.

The following subjects are covered: Introduction to sailing–basic terminology and nomenclature concerning traditional sailing vessels; Navigation–instruction on "dead reckoning," compass and chart orientation; San Francisco Bay Maritime History–historical information concerning the ships, boats, and the sailors of the Barbary Coast; San Francisco Bay Environment- A "past and present" view of man's influences on the Bays' marine life and habitat. Once aboard the vessel, the students interact to achieve common goals. The on board curriculum incorporates hands-on experience for each student relating back to the information learned in the classroom.

There are three duty watches on board: Deck (sail handling), Helm (steering), and Engineering (science, history, etc.). By rotating these watches, every student has a turn at the helm, braces a yard, and participates in an environmen-

→

RENDEZVOUS continued

tal experiment.

The program is conducted in an historic setting, with Captain and ship's officers in period dress, circa 1860.

The *Rendezvous* Maritime Education Program includes: A classroom curriculum package complete with reference materials; 4 hour sail on San Francisco Bay with a U.S. Coast Guard certified captain and 3 qualified staff; Full lunch and beverage program; an optional classroom demonstration. (Call for pricing).

Rig Brigantine.
Contact Drew Harper, Associate Director, Maritime Education Programs, Rendezvous Charters, Pier 40, South Beach Harbor, San Francisco, CA 94107; (415) 543-7405, fax (415) 543-7405.
Specs LOA: 79'6". LOD: 51'. LWL: 43'. Beam: 15'2". Rig height: 82'. Freeboard: 4'5". Sail Area: 2,100 sq. ft. Tons: 51 grt. Power: Detroit diesel. Hull: Douglas fir on white oak. Built: 1933; Seattle, WA. Designer: n/a. Builder: Howards & Sons.
Coast Guard cert. Yes: 49 passengers, 7 crew.
Crew 7. **Trainees** 49. Age: n/a. Sex: n/a.
Program type Maritime education and environmental concerns.
Homeport San Francisco.
Season Year round.
Cost Children: $37, adults: $17, teachers: free.

ROBERTSON II

Robertson II is the flagship of the SALTS fleet and one of the last Canadian fishing schooners built for the trade. Launched in 1940 in Nova Scotia, she represents a valuable link with Canada's maritime past. Massively constructed of pine and oak, she originally worked the Grand Banks with 20 men and eight dories. In 1974, she set sail for Victoria to start life again as a sail training vessel for young people. Over the past years she has been extensively refitted and returned to her historic rig.

Unlike her sister training ship, Pacific Swift, she remains in Pacific Northwest waters throughout the sailing season, March to October. Spring and fall are taken up with group sail training trips

→

involving schools, scouts, and similar youth programs. At the heart of SALTS' programs lie the extended sailing trips which take place during the summer months. Young people from all walks of life come together and learn to live and work as a team despite differing social and economic backgrounds. Ten days in duration, each trip is made up of twenty to thirty trainees, plus the regular ship's crew of master, mate, and watch officers. Trainees participate in every facet of shipboard life from bosun's chores to helmsmanship. In addition to the routine of the watch system, specific instruction in navigation and piloting, seamanship, small boat handling and other nautical basics are provided. The itinerary is planned to take full advantage of winds and tides; a typical passage could include a visit to Desolation Sound and some of British Columbia's spectacular fjords and remote island groups.

Rig Gaff topsail schooner, two-masted.
Contact Capt. Martyn J. Clark, Executive Director, Sail and Life Training Society (SALTS), P.O. Box 5014, Station B, Victoria, British Columbia V8R 6N3 Canada; (604) 383-6811; fax (604) 383-7781.
Specs Sparred length: 130'. LOA: 105'. LOD: n/a. LWL: 98'. Draft: 12'. Beam: 22'. Rig height: 105'. Freeboard: n/a. Sail area: 5,637 sq. ft. Sail no.: n/a. Tons: 150. Power: diesel. Hull: wood. Built: 1940; Shelburne, Nova Scotia. Designer: McKay. Builder: McKay.
Coast Guard cert. Canadian Passenger Vessel and Sail Training Vessel.
Crew 5. Trainees 30 (overnight). Age 13-25. Sex co-ed.
Program type Maritime history and nautical instruction.
Affiliated institutions n/a.
Homeport/waters Victoria, B.C./ Pacific Northwest.
Season March to October.
Cost Can$55 per day per trainee.

ROSE, "HMS"

Rose is the first and only Class-A tall ship in the United States to be U.S. Coast Guard certified as a Sailing School Vessel. As such, she may embark up to 100 persons for educational day sails and up to 49 people overnight on an oceans route. Rose signs on sail trainees (or participants) each season to 'learn the ropes' as she sails to various ports. Sail training sessions may range from several days to weeks or even months in duration. Special one-day programs are often scheduled for corporate, civic, educational, religious and other groups. Participants in the ship's programs have ranged in age from grade school students to senior citizens.

Rose is a full-rigged ship: three

ROSE, "HMS" contnued

masts with square sails on all. She carries 13,000 square feet of sail made entirely from recycled plastic beverage bottles and plastic car fenders – the first such recycling project ever attempted.

The original *HMS Rose* was a 24-gun frigate built in Hull, England, in 1757 in anticipation of the Seven Years' War (also known as the French and Indian War) during which Americans and British fought side by side, and even George Washington wore the 'redcoat' of a commissioned British officer. *Rose's* link with history is tangible to all who walk her wooden decks or run her rigging through their hands.

The new *Rose* was built in 1970 to celebrate the American Bicentennial and was berthed mostly on the Newport, Rhode Island, waterfront until 1984, when she was purchased by the "HMS" Rose Foundation of Bridgeport, Connecticut. Since 1985, the ship has been entirely rebuilt to meet or exceed all safety requirements for a vessel of her class and size. In addition to her sail training mission, America's largest wooden tall ship is available for harbor festivals, dockside receptions, films, advertising and promotional projects, international voyages, invasions and other maritime events.

Rig Full-rigged ship, three-masted.
Contact Richard Bailey, "HMS" Rose Foundation, Inc., One Bostwick Ave., Bridgeport, CT 06605; (203) 335-0932, (203) 335-1433; fax (203) 335-6793.
Specs Sparred length: 179'. LOA: 135'. LOD: 125'. LWL: 105'. Draft: 13'. Beam: 32'. Rig height: 130'. Freeboard: 13'. Sail area: 13,000 sq. ft. Sail no.: 17. Tons: 500. Power: twin diesels. Hull: wood. Built: 1970: Lunenberg, Nova Scotia; rebuilt: 1985-87; Bridgeport, CT and Fairhaven, MA. Designer: original design by Hugh Blades, British Admiralty, modern revisions by Phil Bolger. Builder: Smith & Rhuland.
Coast Guard cert. Dual certificate - Sailing School Vessel (Subchapter R) and Attraction Vessel.
Crew 18. Trainees 31 (overnight), up to 80(day). Age: grade school to adult. Sex co-ed.
Program type An eighty-page manual guides each participant through crew-assisted interactive sail training including instruction in helmsmanship, shipboard safety, sail and line handling, sail evolutions, watchstanding and marlinespike seamanship; custom programs in maritime history and environmental studies for educational institutions; corporate team building programs and general admission sea adventure education for adults. Write or call for specific schedule and availability of dates for custom programs.
Affiliated institutions Rhode Island College *et al.*
Homeport/waters Bridgeport, CT/ East Coast (summer); overseas.
Season Year-round (subject to availability).
Cost approximately $110 per person, per day.

ROSEWAY

Rig Gaff schooner, two-masted.
Contact Capt. George Sloane, Schooner Roseway, P.O. Box 696, Camden, ME 04843; (207) 236-4449.
Specs Sparred length: 137'. LOA: 112'. LOD: n/a. LWL: 89'. Draft: 13'. Beam: 25'. Rig height: 110'. Freeboard: 6'. Sail area: 5,600 sq. ft. Sail no.: n/a. Tons: 97 grt. Power: n/a. Hull: n/a. Built: n/a. Designer: n/a. Builder: n/a.
Coast Guard cert. Passenger Vessel (Subchapter T).
Crew 7. Trainees 36 (overnight); 75 (day). Age varies. Sex co-ed.
Program type Navigation practicum on North/South passages.

ROYALISTE

During the 1995 season, *Royaliste* will sail with trainees between the ages of fourteen and eighteen and introduces them to the maritime history of the Great Lakes, with special reference to the period of the War of 1812. Along with the maritime history component, the trainees are taught basic seamanship and maritime skills through level I of the ASTA Syllabus and Logbook course of instruction.

In 1995, *Royaliste* will sail as part of a squadron from Kingston down the St. Lawrence River to Louisbourg, Cape Breton Island, Nova Scotia to partake in the historical reenactment and celebrate the 250th anniversary of the Louisbourg fortress.

Rig Square topsail ketch.
Contact Vernon Fairhead, RR 1, Shawville, Québec J0X 2Y0 Canada; (819) 647-5544.
Specs Sparred length: 70'. LOA: 50'. LOD: 46'. LWL: 40'. Draft: 6'6". Beam: 14'. Rig height: 60'. Freeboard: 3'6". Sail area: 1,700 sq. ft. Sail no.: n/a. Tons: 22 grt. Power: 85 hp Perkins diesel. Hull: wood. Built: 1970; Nova Scotia. Designer: J.D. Rosborough. Builder: A.F. Theriault.
Coast Guard cert. Uninspected yacht.
Crew 3; 1 instructor. Trainees 9 (overnight); 20 (day). Age 14-18. Sex co-ed.
Program type Marine biology, historic naval reenactments, English and French, and nautical science (ASTA Syllabus and Logbook level I).
Affiliated institutions CSTA, Canadian War Museum.
Homeport/waters Kingston, Ont./ Great Lakes, St. Lawrence River.
Season Inquire.
Cost Can$45 per trainee per day.

SCHOONER PILGRIM

Pilgrim offers a unique hands-on opportunity for students of all ages. Programs include varied curriculums in maritime history, nautical science, and environmental studies. The *Pilgrim* also offers private charters, and has participated in historical reenactments.

The *Pilgrim's* main objective however lies in creating an interest and appreciation of our marine heritage and sea environment. The captain and crew wish to instill in their students the importance of responsibility, teamwork, and leadership. They welcome the challenge of fulfilling the dreams of would be sailors through one of *Pilgrim's* programs or one designed especially for your group.

Pilgrim recently has participated in "Sail Toronto 94" and "Oswego Harbourfest", and her crew invites all who wish to learn aboard under sail.

Rig Square topsail schooner.
Contact Capt. Gary Kurtz, Schooner Pilgrim, Pilgrim Packet Company, P.O. Box 491, Kendall, NY 14476; (716)-682-4757.
Specs Sparred length: 68'. LOA: n/a. LOD: 52'. LWL: 44'3". Draft: 6'. Beam: 15'. Rig height: 57'. Freeboard: 3'6". Sail area: 2,600 sq. ft. Sail no.: n/a. Tons: 33 gross. Power: 85 hp diesel. Hull: Steel. Built: 1987. Designer: Wood. Builder: Marine Metals.
Coast Guard cert. Uninspected yacht, Attraction Vessel.
Crew 2. Trainees 6 (overnight); 6 (day). Age all ages depending upon program. Sex co-ed.
Program type Maritime history, environmental, nautical science, historical reenactments, private charters.
Affiliated institutions n/a.
Homeport/waters Kendall, NY/ Lake Ontario and St. Lawrence River.
Season May-October.
Cost Inquire.

The information here is provided as a service only and no warranty or endorsement of any individual programs or vessels by the American Sail Training Association is intended or implied. ASTA is not an agent for any vessels or programs and does not control, inspect or approve vessels or programs. All information in this directory is provided by the owners. Before booking or boarding, confirm important facts with the vessel's owner, including the status of safety certificates, equipment, and the suitability of the vessel or program to your abilities and needs.

SEA LION

The Buffalo Maritime Society, Inc., offers the *Sea Lion* to youth of all ages as an example of 17th century maritime history. Rigged in hemp with flax linen sails, she is considered one of the most authentic of her kind in the world.

As an attraction vessel, we provide on-board exhibits and shore-based training to a variety of children's groups. While at sea, we rotate an all volunteer crew through programs including navigation and piloting, marlinespike seamanship, and maritime history. All our programs focus on teamwork and self-esteem and our participants are encouraged to apply these skills to their own lifestyles.

In addition, the *Sea Lion* promotes dock-side activities such as theater, music and art. We encourage the students to be creative and display their achievements to the public.

Rig Bark, three masted, (lateen, mizzen).
Contact Timothy Downey, Pres., Buffalo Maritime Society, Inc., 90 Liberty Terrace, Buffalo, NY 14215; (716) 834-3922.
Specs Sparred length: 62'. LOA: n/a. LOD: n/a. LWL: 42'1". Draft: 6'6". Beam: 13'. Rig height: 52'. Freeboard: n/a. Sail area: 1,300 sq. ft. Sail no.: 6. Tons: 48.6 grt. Power: none. Hull: white oak. Built: 1986. Designer: William A. Baker. Builder: Sea Lion Project, Ltd., Chautauqua County, NY.
Coast Guard cert. MSO certified; Attraction Vessel.
Crew 12 (all volunteer); 4 instructors. Trainees: rotated through crew. Age 14 and over. Sex co-ed.
Program type Marine biology, maritime history, environmental, adjudicated youth, youth-at-risk.
Affiliated institutions n/a.
Homeport/waters Buffalo, NY/ Western region of Lake Erie, Lake Ontario.
Season May 15th to September 15th.
Cost None.

SANTA MARIA

Complete vessel information on the *Santa Maria* was not available at press time.

Please see the Columbia Santa Maria, Inc. listing under the Directory of Programs.

SHENANDOAH

While the *Shenandoah* is not a replica, the vessel's design has a strong resemblance to that of the U.S. Revenue Cutter *Joe Lane* of 1851. For her first twenty-five years, the rakish square topsail schooner was painted white, but she now wears the black and white checkerboard paint scheme of the nineteenth-century Revenue Service. Every summer *Shenandoah* plies the waters of southern New England and Long Island Sound visiting the haunts of pirates and the home ports of whaling ships.

Rig Square topsail schooner, two-masted.
Contact Capt. Robert S. Douglas, Coastwise Packet Co., Inc., P.O. Box 429, Vineyard Haven, MA 02568; (508) 693-1699.
Specs Sparred length: 152'. LOA: 108'. LOD: n/a. LWL: 101'. Draft: 11'. Beam: 23'. Rig height: 94'. Freeboard: 3' (amidships). Sail area: 7,000 sq. ft. Sail no.: n/a. Tons: 85 grt. Power: no auxiliary power. Hull: wood. Built: 1964. Designer: Robert S. Douglas. Builder: Harvey F. Gamage, South Bristol, ME.
Coast Guard cert. passenger vessel (Subchapter T).
Crew 9. Trainees 30 (overnight); 35 (day). Age 12-20. Sex male only or female only.
Program type Windjammer cruises and school ship.
Affiliated institutions n/a.
Homeport/waters Vineyard Haven, MA/ Long Island to Nantucket.
Season June to September.
Cost $75 per person per day; group rates: 30 people for six days, $12,000 (June and September), $15,000 (July and August).

Discover your own potential...

We hope you will use this Directory to discover your own potential for becoming involved with ASTA, TALL SHIPS, and with sail training.

SHERMAN ZWICKER

Rig Gaff schooner, two-masted.
Contact Bob Ryan, Grand Banks Schooner Museum, Box 123, Boothbay, ME 04537; (207) 633-4727.
Specs Sparred length: n/a. LOA: 142'. LOD: n/a. LWL: n/a. Draft: 14'. Beam: 26'. Rig height: 86'. Freeboard: n/a. Sail area: n/a sq. ft. Sail no.: n/a. Tons: n/a. Power: 320 hp diesel. Hull: wood. Built: 1942; Lunenberg. Designer: traditional. Builder: Smith and Rhuland.
Coast Guard cert. Not documented (foreign built).
Crew 3. Trainees 12-20. Age all. Sex co-ed.
Program type Seamanship.

SOUNDWATERS

SoundWaters is a non-profit environmental organization dedicated to the restoration and preservation of Long Island Sound. Its most visible platform is the *SoundWaters*, a floating classroom on Long Island Sound. *SoundWaters'* education program offers a multi-disciplinary approach to education and includes graduate-credit courses for educators.

The *SoundWaters* sails port-to-port in Connecticut and Westchester County and Long Island, New York, from April 15 to November 15. The floating classroom program introduces adults and children to the ecological wonders of Long Island Sound through history, marine sciences, ecology and sail training. The eco-story, a ten-lesson curriculum that integrates Long Island and environmental concerns into history, social science, mathematics and language arts lessons, is available to classroom teachers who sail with *SoundWaters*.

SoundWaters' Eco-Mariner program offers summer sail training and marine ecology of Long Island Sound aboard SoundWaters. One-week day sessions are scheduled in July and August for twelve to fourteen-year-olds. The program includes instruction in basic seamanship and ship handling; navigation and nautical knots; weather forecasting and marine ecology. Participants take turns at the helm; raise, trim and set sails; learn to chart a course, set a trawl, discover the ancient art of knot-tying and participate fully in the sailing of the *SoundWaters*.

→

SOUNDWATERS continued

Field experience may include exploring a salt marsh, sailing to a local lighthouse or visiting an oyster farm on Long Island Sound. A one-week Special Eco-Mariner Program has been adapted for teens and young adults with special needs. The Celestial Mariner Program is a 7-day overnight camp that not only includes sail training and marine ecology but emphasizes camp life, with responsibilities, camp fires, games, and outdoor cooking. Campers sleep on islands and beaches.

Much more than a summer camp, the Eco-Mariner Programs are designed to teach young people valuable life skills and to develop an awareness of Long Island Sound's marine ecosystems and environment. The sessions are limited to twenty-five students. A teacher enrichment sail training course is also offered.

The expert *SoundWaters* education staff includes environmental educators, crew and a master-licensed captain. College graduates with expertise in ecology, marine sciences or sailing are encouraged to apply for seasonal employment. A licensed passenger vessel, SoundWaters is also available for charter.

Rig Three-masted sharpie (gaff schooner).
Contact SoundWaters, Four Yacht Haven West Marine Center, Washington Blvd., Stamford, CT 06902; (203) 323-1978.
Specs Sparred length: 80'. LOA: 64'10". LOD: n/a. LWL: 50'10". Draft: 2'9" (board down); 8'8" (board down). Beam: 16'. Rig height: 54'. Freeboard: 3'6". Sail area: 1,510 sq. ft. Sail no.: 4. Tons: 31 grt. Power: 130 hp Perkins diesel. Hull: steel. Built: 1986. Designer: William A. Wood, Annapolis, MD. Builder: Marine Metals, Norfolk, VA.
Coast Guard cert. passenger vessel (Subchapter T).
Crew 3; 7 instructors. Trainees 42 (day). Age 8+. Sex co-ed.
Program type Marine biology, English, environmental studies, special education, and full curriculum academics for middle and highschool and college students and adults.
Affiliated institutions n/a.
Homeport/waters Stamford, CT/ Long Island Sound.
Season April to November.
Cost $25 per person. SoundWaters Floating Classroom 3-hour group educational sail, $600-$950; Eco-Mariner Program, one-week sail training and marine ecology program, $275; Special Eco-Mariner Program, one-week sail training and marine ecology camp for teens and young adults with special needs; Celestial Mariner Program, 7-day overnight sail training and marine ecology camp.

ASTA's Mission is...

"To encourage character building through sail training, promote sail training to the American public, and support education under sail."

SPIRIT OF MASSACHUSETTS

Spirit of Massachusetts is modeled after the fishing schooner *Fredonia*, which was designed by Edward Burgess in 1889 and was popular for its beautiful appearance and speed through the water. The design is typical of the Gloucester fishing schooners of the late nineteenth and early twentieth centuries, the "fast and able" vessels which plied the rich Grand Banks and Georges Bank.

New England Historic Seaport, a non-profit corporation, has been conducting sail training programs since 1979. At first, this was done aboard chartered vessels. Then, in April of 1983, the keel of a new ship of their own was laid. A year later, *Spirit of Massachusetts* was launched. A wide variety of timber from many regions of the United States was used in the construction, including greenheart, white oak, long-leaf yellow pine, hackmatack and tall Douglas fir for the masts. She was also authentically rigged using the finest natural fibers available. While traditional in design and construction, *Spirit of Massachusetts* was built to meet all current safety requirements, and she is fully licensed by the U.S. Coast Guard to carry passengers.

On *Spirit of Massachusetts*, students participate in the operation of a traditional vessel, learning many skills including basic seamanship and navigation, with an introduction to the ocean's resources. In addition, each program has a unique theme. The skills acquired in sea experience under sail are personal ones: leadership, self-reliance, confidence and flexibility to successfully meet a variety of challenges both afloat and ashore.

Rig Topsail schooner, two-masted.
Contact Gary Cohen/ Stephen Wedlock, New England Historic Seaport, Building 1, Charlestown Navy Yard, Boston, MA 02129; (617) 242-1414.
Specs Sparred length: 125'. LOA: n/a. LOD: 100'. LWL: 80'. Draft: 10'. Beam: 24'. Rig height: 103'. Freeboard: n/a. Sail area: 7,000 sq. ft. Sail no.: n/a. Tons: 90. Power: 235 hp diesel. Hull: wood. Built: 1983-84; Boston, MA. Designer: Melbourne Smith and Andrew Davis. Builder: New England Historic Seaport.
Coast Guard cert. Sailing School Vessel (Subchapter R) and Passenger Vessel (Subchapter T).
Crew 7-9. Trainees 22. Age 14+. Sex co-ed.
Program type Educational.
Affiliated institutions Area schools.
Homeport/waters Boston, MA/ Atlantic Ocean and Caribbean.
Season Year-round.
Cost Varies by voyage.

ST. LAWRENCE II

The STV *St. Lawrence II* is a purpose-built sail training vessel operating primarily on the Great Lakes. She has been sailing since 1956 and her owners believe that hard work and responsibility at a young age creates better citizens for the future. She has a complement of twenty-nine, comprised of eighteen new trainees, three petty officers, bosun's mate, bosun, chef, three watch officers, and an executive officer, all between the ages of thirteen and eighteen. The captain is the only adult aboard.

Trainees in the *St. Lawrence's* hands-on program are encouraged to learn by doing, and progress is monitored by the new Canadian Sail Training Association grade standards. Officers are graduates of Brigantine, Inc.'s winter training program in which they attend lectures on seamanship, navigation and safety, and ship's systems, while doing the bulk of the maintenance on the ship. Every year the ship sails over 4,000 miles, spends in excess of forty full nights at sea and introduces one hundred fifty trainees to the rigors of life aboard ship, while visiting numerous ports all over the Great Lakes. Brigantine, Inc., also has a lead-up program for eleven- to thirteen-year-olds providing three-day cruises on Lake Ontario and the St. Lawrence River.

Rig Brigantine.
Contact Brigantine, Inc., 53 Yonge St., Kingston, Ont. K7M 6G4 Canada; (613) 544-5175.
Specs Sparred length: 72'. LOA: 60'. LOD: n/a. LWL: 45'. Draft: 8'. Beam: 15'. Rig height: 54'. Freeboard: 4'4". Sail area: 2,560 sq. ft. Sail no.: n/a. Tons: 34 grt. Power: 165 diesel. Hull: steel. Built: 1955; Kingston, Ontario. Designer: Francis A. MacLachlan. Builder: Kingston Shipyards.
Coast Guard cert. n/a.
Crew 2 adult, 9 youth. Trainees 18 (overnight), 29 (day). Age 13-18 (sometimes 11-adult). Sex co-ed.
Program type n/a.
Affiliated institutions n/a.
Homeport/waters Kingston, Ont./ Lake Champlain and adjacent waters.
Season April to November (sailing); October to March (winter program).
Cost Can$45 per person per day; Can$1,200 per day for group of 18.

STEPHEN TABER

Rig Gaff schooner.
Contact Capts. Ken and Ellen Barnes, Schooner *Stephen Taber*, 70 Elm St., Camden, ME 04843; (800) 999-7352.
Specs Sparred length: 115'. LOA: 78'. LOD: n/a. LWL: 68'. Draft: 5'. Beam: n/a. Rig height: 93'. Freeboard: n/a. Sail area: n/a sq. ft. Sail no.: n/a. Tons: n/a. Power: n/a. Hull: n/a. Built: n/a. Designer: n/a. Builder: n/a.
Coast Guard cert. n/a.
Crew n/a. Trainees n/a. Age n/a. Sex n/a.
Program type n/a.

SUNDERLAND

Pacific Northwest Passages is a nonprofit adventure-based program designed to provide engaging, challenging and meaningful experiences for today's youth. Adventure-based programs that provide challenges in a supervised and supportive environment have been shown to have a significant impact on breaking down destructive anti-social behavior in youth. Programs of this nature also reinforce efforts of youth to become constructive participants in society.

The 82' schooner *Sunderland* is the core of our program. The routine of group living, daily maintenance and the challenge of sailing this vessel provides a context for positive change. Life aboard a sailing vessel has the unique potential for awakening in youth new ways of thinking and acting as they respond to its rigors and demands.

Pacific Northwest Passages exists to help kids. The environment of the ship and the experience of each voyage provides opportunities for personal change. For example, if a group wants to work on conflict resolution we can emphasize situations which guide the group through different conflict resolution strategies. Reflective discussions afterward help integrate the experience for future performances. Pacific Northwest Passages is designed to work with existing youth agencies.

Rig Gaff schooner, two-masted.
Contact Pacific Northwest Passages, P.O. Box 485, Langley, WA 98260; (206) 321-4840.
Specs Sparred length: 102'. LOA: n/a. LOD: 82'. LWL: 70'. Draft: 11'. Beam: 19'6". Rig height: 60'. Freeboard: 5'. Sail area: 3,400 sq. ft. Sail no.: n/a. Tons: 72 grt. Power: 100 hp 1935 alpha diesel. Hull: White Oak and English Elm. Built: 1885. Designer: n/a. Builder:

*S*UNDERLAND continued

Samuel Richards, Lowestoft, England.
Coast Guard cert. pending.
Crew 4; 3 instructors. Trainees 20. Age 7-19. Sex co-ed.
Program type Special education and drug rehabilitation for adjudicated youth and youth-at-risk.
Affiliated institutions n/a.
Homeport/waters Langley, Whidbey Island, WA/ Puget Sound.
Season The program expects to operate in 1995 pending USCG certification.
Cost n/a.

*S*USAN CONSTANT

"On Saturday, the twentieth of December in the yeere 1606, the fleet fell from London," wrote George Percy, who kept an account of the voyage to Virginia. Three small ships — *Susan Constant* of 120 tons, *Godspeed* of 40 tons and *Discovery* of 20 tons — were underway on a voyage of colonization to the new world. On May 13, 1607, the colonists chose a site on the banks of the James River, naming it for their king. Jamestown was the first successful permanent English colony in North America

Today at Jamestown Settlement, a living history museum which recreates America's first permanent English colony, the three ships have been accurately recreated and serve as working exhibits.

To further the educational mission of the museum, a volunteer sail training program is offered to individuals of all ages. *Susan Constant* and *Godspeed* embark on several sail training and educational outreach voyages each year. Participants are trained in sailing a seventeenth-century merchant vessel including handling square sails, marlinespike seamanship, navigation, safety procedures, watch standing and maritime history.

Rig Bark, three-masted (lateen mizzen).
Contact Eric Speth, Maritime Program Manager, Jamestown-Yorktown Foundation, PO Drawer JF, Williamsburg, VA 23187; (804) 229-1607; fax (804) 253-7350.
Specs Sparred length: n/a. LOA: 116'. LOD: 83'. LWL: 77'. Draft: 11'6". Beam: 24'10". Rig height: 95'. Freeboard: n/a. Sail area: 3,902 sq. ft. Sail no.: n/a. Tons: 120. Power: diesel. Hull: wood. Built: Williamsburg, VA. Designer: Stanley Potter. Builder: Allen C. Rawl.
Coast Guard cert. n/a.
Crew n/a. Trainees n/a. Age n/a. Sex n/a.
Program type Seamanship and maritime history.
Affiliated institutions Jamestown Settlement, Williamsburg, VA.
Homeport/waters Jamestown, VA/ James River and Chesapeake Bay.
Season March-November.
Cost n/a.

SWIFT OF IPSWICH

The Los Angeles Maritime Institute (LAMI), the educational affiliate of the Los Angeles Maritime Museum, operates the square topsail schooner *Swift of Ipswich*. LAMI staff members are noted for their expertise in the development of personal and "human skills" such as communication, cooperation, teamwork, persistence, self-reliance and leadership along with their ability to teach the art of operating and maintaining a vessel at sea. Staff and crew share a commitment to knowing and understanding the natural world and questioning the human role in nature. Programs are an outgrowth of those operated for eighteen years with students and staff from the Alternative/Magnet Schools of the Los Angeles Unified School District. Three different programs are offered.

The TOPSAIL Youth Program is a basic outreach program, with participants recommended by people who work with youth, including educators, youth leaders and clergy. Cost is on an ability-to-pay basis. It is our goal never to turn a youth away for lack of money. TOPSAIL begins with a series of day-sails followed by a five-day voyage which is planned and organized by the participants, complete with purpose, destination, itinerary, meal planning and provisioning. Upon completion of the two-week basic program participants are encouraged to continue as active members of the *"Swift* Family." Subsequent activities can include *Swift* expeditions, shore-based classes and projects by LAMI, and other institutions, organizations and businesses.

SWIFT EXPEDITIONS are more advanced and challenging voyages with specific purposes, goals and duration.

COOPERATIVE PROGRAMS afford other organizations such as youth groups, churches, schools, community groups, clubs and museums the opportunity to participate in the experience, fun and challenge a voyage on *Swift* can offer. The purposes, destinations, duration and logistics for each voyage are developed cooperatively with the sponsoring organization.

The Los Angeles Maritime Museum and all of its affiliates take pleasure in offering hospitality on an as-available basis to visiting tall ships and other "educationally significant" vessels. Please advise us of your plans and needs as early as possible. Dock space is limited and must be arranged in advance in order to allow for appropriate accommodations.

Rig Square topsail schooner.
Contact Mr. James L. Gladson, Los Angeles Maritime Institute, Berth 84, Foot of Sixth St., San Pedro, CA 90731; (310) 548-2902.
Specs Sparred length: 90'. LOA: 70'. LOD: 66'. LWL: 62'. Draft: 10'. Beam: 18'. Rig height: 74'. Freeboard: 5'. Sail area: 5,166 sq. ft. Sail no.: none. Tons: 46 grt. Power: diesel. Hull: wood. Built: 1938; Ipswich, MA Designer: Howard I. Chappelle. Builder: William A. Robinson.

SWIFT OF IPSWICH continued

Coast Guard cert. Passenger Vessel (Subchapter T).
Crew 6. Trainees 31 (overnight); 49 (day). Age 12+. Sex co-ed and single-sex crews.
Program type Educational sailing adventures for "at-risk" youth and other youth or adult groups.
Affiliated institutions n/a.
Homeport/waters Los Angeles, CA/ coastal California and offshore islands.
Season Year-round.
Cost Inquire.

SYLVINA W. BEAL

The *Sylvina W. Beal* was built in East Boothbay, Maine, in 1911, as a mackerel seiner and was later used as a fisheries' cargo carrier. In 1981, she was converted to a windjammer passenger schooner, and is now used for educational and vacation trips out of Mystic, Connecticut, from May through October, and St. Lucia, November through March. If you are interested in more detailed information call 800-333-MYST.

Rig Gaff schooner, two-masted.
Contact Capt. Geoffrey P. Jones, Schooner *Sylvina W. Beal*, Mystic Nautical Heritage Society, 120 School Street, Mystic, CT 06355; (800)-333-MYST.
Specs Sparred length: 84'. LOA: 80'. LOD: 77'. LWL: 70'. Draft: 8'. Beam: 17'. Rig height: 56'. Freeboard: 4'. Sail area: 2,200 sq. ft. Sail no.: n/a. Tons: 46 grt. Power: 60 hp. Hull: wood. Built: 1911; East Boothbay, ME. Designer: Frank J. Adams Yard. Builder: Frank J. Adams Yard.
Coast Guard cert. Passenger Vessel (Subchapter T).
Crew 4. Trainees 18 (overnight), 30 (day). Age 14+. Sex co-ed.
Program type Sail Training: For schools, scouts, etc. Also, marine biology, maritime history, Literature of the Sea, and environmental studies for colleges and schools.
Affiliated institutions University of Massachusetts (Boston).
Homeport/waters Mystic, CT/ From Lubeck, ME to Sandy Hook, NJ. Also, St. Lucia in the winter.
Season: Year-round.
Cost $750-$1,300 per day for full boat charter depending on the time of year, number of days, and type of program.

TABOR BOY

Tabor Boy has been engaged in sail training as a seagoing classroom for Tabor Academy students since 1954. Offshore voyaging and oceanographic studies go together in the curriculum, with cruises to destinations as distant as Mexico and Panama adding adventure to the experience. Many Tabor Academy graduates go on to the U.S. Merchant Marine, Navy or Coast Guard academies.

The schooner also offers seven summer orientation voyages for newly enrolled freshmen and sophomore students. During this time, trainees are fully involved in sail handling, ship operation, navigation, seamanship, and oceanographic studies. Harbor festivals and port visits along the New England coast are highlights of time spent ashore.

Rig Dutch pilot schooner, two-masted.
Contact Capt. James Geil, Tabor Academy, Marion, MA 02738; (508) 748-2000.
Specs Sparred length: 115'. LOA: 92'. LOD: 84'. LWL: 82'6". Draft: 10'6". Beam: 21'9". Rig height: 95'. Freeboard: n/a. Sail area: 3,600 sq. ft. Sail no.: "2". Tons: 99.9. Power: 330 hp diesel. Hull: iron. Built: 1914; Amsterdam, The Netherlands. Designer: n/a. Builder: N.V. Boelles Scheepswerven & Machinefabrik.
Coast Guard cert. Sailing School Vessel (Subchapter R).
Crew 6. Trainees 16. Age 14-18. Sex co-ed.
Program type High school; seamanship and oceanography for students.
Affiliated institutions Tabor Academy.
Homeport/waters Marion, MA/ coastal New England (summer); offshore Atlantic Ocean (school year) and Caribbean Sea.
Season n/a.
Cost Covered by regular tuition plus a nominal cruise fee to offset expenses.

The information here is provided as a service only and no warranty or endorsement of any individual programs or vessels by the American Sail Training Association is intended or implied. ASTA is not an agent for any vessels or programs and does not control, inspect or approve vessels or programs. All information in this directory is provided by the owners. Before booking or boarding, confirm important facts with the vessel's owner, including the status of safety certificates, equipment, and the suitability of the vessel or program to your abilities and needs.

TECUMSETH

H.M.S. Tecumseth is a replica of the war schooner *Tecumseth* that served with the Royal Naval Establishment at Penetanguishene. Used for defense and transport duties from the Royal Navy Base, she was an important addition to the naval forces on the Upper Lakes.

Living history takes place aboard *Tecumseth* as on the *Bee*, where you are sworn into the Royal Navy, trained, and shipped out aboard a Royal Navy ship.

A modern ship with up-to-date safety features, yet the mirror of her 1815 namesake, *Tecumseth* will take you back in time to the days of the Nelson and the Wooden walls. Once aboard, you become one of the crew and make the ship come alive. Programs are open to anyone aged ten and older. The *Tecumseth* takes a maximum of 45 trainees per sail. No previous experience is necessary.

Rig Topsail schooner.
Contact Chris Bagley, Marine Coordinator, Discovery Harbour, P.O. Box #1800, Penetanguishene, Ontario, Canada, L0K 1P0; (705) 549-8064.
Specs Sparred length: 125'. LOA: 80'. LOD: 70'. LWL: 63'. Draft: 8'. Beam: 29'. Rig height: 90'. Freeboard: n/a. Sail area: 4700 sq. ft. Sail no.: 8. Tons: 146. Power: 185 hp diesel. Hull: steel. Built: 1991-1994. Designer: Bob Johnston. Builder: Kanter Yachts, St. Thomas, Ontario.
Coast Guard cert. n/a.
Crew Staff and volunteers: 12. Age 13-25. Sex n/a.
Program type Seamanship.
Affiliated institutions n/a.
Homeport/waters Penetanguishene, Georgian Bay & Lake Huron, ONT.
Season June-September.
Cost Approximately $20 per person per 2 hour sail.

TOLE MOUR

Tole Mour operates in support of OceanQuest Hawaii, a nonprofit joint venture between Marimed Foundation of Hawaii and VisionQuest National Ltd. of Arizona. OceanQuest Hawaii is a year-round, open ocean program for adjudicated and/or emotionally impaired adolescents from Hawaii and several Mainland states. Marimed, which owns *Tole Mour*, is responsible for vessel operations and maintenance and for the maritime skills training and vocational education of the cadets enrolled in the program. Vision-Quest is responsible for the treatment and schooling of cadets, for pre-voyage orientation of cadets, and for matters relating to quality assurance. Marimed handles community reintegration and after care for Hawaii youth; VisionQuest handles community reintegration and after care for youth from the Mainland.

OceanQuest Hawaii is part of an 18 month comprehensive treatment and training program for youth who are referred by courts or other state agencies and who might otherwise be incarcerated or hospitalized. The ship-based phase of the program is preceded by a camp-based orientation that includes one or more wilderness "quests;" it is followed by six months of intensive, community-based tracking and after care.

Tole Mour makes regular passages between Hawaii and the New England and Mid Atlantic states via Panama. She spends the Winter and Spring in Hawaii an California and the Summer and Fall on the East Coast and/or Great Lakes. Cadets typically remain on board for four to eight months and make at least one offshore passage of two weeks or more.

Rig Square topsail schooner, three-masted.
Contact Mr. David D. Higgins, Marimed Foundation, 1050 Ala Moana Boulevard, Building D, Honolulu, Hawaii 96814; (808) 593-2586.
Specs Sparred length: 156'. LOA: 131'. LOD: 125'. LWL: 101'. Draft: 13'6". Beam: 30'10". Rig height: 110'. Freeboard: n/a. Sail area: 8,500 sq. ft. Sail no.: n/a. Tons: 230 gross. Power: 575 hp Deutz. Hull: steel. Built: 1988; Seattle, WA. Designer: Ewbank, Brooke Associates, New Zealand. Builder: Nichols Brothers.
Coast Guard cert. Sailing School Vessel (Subchapter R).
Crew and staff 21. Trainees 28 (overnight). Age 14-18. Sex male.
Program type Treatment, education, and vocational skills training for court-referred adolescents.
Affiliated institutions VisionQuest National, Ltd.
Homeport/waters Honolulu, Hawaii/ Pacific, Atlantic, Caribbean.
Season Year-round.
Cost Inquire.

VICTORY CHIMES

Built in Bethel, Delaware, in 1900, the three-masted schooner *Victory Chimes* is the only American built Class-A Tall Ship with a United States Coast Guard certificate to carry passengers for hire. She is the largest pure sailing vessel under the American flag and the only original three-master still working in America. Recently nominated for National Historic Landmark status, the Victory Chimes has been quietly supporting herself and a small succession of private owners for the past ninety-five years. She has never been part of a foundation nor has she ever received any grants or endowments. She has been and continues to be a well maintained working vessel. Her current caretakers/owners, Captain Kip Files and Captain Paul DeGaeta, offer Windjammer style vacations on Penobscot Bay, Maine. At over 200 gross tons, the Victory Chimes attracts career minded professional crew and carries a crew of nine.

Former name ex-*Edwin and Maud.*
Rig Gaff schooner, three-masted.
Contact Victory Chimes, P.O. Box 1401, Rockland, ME 04841; (207) 594-0755; (207) 265-5651; (800) 745-5651.
Specs Sparred length: 170'. LOA: 132'. LOD: 132'. LWL: 127'. Draft: 7'5". Beam: 25'. Rig height: 87'. Freeboard: 11'. Sail area: 7,100 sq. ft. Sail no.: n/a. Tons: 208 grt. Power: yawl boat with 135 hp engine. Hull: wood. Built: 1900; Bethel, DEl. Designer: J.M.C. Moore. Builder: George K. Phillips & Co., J.M.C. Moore, Master Builder.
Coast Guard cert. Passenger Vessel (Subchapter T).
Crew 9. Trainees 44. Age 16-75. Sex co-ed.
Program type Maritime history, marine biology and environmental studies for high school students and adults; windjammer cruises.
Affiliated institutions Passenger Vessel Association.
Homeport/waters Rockland, ME/ coastal Maine.
Season June through September.
Cost Inquire.

Development of Curricula...

One of ASTA's primary goals is to provide sail training programs with the guidelines necessary for developing programs that educational institutions will recognize, and to involve educators more in the development of appropriate curricula for shipboard education.

VIRGINIA

Built in 1913, *Virginia* is a Q-Class sloop designed to race under the Universal Rule developed by Nathaniel Herreshoff in 1901. Indeed the Q-Class boats were so fast that they were required to sail as a separate class within the Universal Rule. One of the few yachts named to the National Register of Historic Places (1991), *Virginia* has been actively sailed throughout her long career and is a three-time winner of the Chicago-Mackinac Race, winner of the Milwaukee, South Shore Yacht Club "Virginia Series" — which takes its name from the boat — and more than thirty smaller cups. *Virginia* is still actively sailed and raced in Southern California. In 1990, *Virginia* won first place in class and first to finish in the Newport to Ensenada Race. In 1992, *Virginia* was first in class and first overall in the Long Beach-Dana Point race, and won the Dana Point series.

Students learn the fundamentals and fine points of helmsmanship, sail trim and yacht racing, and also practice all the crew positions for rigging, setting, jibing and dousing a spinnaker.

Rig Sloop.
Contact Daniel Heagney, Virginia Program Director, Nautical Heritage Society, The Dana Lighthouse, 24532 Del Prado, Dana Point, CA 92629; (714) 661-1001.
Specs Sparred length: 43'10". LOA: 43'10". LOD: n/a. LWL: 27'6". Draft: 6'. Beam: 8'6". Rig height: 56'. Freeboard: 2'. Sail area: 851 sq. ft. Sail no.: 47793. Tons: 14 grt. Power: n/a. Hull: wood. Built: 1913; City Island, New York. Designer: William Gardner. Builder: Wood & McClure Shipyard.
Coast Guard cert. Sailing School Vessel (Subchapter R) and uninspected yacht.
Crew 6-8; 1-2 instructors. Trainees 6 (day). Age adults. Sex co-ed.
Program type Beginning through advanced sailing and ocean racing.
Affiliated institutions n/a.
Homeport/waters Dana Point, CA/ coastal southern California.
Season Year-round.
Cost $105 per student for 12-hour Introduction to Sailing; $155 for 18-hour Traditional Sailing; $255 for 30-hour Advanced Sailing.

VOYAGER

Voyager was designed and built by Frank Fulchiero. She is a replica of a nineteenth-century packet schooner. Her charms are captured below decks by the varnished woods and polished brass fittings in the main saloon and cabins. Her ten private cabins are fitted with mahogany upper and lower berths, reading lamps, and sinks with running water, a luxury surpassed only by a hot-water shower — a rare treat found on few other schooners.

Voyager is licensed to carry forty nine passengers for day sails and up to twenty overnight. Cruises lasting from three hours to several weeks duration can be tailored to the special needs of interested parties.

Rig Gaff schooner, two-masted.
Contact Capt. Jay Scott, Owner, 500 River Place, Apt. 5109, Detroit, MI 48207; (810) 637-0061.
Specs Sparred length: 95'. LOA: 65'. LOD: 65'. LWL: 61'. Draft: 9'. Beam: 21'. Rig height: 82'. Freeboard: 4'. Sail area: 2,200 sq. ft. Sail no.: n/a. Tons: 63 grt. Power: diesel. Hull: n/a. Built: 1986; Reedville, VA. Designer: Frank Fulchiero. Builder: Jenning Boat Yard and Frank Fulchiero.
Coast Guard cert. Passenger Vessel (Subchapter T).
Crew 4-6 instructors. Trainees 20 (overnight); 49 (day). Age any. Sex co-ed.
Program type Marine biology, maritime history and environmental science.
Affiliated institutions n/a.
Homeport/waters Detroit, MI/Great Lakes and the Caribbean (winter).
Season Year-round.
Cost Inquire.

The information here is provided as a service only and no warranty or endorsement of any individual programs or vessels by the American Sail Training Association is intended or implied. ASTA is not an agent for any vessels or programs and does not control, inspect or approve vessels or programs. All information in this directory is provided by the owners. Before booking or boarding, confirm important facts with the vessel's owner, including the status of safety certificates, equipment, and the suitability of the vessel or program to your abilities and needs.

WELCOME

The square topsail sloop *Welcome* is undergoing complete restoration at the Great Lakes Maritime Academy in Traverse City, Michigan, by volunteer builders of the Maritime Heritage Alliance. The *Welcome* replicates faithfully the original sloop, built in 1775 at Mackinaw City, which hauled cargo, and was later sold to the British military. Armed with cannon and marines, she guarded the strategically vital Straits of Mackinaw until her loss in 1781. The restoration site welcomes visitors to see traditional shipbuilding techniques applied to this lovely vessel. After completion, *Welcome* will sail again and visit ports throughout the Great Lakes, crewed by Maritime Heritage Alliance members.

Rig Topsail sloop.
Contact Linda Strauss, Director of Operations, Maritime Heritage Alliance, P.O. Box 1108, Traverse City, MI 49685-1108; (616) 946-2647.
Specs Sparred length: 90'. LOA: 56'. LOD: n/a. LWL: 49'. Draft: 8'. Beam: 16'. Rig height: 96'. Freeboard: 6'. Sail area: n/a sq. ft. Sail no.: n/a. Tons: 45 grt. Power: Volvo Diesel. Hull: wood. Built: Mackinaw City, MI. Designer: Fred Ford. Builder: Ted McCutcheon.
Coast Guard cert. Attraction Vessel.
Crew 5. Trainees 11. Age 13+. Sex co-ed.
Program type Maritime history for students of all ages.
Affiliated institutions The Association for Great Lakes History, ASTA.
Homeport/waters Traverse City, MI/ northern Great Lakes.
Season May to October.
Cost Maritime Heritage Alliance membership.

Rallies...

Rallies occur every year in various locations with a variety of ASTA member vessels participating. In addition, ASTA has worked with the STA and other national sail training associations in the organization of sail training races and cruises-in-company in connection with international events of major significance.

WESTWARD *(see also Corwith Cramer)*

SEA's educational programs include SEA Semester (college level, 12 weeks long), SEA Summer Session (college level, 8 week long) and SEA Seminars for high school students, teachers and adults. Nearly all of these programs include a seagoing component on board the sailing school vessels *Westward* and *Corwith Cramer*. SEA programs attract outstanding educators and a variety of motivated and adventuresome students who are admitted by competitive selection.

SEA Semester (six sessions each year) offers college students a comprehensive undergraduate marine education and combines classroom study ashore in Woods Hole with an offshore voyage aboard a sailing vessel fully equipped for oceanographic research. Students spend the first half of SEA Semester (and SEA Summer Session) at SEA's Woods Hole campus receiving classroom and laboratory instruction in three 3-credit ocean-related courses: Oceanography, (scientific processes in the oceans); Nautical Science (navigation, ship operations, meteorology); and Maritime Studies (maritime history, literature, art and contemporary maritime affairs). During the second half of the program, students sail aboard the Westward and the *Corwith Cramer*, where theories and problems raised ashore are tested in the practice of oceanography and ship operations at sea.

Students are enrolled in two sequential 4-credit courses: Practical Oceanography I and Practical Oceanography II. (During SEA Summer Session, students are enrolled in one 3-credit, Practical Oceanographic Research.) Aboard ship, students stand eight hours of watch in the lab and on deck and are carried out at sea while the vessel is underway. Students earn a full term's academic credit (17 semester hours) for their participation in SEA Semester.

SEA Seminars: SEA offers a variety of shorter programs for high school students (three-week summer seminars, *Science at SEA* and *The Oceanography of the Gulf of Maine*), teachers (SEA Experience: an intensive five-week summer seminar for teachers of grades K through 12) and lifelong learners (Elderhostel). Seminars are offered primarily in summer months.

Rig Staysail schooner, two-masted.
Contact Sea Education Association (SEA) Inc., P.O. Box 6, Woods Hole, MA 02543; (508) 540-3954, (800) 552-3633; fax (508) 457-4673.
Specs Sparred length: n/a. LOA: 125'. LOD: 99'. LWL: 84'. Draft: 12'6". Beam: 22'. Rig height: 105'. Freeboard: n/a. Sail area: 7,000 sq. ft. Sail no.: n/a. Tons: 114. Power: 350 hp diesel. Hull: steel. Built: 1961; Lemwerder, Germany. Designer: Eldridge-McInnis. Builder:

Abeking & Rasmussen.
Coast Guard cert. Sailing School Vessel.
Crew 10 instructors (6 professional mariners and 4 scientists). Students: 24 college students in SEA Semesters. SEA Seminars include high school students and teachers. Co-ed.
Program type Ocean studies including oceanography, nautical science and maritime history and literature.
Affiliated institutions Boston University, Colgate University, College of Charleston, Cornell University, Drexel University, Eckerd College, Franklin & Marshall College, Rice University, University of Pennsylvania. More than 150 additional colleges and universities award credit for SEA programs.
Homeport/waters Woods Hole, MA/ worldwide.
Season Year-round.
Cost Inquire.

WILLIAM H. ALBURY

The Schooner *William H. Albury* is in it 21st year under Captain Maggio's command. She has represented the Bahamas in the Tall Ships/ OpSail events of 1976, '80, and '82. She is the last Bahamian Schooner in existence and operates from and is maintained at her birthplace of Man of War Cay. Sail Training passages are carried out in Abaco Sound.

Rig Gaff schooner, wood, two-masted.
Contact Capt. Joseph A. Maggio, Schooner Heritage of Miami, Inc., 3145 Virginia St., Coconut Grove, FL 33133; (305) 442-9697.
Specs Sparred length: n/a. LOA: 70'. LOD: 56'. LWL: 49'. Draft: 6'. Beam: 13'. Rig height: 64'. Freeboard: n/a. Sail area: 2,100 sq. ft. Sail no.: TS/BH. Tons: 24. Power: 150 hp Detroit Diesel: GM453. Hull: wood. Built: 1963, Man O War Cay, Abaco, Bahamas. Builder: William H. Albury and his shipwrights. Design: Bahamian Banks Schooner.
Coast Guard cert. Sailing School Vessel (Subchapter R).
Crew Master, mate. Trainees (12 overnight; 30 daysails). Age 13-73. Sex both. Trainees and crew operate vessel under captain and mate.
Program type High Adventure Sea Exploring.
Affiliated institutions Boy Scouts of America.
Homeport/waters Man O War Cay, Abaco, Bahamas/ All waters/harbors of the Bahamas. Biscayne Bay, Florida Keys, and Bahamas.
Season Year-round.
Cost 1994: $450 per person.

WILLIAM H. THORNDIKE

The schooner *William H. Thorndike*, corporate flagship of Meredith, NH-based Annalee Mobilitee Dolls Inc., has arrived back in her home port in New England after twenty years away. Leaving San Diego in the fall of 1993, she headed to New England on a route that took her through the Panama Canal, on towards Antigua, then to Bermuda, and finally homeward to the New England coast.

While docked in San Francisco during the summer of 1993, the boat sailed in the 1st annual Parade of Tall Ships® on the west coast. While in Antigua, the *William H. Thorndike* participated in the 1994 Antigua Classic Yacht Regatta and won two first place prizes: First Place in the Schooner Class for the three days of racing, and First Prize in the competition for Most Photogenic Schooner designation. The vessel is also the recent recipient of a trophy for sportsmanship "over and above the call of duty" at the 7th Annual Camden Wooden Yacht Regatta.

Committed to seamanship, sail training, and good sportsmanship, the captain and crew of the *William H. Thorndike* enjoy competing in the many regattas that occur throughout the year.

The *William H. Thorndike* is a member of the Master Mariners Association, a group made up of traditional vessels that fosters camaraderie through social gatherings of the ships and light-hearted competition. All on board the *William H. Thorndike* invite those interested in seamanship and sail training to contact them to find out more about sailing opportunities on board the *William H. Thorndike*.

Former name ex-*Tyrone*.
Rig Gaff schooner.
Contact Townsend Thorndike, 50 Reservoir Road, P.O. Box 708, Meredith, NH 03253-0708; (603) 279-3333 ext. 3120.
Specs Sparred length: 75'. LOA: 65'. LOD: 65'. LWL: 50'. Draft: 8'6". Beam: 15'. Rig height: 60'. Freeboard: n/a. Sail area: n/a. Sail no.: G39. Tons: 43. Power: diesel. Hull: wood. Built: 1939. Designer: Sam Crocker. Builder: Sims Brothers, doc. # 239013.
Coast Guard cert. n/a.
Crew 4 **Trainees:** 6 **Age:** n/a. **Sex:** co-ed
Program type Seamanship.
Affiliated institutions n/a.
Homeport/ waters New Hampshire/unlimited.
Season n/a.
Cost Inquire.

YANKEE CLIPPER

For sixty-four years, Ship 97 has trained youth between the ages of fourteen and eighteen in nautical skills such as sailing, seamanship, navigation, aquatics, communications and leadership, as well as citizenship and character building. *Yankee Clipper* participated in ASTA activities in both Vancouver and Seattle during the Captain Cook Bicentennial in 1978, in the Expo '86 "Salute to the Sailor" events and as a member of the 1989 Washington Centennial flotilla of classic vessels. In 1983, 1984 and 1987, *Yankee Clipper* was awarded the Old Timers Trophy for the best classic sailboat in the Seattle Yacht Club Opening Day Parade. The Ship also uses a 14' C-Lark and Lido, and 10' Sea Scouter sailing dinghies. Meetings are held weekly, overnight cruises monthly and longer cruises in the summer.

Rig Gaff ketch.
Contact John E. Kelly, Sea Scout Ship No. 97, 5271 Forty-fifth Ave., S.W., Seattle, WA 98136; (206) 932-0971.
Specs Sparred length: 54'. LOA: 44'. LOD: n/a. LWL: 42'. Draft: 5'. Beam: 11'. Rig height: 46'. Freeboard: 3'. Sail area: 1,000 sq. ft. Sail no.: n/a. Tons: n/a. Power: 100 hp diesel. Hull: n/a. Built: n/a. Designer: n/a. Builder: n/a.
Coast Guard cert. Passenger Vessel (Subchapter T).
Crew 14; 4 instructors. Trainees 14 (overnight); 20 (day). Age 14-21. Sex co-ed.
Program type Nautical skills training for Sea Scouts.
Affiliated institutions Boy Scouts of America.
Homeport/waters Seattle, WA/ Puget Sound and British Colombia.
Season Year-round.
Cost Scout dues plus direct cost (no paid crew or officers).

ZODIAC

The circumstances of *Zodiac's* design, construction and livelihood are woven like thread through the fabric of the twentieth century. As *Zodiac*, she was designed to reflect the highest achievement of naval architecture under working sail. Yet she was fundamentally a yacht. Built in 1924 for the Johnson & Johnson Pharmaceutical Company, she raced the Atlantic from Sandy Hook, New

→

ZODIAC continued

Jersey, to Spain, in 1928. The crash of 1929 effectively ended the economic order which supported the giddy days of the great schooner yachts, and *Zodiac* was sold to the San Francisco Bar Pilots Association in 1931.

Renamed *California*, she began a proud 40 years off the Golden Gate. She was the largest schooner ever operated by the Bar Pilots, and worked in that capacity through wartime and in peace until 1972. She was purchased again in 1975 by a group of young craftsmen experienced in wooden boat restoration who stepped a new 105' main mast and 95' foremast in 1982, bent on 7,000 square feet of new Dacron sails and restored her maiden name, *Zodiac*.

In 1982, she was placed on the National Register of Historic Places, the official list of the nation's cultural treasures worthy of preservation as a tangible reminder of the maritime history of the United States. Certified by the U.S. Coast Guard as a passenger vessel, she operates in Puget Sound, the San Juan Islands and Canadian Gulf Island, and is the largest working boat on the West Coast. *Zodiac* offers hot showers, large bunks, heated lounge and fo'c's'le and is ideal for the sail training and education sessions that are popular with a wide range of people, including Elderhostels.

Thirteen Elderhostel sessions in early spring and late fall keep the volunteer crew on their toes teaching sailing, navigation, Northwest Indian Culture, legends of the Pig War Island and geology and natural resources of the San Juan Islands. Summer sessions are open to sailing enthusiasts sixteen years and older who want to learn to handle the great sails and stand watches on the helm and in the chart room.

Former name ex-*California*, ex-*Zodiac*.
Rig Gaff schooner, two-masted.
Contact Karl Mehrer and Tim Mehrer, Vessel Zodiac Corp., P.O. Box 322, Snohomish, WA 98290; (206) 483-4088, (206) 325-6122.
Specs Sparred length: 158'. LOA: 127'. LOD: 127'. LWL: 101'. Draft: 16'. Beam: 25'. Rig height: 105'. Freeboard: 5' (amidships). Sail area: 7,000 sq. ft. Sail no.: n/a. Tons: 145 grt. Power: 700 hp diesel. Hull: wood. Built: 1924; East Boothbay, ME. Designer: William Hand, Jr.. Builder: Hodgdon Bros.
Coast Guard cert. Passenger Vessel (Subchapter T).
Crew 8. Trainees 20 (overnight); 49 (day). Age 16+. Sex co-ed.
Program type Sail training and education for youth of all ages, maritime history, environmental studies and Elderhostel for adults.
Homeport/waters Seattle, WA/ Puget Sound, San Juan Islands, Canadian Gulf Islands.
Season Year-round
Cost $2,500 per day.

Directory of
Sail Training
Programs
in the United States & Canada

The following list of sail training organizations includes organizations that own or operate sail training vessels as well as organizations that promote, support or develop sail training programs. Program descriptions for organizations that own vessels can be found in the entries for individual vessels in the preceding section. Member organizations are indicated by the ASTA® logo next to their name, and their entries usually include a narrative description of the program they offer.

The information here is provided as a service only and no warranty or endorsement of any individual program or vessel by the American Sail Training Association is intended or implied. ASTA is not an agent for any vessels or programs and does not control, inspect or approve vessels or programs. All information in this directory is provided by the owners. Before booking or boarding, confirm important facts with the vessel's owner, including the status of safety certificates, equipment, and the suitability of the vessel or program to your abilities and needs.

ActionQuest/ActionSail Programs

Capt. James Stoll, ActionQuest Programs, PO Box 5507, Sarasota, FL 34277; (813) 924-6789, fax (813) 924-6075.

ActionQuest Programs offers ActionSail as an opportunity for teens ages thirteen to nineteen to learn sailing while living aboard and cruising throughout the British Virgin and Leeward Islands. Shipmates sail in a fleet and rotate positions daily, acting as skipper, mate, navigator, cook, ship's husband, sail trimmer and bosun. Each sailor is fully involved in ship operation and seamanship while receiving certification training in diving, windsurfing, water skiing, celestial navigation and other maritime skills. Harbor visits and shore excursions while in port, and Motive Power programs offered in the evenings aboard, assist young adults to recognize, organize and accomplish their goals.

ActionQuest uses various sailing vessels in their program and operates during the summer months. Cost per session (three to six weeks) runs from $3,000 to $6,000. The programs use the British Virgin Islands and St. Maarten as home ports and sail the Virgin and Leeward Islands. Licensed skippers interested in summer employment are encouraged to apply.

Alexander & Alexander

J. Withers Davis, Alexander & Alexander, 111 Market Pl., Baltimore, MD 21202; (410) 547-2800; fax (410) 547-2914.

Alexandria Seaport Foundation

Alexandria Seaport Foundation, 1000 South Lee St., Jones Point Park, Alexandria, VA 22314; (703) 549-7078. *(Alexandria, Federalist)*

The Alexandria Seaport Foundation provides speakers for community organizations interested in maritime topics, and acquires artifacts and historic vessels for its collections.

Annalee Mobilitee Dolls, Inc.

Townsend Thorndike, 50 Reservoir Road, Box 708, Meredith, NH 03253; (603) 279-3333. *(William H. Thorndike)*

Apalachicola Maritime Museum

Pam Vest, Executive Director, Apalachicola Maritime Museum, Inc., PO Box 625, Apalachicola, FL 32329-0625; (904) 653-8708. *(Governor Stone)*

The Aquaculture Foundation

Capt. Wendell Corey, Executive Director, The Aquaculture Foundation, Captain's Cove, 1 Bostwick Ave., Bridgeport, CT 06605; (203) 367-3327. *(Black Pearl, John E. Pfriem)*

Artisans School

Emory H. Niles, Director of Admissions, The Artisans School, PO Box 539, Rockport, ME 04856; (207) 236-6071; FAX (207) 236-8367.

The Artisans School is a two-year college for creative people. Our associate degree program is interdisciplinary and combines the best aspects of academic and apprenticeship training.

The program centers around a series of learning projects for which students assume responsibility for design, planning, construction, and leadership. The projects are typically watercraft: historical reproduction, high-tech racing yachts, or experimental prototypes that explore uncharted areas of environmental design. Students also make tools, furniture, structural projects, and design exercises. A complement of academic courses is interwoven to expand on the theoretical dimension to these projects and to provide a foundation in writing, business, math and humanities. A high student-to-teacher ratio (currently 4:1) allows for an exceptional degree of individual instruction and attention.

The Artisans School grants an Associate of Science degree following successful completion of the course of study.

Baltimore Operation Sail, Ltd.

(Name to change to Sail Baltimore on Jan. 1, 1995.)
Carmel G. Locey, Executive Director, Baltimore Operation Sail, Ltd., Suite B, 200 West Lombard St., Baltimore, MD. 21201-2517; 410 752-8632; FAX 410 385-0361.

Baltimore Operation Sail, a 501(c)(3) non-profit volunteer organization founded in 1975, is a community service organization located in Baltimore whose mission is to offer maritime educational experiences to the general public, visitors, local citizens, children and disadvantaged youth; to stimulate the economy of the City of Baltimore and surrounding communities; to increase regional tourism to provide a forum and network for encouraging business development opportunities in an international arena; and to foster international cultural exchange.

The Board of Directors of Baltimore Operation Sail accomplishes its mission through recruiting, planning and hosting visits of various types of ships—tall, naval, non-naval vessels of historic interest and other non-commercial vessels whose presence in the harbor offer educational and cultural experiences.

Baltimore Operation Sail also produces special events designed to attract people to the city's waterfront. Utilizing the skills of the board, staff and volunteers, which include event marketing, management and publicity, Baltimore Operation Sail has produced several successful tall ships events and water parades over the past twenty years. We work in partnership with ASTA, the Baltimore Office of Promotion, area yacht clubs and local corporations to produce these quality events.

BOAT/U.S. Foundation

James F. Ellis, BOAT/US Foundation, 880 South Pickett St., Alexandria, VA. 22304; (703) 823-9550; FAX (703) 461-2855.

The BOAT/U.S. Foundation is a national non-profit boating safety organization which operates a toll-free CourseLine for information on free boating courses (800) 336-2628; in Virginia, (800) 245-2628. BOAT/U.S. researches boating accidents and safety issues, produces and distributes free safety literature, maintains a national recreational boating reference library, promotes boating education and tests safety products.

Boston Nautical Heritage Group

Barry L. Nickerson, P.O. Box 379, Stoughton, MA 02072-0379; (617) 344-1749.

Boy Scouts of America

Bill Rogers, Associate Director, Exploring, Boy Scouts of America, 1325 West Walnut Hill Lane, PO Box 152079, Irving, TX 75015-2079; (214) 580-2423; fax (214) 580-2502.

Brigantine, Inc.

Brigantine, Inc., 53 Yonge St., Kingston, Ontario K7M 6G4 Canada; (613) 544-5175. *(St. Lawrence II)*

Buffalo Maritime Society, Inc.

Timothy Downey, President, Buffalo Maritime Society, Inc., 90 Liberty Terr., Buffalo, NY 14215; (716) 834-3922. *(Sea Lion)*

California Maritime Academy

Todd Roberts, Sail Club President, California Maritime Academy, PO Box 1392, Vallejo, CA 94590; (707) 648-4200.

Canadian Sail Training Association (CSTA)

Chris M. Bagley, Canadian Sail Training Association, PO Box 709, Ottawa, Ontario K1P 5P8 Canada; (705) 728-8265.

The Canadian Sail Training Association is dedicated to developing character and fostering an appreciation of our maritime heritage and environment in Canadians young and old alike. Since its beginnings, the CSTA has provided an information and resource network for Canadian sail training programs from coast to coast and on the Great Lakes. The active involvement of our member organizations provides a base for us to raise public and media awareness about sail training and how it can make a difference in people's lives.

Through its members, the CSTA provides leadership and guidance in sail training opportunities for young people and some not so young. It is working towards setting and maintaining standards in sail training and also helps organize and publicize events.

Canvasback Missions, Inc.

Canvasback Missions, Inc., 140 W. Industrial Way, Suite B, Benicia, CA 94510; (707) 746-7828; fax (707) 747-1861. *(Canvasback)*

Challenge, Inc.

Challenge, Inc. Bert Rogers, Program Director, or Arden Brink, Executive Director, 99 Commercial St., Bath, ME 04530-2564; (207) 443-6222, fax (207) 443-6260. *(Harvey Gamage)*

Chesapeake Bay Maritime Museum

Mary Ellen Olcese, Education Department for Programs, Chesapeake Bay Maritime Museum, PO Box 636, St. Michaels, MD 21663; (301) 745-2916.

Class Afloat/Ecole-en-Mer

Marie-Josee Valiquette, Director of Admissions, Class Afloat/Ecole-en-Mer, 1812 Maritime Mews, Vancouver, British Columbia V6H 3X2 Canada; (604) 682-4353; FAX 604 682-5399

Classic Windjammer Co., Inc.

Classic Windjammer Co., Inc., PO Box 459, Madison, NJ 07940; (201) 966-1684. *(Richard Robbins)*

Coastwise Packet Co., Inc.

Capt. Robert S. Douglas, Coastwise Packet Co., Inc., PO Box 429, Vineyard Haven, MA 02568; (508) 693-1699. *(Shenandoah)*

Columbus Santa Maria, Inc.

50 W. Gay St., Columbus, OH 43215; (614) 645-8760. *(Santa Maria)*
Rig Nao
Contact Andy Politz, Bo'sun, 50 W. Gay St., Columbus, OH 43215; (614) 645-8760.
Specs Sparred length: n/a. LOA: 113'. LOD: 98'. LWL: 72'. Draft: 5'6". Beam: 26'. Rig height: 89'. Freeboard: n/a. Sail area: n/a. Sail no.: n/a. Tons: n/a. Power: n/a. Hull: n/a. Built: n/a. Designer: n/a. Builder: n/a.
Coast Guard cert. n/a.
Crew The Santa Maria does not sail so has no crew in the traditional sense. Trainees: n/a. Age: n/a. Sex: n/a.
Program type Historic tours, sail training (day and overnight), boatbuilding, small craft handling, high school independent study courses, sail-a-day, navigation, anchoring, sounding, etc., others available.
Affiliated institutions Columbus Santa Maria, Inc.
Homeport/waters Columbus, Ohio
Season Closed January 1 through March 30
Cost Prices vary, please inquire

The *Santa Maria* is a full-scale museum quality representation of Christopher Columbus' flagship. She is berthed in the Scioto River in downtown Columbus, Ohio, the largest city in the world named for Christopher Columbus. The *Santa Maria* was built for Columbus' 1992 Quincentennial Celebration from Martinez Hidalgo's plans as adapted and provided by the Kingdom of Spain. While she is rigged to sail, she is primarily operated as a dockside exhibit and educational vessel due to space limitations of the Scioto River.

The *Santa Maria* is owned and operated by Columbus Santa Maria, an Ohio charitable not-for-profit organization. In addition to being open to the public for daily tours, a wide variety of educational programs are offered for youth and adults. Small boatbuilding and rowing programs complement the sail handling courses offered on the ship.

Conventures, Inc.

Dusty S. Rhodes, President, Boston Seaport Festival, Conventures, Inc., 250 Summer St., Boston, MA 02210; (617) 439-7700; fax (617) 330-1732.

Conventures, Inc., New England's leading special events management firm, is proud to support the American Sail Training Association. Creators and managers of Sail Boston 1992, the largest tall ships event in New England history, Conventures continues its mission to promote a great awareness and appreciation of Boston's maritime heritage.

The fifth annual Boston Seaport Festival is scheduled to take place at the Boston National Historical Park at Charlestown Navy Yard on August 17-20, 1995. The event encompasses an ASTA Rally and includes a full weekend of events for the captains and crews of participating vessels. On-going entertainment, children's interactive exhibits and games, marine craft displays and local seafood restaurant participation highlight the festival. Having drawn over 50,000 people each year, the Boston Seaport Festival has become one of the summer's main events at the Navy Yard. Conventures has initiated a Visiting Ships Program in Boston Harbor and was pleased to host the *Libertad*, Argentina's naval training ship, in July. The Seaport Festival brought an additional eight ships, including the *Tole Mour* from Hawaii, the *Gazela* from Philadelphia and the *HMS Bounty* from Fall River. The *Danmark* sailed into Boston September 22-28, 1994.

Conventures is dedicated to assisting all sail training vessels and sail training programs with logistical help for any scheduled port calls in Boston throughout the sailing season. Conventures is also able to offer assistance to vessels who seek sponsorship or other fund raising opportunities while in port. In the spirit of Sail Boston 1992, Conventures looks forward with great anticipation to maintaining an active role in sail training ships, programs, and events around the world.

Corpus Christi Museum of Science

David W. Hiott, Fleet Capt., Las Carabelas Columbus Fleet Association, 1900 North Chaparral, Corpus Christi, TX 78401; (512) 883-2882. (*Nina, Pinta, Santa Maria*)

Crosscurrent Voyages

Capt. Rod Phillips, Crosscurrent Voyages, 92 Seabreeze Dr., Richmond, CA 94804; (510) 234-8202. (*Nehemiah*)

Delaware Bay Schooner Project

Ms. Meghan Wren, Delaware Bay Schooner Project, PO Box 57, Dorchester, NJ 08316; (609) 785-2060. *(A. J. Meerwald/Clyde A. Phillips)*

Dirigo Cruises

Eben Whitcomb, Dirigo Cruises, 39 Waterside Lane, Clinton, CT 06413-2194; (203) 669-7068.

Discovery Harbour

Chris M. Bagley, Marine Coordinator, Discovery Harbour, PO Box 1800, Penetanguishene, Ontario L0K 1P0 Canada; (705) 549-8064. *(Bee, Tecumseth)*

Downeast Windjammer Cruises

Downeast Windjammer Cruises, Capt. Steven F. Pagels, P.O. Box 8, Cherryfield, ME 04622; (207) 288-4585 (summer), (207) 546-2927 (winter). *(Francis Todd, Natalie Todd)*

Durlach Associates

John Durlach, Mark Durlach, Durlach Associates, 218 King St., Suite 200, Charleston, SC 29401; (803) 723-2801.

Durlach Associates works with the City of Charleston to promote tall ships events and attract tall ships to the city of Charleston.

Elizabeth II State Historic Site

Elizabeth II State Historic Site, PO Box 155, Manteo, NC 27954; (919) 473-1144. *(Elizabeth II)*

Fall River Area Chamber of Commerce & Industry

Robert J. Boiselle, President, Fall River Area Chamber of Commerce & Industry, 200 Pocasset Street, Fall River, MA 02721; (508) 676-8226

Fall River Celebrates America is an annual four-day waterfront festival sponsored by the Fall River Area Chamber of Commerce & Industry that is held the second weekend in August at Battleship Cove in Fall River, Massachusetts. The Celebration includes a parade of sail led by the tall ship, *HMS Bounty;* an international food fair; water ski shows; concerts and entertainment by nationally acclaimed entertainers; a six-division parade; traveling amusement park; children's activity center; beach volleyball tournament arts, crafts and collectibles fair; sailing regatta and more! A highlight of the festival is a spectacular fireworks display on Saturday evening.

Fall River Celebrates America increases awareness and knowledge of the historic Fall River waterfront, promotes maritime events, provides educational experiences in the area of maritime training through exhibits and demonstrations, promotes tourism and attracts more than 500,000 people to Battleship Cove.

Please contact: Donna Futoransky, Managing Director of Fall River Celebrates America, Fall River Area Chamber of Commerce & Industry, 200 Pocasset St., Fall River, MA 02720; (508) 676-8226.

Friends of Argus

Commodore Bill Cunningham, 1931 West Coast Highway, Newport Beach, CA 92633; (714) 642-5031. (*Argus*)

Gloucester Adventure, Inc.

Benjamin S. Hersey, Gloucester Adventure, Inc., PO Box 1306, Gloucester, MA 01931-1306; (508) 281-8079. (*Adventure*)

Grand Banks Schooner Museum

Bob Ryan, Grand Banks Schooner Museum, Box 123, Boothbay, ME 04537; (207) 633-4727. (*Sherman Zwicker*)

Gray's Harbor Historical Seaport

Les Bolton, Gray's Harbor Historical Seaport, PO Box 2019, Aberdeen, WA 98520; (206) 532-8611. (*Lady Washington*)

Great Lakes Maritime Academy

RAdm. David C. Brown, USMS, Superintendent, Great Lakes Maritime Academy, 1701 East Front St., Traverse City, MI 49686; (616) 922-1200, (800) 748-0566 ext. 1203.

Great Lakes Schooner Co. Ltd.

Great Lakes Schooner Co. Ltd., 249 Queen's Quay West, Suite 111, Toronto, Ontario M5J 2N5; (416) 591-5355, (800) 267-3866, (800) 267-3866, fax (416) 591-5377. (*Challenge*)

Hands On Sail Training, Inc.

Capt. Dutch Shultis, 3 Church Cir. # 234, Annapolis, MD 21401; (410) 268-0647.

Harbourfront Centre

Fred Addis, Marine Programmer, Harbourfront Centre, 410 Queen's Quay West, Toronto, Ontario M5V 2Z3 Canada; (416) 973-4119; FAX (416) 973-8729.

Historic St. Mary's City Commission

Capt. Will Gates, Historic St. Mary's City Foundation, PO Box 39, St. Mary's City, MD

20686; (301) 862-0982. *(Maryland Dove)*

Historic Ships Consortium

Mark Newell, Historic Ships Consortium, P.O. Box 984, Augusta, GA 30901; (803) 279-8216.

HMS Rose Foundation, Inc.

Richard Bailey, "HMS" Rose Foundation, Inc., One Bostwick Ave., Bridgeport, CT 06605; (203) 335-0932, (203) 335-1433; FAX (203) 335-6793. *(Rose)*

Hudson River Sloop Clearwater, Inc.

Capt. Betsy Garthwaite, Hudson River Sloop *Clearwater*, Inc., 112 Market St., Poughkeepsie, NY 12601-4095; (914) 454-7673. *(Clearwater)*

Inland Seas Education Association

Inland Seas Education Association, P.O. Box 218, 101 Dame St., Millside Building, Suttons Bay, MI 49682-0218; (616) 271-3077. *(Inland Seas)*

Jamestown-Yorktown Foundation

Capt. Eric Speth, Maritime Program Manager, Jamestown-Yorktown Foundation, PO Drawer JF, Williamsburg, VA 23187; (804) 229-1607; FAX (804) 253-7350. *(Godspeed, Susan Constant)*

Kalmar Nyckel Shipyard

Peggy Tigue-Fillos, Kalmar Nyckel Shipyard, 823 East 7th St., Wilmington, DE 19801; (302) 429-7447.
The Kalmar Nyckel Foundation has embarked on an enthusiastic project to build a working replica of the 1629 Dutch Pinnance. *Kalmar Nyckel*, which landed the first Swedes and Finns in 1638. We have also established a working colonial shipyard and nautical museum. The *Kalmar Nyckel* Project is a complex of historical, cultural and educational facilities and programs. The *Kalmar Nyckel* Project is scheduled for lofting (the first phase of our building project) in the Fall of 1994, with a completion date in 1996.

Leif Ericson Viking Ship Co.

Capt. David Segermark, Leif Ericson Viking Ship Co., 144 Ridgefield Rd. Newtown Square, PA 19073; (610) 356-3723. *(Norseman)*

Living Classrooms Foundation

James Bond, Executive Director, Living Classrooms Foundation, The Lighthouse at Pier 5, 717 Eastern Ave., Baltimore, MD 21202; (410) 685-0295; FAX (410) 752-8433. *(Lady Maryland)*

The Longship Company, Ltd.

Bruce Blackistone, The Longship Company, Ltd., Oakley Farm, Avenue, MD 20609; (301) 769-2627. *(Fyrdraca, Gyrfalcon)*

Los Angeles Maritime Institute

Mr. James L. Gladson, Los Angeles Maritime Institute, Berth 84, Foot of Sixth St., San Pedro, CA 90731; (310) 548-2902. *(Swift of Ipswich)*

Louisbourg Harbour Committee, Town of

P.O. Box 88, Louisbourg, Nova Scotia, Canada, B0A 1M0; (902) 733-2014, FAX (902) 733-2838.

Historic Louisbourg, on Cape Breton Island in Nova Scotia, Canada, is both an active fishing harbour and the site of an 18th century French fortress. The harbour is deep, large, and well-protected, and it is surrounded by magnificent natural scenery. Louisbourg will be a busy port in 1995, as the Town of Louisbourg and the world-class Fortress of Louisbourg National Historic Site will commemorate significant events of a colorful past.

The year 1995 marks the 275th anniversary of the official founding of the historic fortress town, the 250th anniversary of the successful New England siege and the 100th anniversary of the coming of the Sydney and Louisbourg Railway. In 1995, Louisbourg looks back to these events as important milestones in the life of this seafaring community. The Town of Louisbourg is inviting ships and sailing enthusiasts to Louisbourg to be part of this historic summer. The Fortress of Louisbourg National Historic Site is planning a Grand Encampment of military enactors from July 27-30. Victor Suthren of the War Museum in Ottawa is enthusiastically organizing a Grand Descent of the St. Lawrence River by Great Lakes sail training vessels to commemorate the event.

Contact the Town of Louisbourg Harbour Committee to learn more about the port of Louisbourg, harbour facilities and services, and the exciting events that are planned for 1995.

M. Friedman Corp.

M. Friedman Corp./The *Gray*, Suite 101, 21 Montauk Ave., New London, CT 06320-4913; (203) 447-0706. *(Gray)*

Mahina Productions, Inc.

John Neal, Director, Mahina Productions, Inc., Box 1596, Friday Harbor, WA 98250; (206) 378-6131, fax (206) 378-4392. (*Mahina Tiare*)

Mahina Productions produces weekend Offshore Cruising Seminars in the U.S., geared for sailors who are considering or planning on making coastal or offshore passages on their own sailboats. Covered in these 20 hour exciting seminars are: Boat Selection, Sail Selection and Repair, Equipment and Outfitting, Cost of Cruising, Working While Cruising, Piloting and Navigation, Provisioning, Women's' Point of View, Anchoring Techniques, Weather and Passage Planning, Cruising Medicine and Safety Equipment and Practices. Presenters include authors John Neal and Barbara Marratt, sail maker Carol Hasse, yacht designer Robert Perry, meteorologist Earl Seagars and more. John Neal and staff have presented 78 weekend Offshore Cruising Seminars since 1976 to over 4,000 students, many of whom have since circumnavigated the globe. The weekend seminar is included for students accepted on offshore sail-training legs aboard *Mahina Tiare*, which operates in the South Pacific.

Rig Ketch
Contact *Mahina Tiare* Sailing Expeditions, John Neal, P.O. Box 1596, Friday Harbor, WA 98250; (206) 378-6131, fax (206) 378-4392.
Specs Sparred length: n/a. LOA: 42'4". LWL: 34'5". Draft: 5'9". Beam: 12'5". Rig height: 55'1". Freeboard: 4'2". Sail area: 824 sq. ft. Sail no.: HR 42-70. Tons: 12. Power: 62 hp Volvo diesel. Hull: fiberglass. Built n/a. Designer: Enderlien/Rassy. Builder: Hallberg Rassy.
Coast Guard cert. n/a.
Crew 1-2 instructors. Trainees 4-5. Age 30-70. Sex co-ed.
Program type Sail, navigation and ocean passage training.
Affiliated institutions n/a.
Homeport/ waters Friday Harbor, WA and Auckland, New Zealand/ South Pacific, coastal Chile and Antarctica.
Season May to November for South Pacific, December-May for Chile and Antarctica.
Cost Inquire.

Mahina Tiare has sailed approximately 9,000 miles a year as a sailing school vessel since 1990 in the North and South Pacific. Since *Mahina Tiare* is a modern vessel, sail handling, navigation and seamanship taught aboard are current with today's practices aboard offshore yachts. However, the important traditions of watch standing, good seamanship, celestial navigation and personal responsibility to the ship and one's shipmates are very much a part of passages aboard *Mahina Tiare*. Many of *Mahina Tiare's* students are planning long distance ocean cruises on their own boats in the future, but have chosen to make their first ocean passage with an experienced (20 years, 115,000 miles) instructor. Celestial navigation, radar navigation, ancient Polynesian navigation and daily weather plotting are a vital part of each cruise.

In June 1994, *Mahina Tiare* left Auckland and sailed to Tahiti, the Austral Islands, to Puerto Montt, Chile, down the coast of Chile, departing January, 1995 for a five week expedition to Antarctica. *Mahina Tiare* will return home to Friday Harbor, WA via coastal Chile, Juan Fernandez Island, Easter Island, Pitcairn Island, the Marquesas, Hawaii and Victoria, B.C. Passage legs range from two to four weeks and applicants must have at least intermediate-level sailing skills. Included in the expedition is tuition at an intensive weekend Offshore Cruising Seminar, conducted five times annually in various locations in the U.S. For a complete brochure on *Mahina Tiare* Sailing Expeditions, contact Armchair Sailor, 2110 Westlake Ave. North, Seattle, WA 98109; (800) 875-0852, fax (206) 285-1935.

Maine Maritime Academy

Capt. Elliot D. Rappaport, or Phil Harman, Director of Waterfront, Maine Maritime Academy, Castine, ME 04420; (207) 326-4311. *(Bowdoin)*

Maine Maritime Museum Apprenticeshop

Maine Maritime Museum Apprenticeshop, 243 Washington St., Bath, ME 04530; (207) 443-1316. *(Chance, Maine)*

Maine Windjammer Cruises

Ray Williamson, Maine Windjammer Cruises, PO Box 617, Camden, ME 04843; (207) 236-2938. *(Grace Bailey, Mercantile, Mistress)*

Marimed Foundation

Mr. David D. Higgins, Marimed Foundation, 1050 Ala Moana Blvd., Building D, Honolulu, Hawaii 96814; (808) 593-2586. *(Tole Mour)*

Marine Sciences Under Sail

Ned Webster, Director, Marine Sciences Under Sail, PO Box 3994, Hollywood, FL 33023; (305) 983-7015.

Maritime and Seafood Industry Museum

Robin Krohn, Manager, Maritime and Seafood Industry Museum, PO Box 1907, Biloxi, MS 39533; (601) 435-6320. *(Glenn L. Swetman, Mike Sekul)*

Maritime Heritage Alliance

Linda Strauss, Director of Operations, Maritime Heritage Alliance, PO Box 1108, Traverse City, MI 49685-1108; (616) 946-2647. *(Madeline, Welcome)*

Maritime Museum of San Diego

Joseph Ditler, Development Director, Maritime Museum of San Diego, 1306 North Harbor Dr., San Diego, CA 92101; (619) 234-9153.

Massachusetts Maritime Academy

Massachusetts Maritime Academy, PO Box D, Buzzards Bay, MA 02532; (508) 759-5761.

Massachusetts Schooner Ernestina Commission

Gregg Swanzey, P.O. Box 2010, State Pier, New Bedford, MA 02741-2010; (508) 992-4900, FAX (508) 984-7719. *(Ernestina)*

Milwaukee Maritime Center

David B. Falzetti, Executive Director, Milwaukee Lake Schooner, Ltd., Milwaukee Maritime Center, 500 North Harbor Dr., Milwaukee, WI 53202; (414) 276-5664, fax (414) 276-8838. *(Milwaukee Lake Schooner)*

Mystic Nautical Heritage Society, Inc.

Capt. Geoffrey P. Jones, Schooner *Sylvina W. Beal* @ Mystic Nautical Heritage Society, 120 School Street, Mystic, CT 06355. *(Sylvina W. Beal)*

Mystic Seaport Museum

Education Department, Mystic Seaport Museum, Box 6000, Mystic, CT 06355-0990; (203) 572-5285. *(Brilliant, Joseph Conrad)*

National Marine Educators Association (NMEA)

National Marine Educators Association, PO Box 51215, Pacific Grove, CA 93950.

The National Marine Educators Association (NMEA) is an organization of about 1,500 teachers and administrators throughout North America and the Pacific who have an interest in marine and aquatic education. The members teach in disciplines as diverse as fine arts and home economics as well as the more traditional biology, chemistry and physics. Through their major publication, *Currents*, the *Journal of Marine Education*, and their newsletter, *NMEA News*, they encourage their members to infuse marine and aquatic topics into their traditional curricula. A national conference held the first week of August each year allows the membership to share recent advances and innovative ideas in marine education. Fifteen regional chapters including coastal North America (Great Lakes included) and the Pacific Islands give the members local opportunities for the exchange of ideas and methods.

National Maritime Historical Society (NMHS)

Mr. Peter Stanford, President, National Maritime Historical Society, PO Box 68, 5 John Walsh Blvd., Peekskill, NY 10566; (914) 737-7878.

The society works to keep America's seafaring history alive through research, archaeological expeditions and ship preservation efforts. They work with museums, historians and various sail training groups and publish a quarterly magazine, *Sea History*.

National Ocean Access Project

National Ocean Access Project, PO Box 33141, Washington, DC 20033; (301) 280-0466.

National Sailing Industry Association

Mr. George Rounds, National Sailing Industry Assoc., Suite 1150, 401 North Michigan Ave., Chicago, IL 60611.

National Trust for Historic Preservation

Richard Moe, Director of Maritime Preservation, National Trust for Historic Preservation, 1785 Massachusetts Ave., N.W., Washington, DC 20036; (202) 673-4105.

The National Trust for Historic Preservation is a private, non-profit organization chartered by Congress to encourage public participation in the preservation of sites, buildings, vessels, objects and activities significant in United States history and culture. The Trust is supported by membership dues, private gifts and matching grants from the U.S. Department of the Interior.

Nauset Sea Explorers

Capt. Michael F. Allard, Nauset Sea Explorers, Boy Scouts of America, Allard Construction, Inc., PO Box 1236, Orleans, MA 02653; (508) 255-5260. *(Picara)*

Nautical Heritage Society

Nautical Heritage Society, The Dana Lighthouse, 24532 Del Prado, Dana Point, CA 92629; (714) 661-1001. *(Californian, Virginia)*

Navy Pier, Chicago, Illinois

Owner: Metropolitan Pier and Exposition Authority, Chicago, IL. Jon Clay Acting CEO, Jerome R. Butler, General Manager. Navy Pier - 600 East Grand Avenue, Chicago, IL 60611; (312) 791-6568, FAX (312) 791-6572.

Navy Pier, a Chicago landmark since 1916, is being redeveloped into a multi-use property featuring a 170,000 square foot convention facility, 48,000 square feet of meeting rooms, theaters, the Chicago Children's Museum, specialty retail and restaurants. In addition to these features, the Pier will offer a multitude of other activities, including a giant Ferris wheel, an outdoor park, a 1500-seat performance pavilion and an enclosed tropical park with spectacular views of Chicago's skyline and Lakefront. Navy Pier provides the perfect location for exhibitions, meetings or special events of any kind. In addition, the Pier will be home to several dinner and sightseeing boats, and in May of 1995 will also have a four-masted schooner which will provide rides to passengers on both an excursion and charter basis. Located just minutes from Chicago's hotel district, the Pier promises to be a "must see" attraction.

The grand opening of the "new" Navy Pier is scheduled for Spring/Summer 1995.

New England Historic Seaport

New England Historic Seaport, Building 1, Charlestown Navy Yard, Boston, MA 02129; (617) 242-1414. (*Spirit of Massachusetts*)

New Jersey Fresh Seafood Festival

Robert Ruffulo, 2915-17 Atlantic Ave., Atlantic City, NJ 08401; (609) 266-0927.

New Netherland Museum

Nick Burlakoff, *Half Moon* Visitor Center and New Netherland Museum, Liberty State Park, Jersey City, NJ 07035; (201) 433-5900. (*Half Moon*)

Norfolk, City of

Ms. Betty A. Webb, Department of Parks and Recreation, City of Norfolk, 501 Boush St., Norfolk, VA 23510; (804) 441-2400; FAX (804) 441-5423. *(Norfolk)*

Norfolk Festevents

Karen Scherberger, Executive Director, Tim Jones, Ship Director, 120 West Main St., Norfolk, VA 23510; (804) 627-7809; FAX (804) 622-8369.

Coordinating and handling all aspects of Norfolk's waterfront ship visits program. Facilities include the new, state-of-the-art NAUTICUS International Pier located at NAUTICUS, The National Maritime Center. Regular ship visits scheduled include tall ships and Government vessels, NAVY, USCG, NOAA. The NAUTICUS International Pier is centrally located and within short walking distance to downtown Norfolk shopping areas, a wide variety of restaurants and nightclubs, the YMCA, harbor and dinner cruise boats, churches, cultural events, such as symphony opera, theater, The Chrysler Museum, and the MacArthur Memorial. It is immediately adjacent to Town Point Park, site of free weekly festivals, concerts and special events, and the Waterside Festival Marketplace with 150 shops and restaurants open 7 days a week. Call or write for more information.

Northern S.T.A.R. (Sail Training and Renewal)

Jack Ewing, Northern S.T.A.R., 2200 E. Mitchell Rd. #199, Petoskey, MI 49770; (616) 547-9674.

The Northern S.T.A.R. program focuses on maritime history, ecological marine biology, and stresses crew experience, expeditionary learning, and early intervention.

Oakland, Port of

Bob Middleton, Public Affairs, Port of Oakland, 530 Water St., Oakland, CA 94607.

Ocean Voyages

Mary T. Crowley, Director, Ocean Voyages, 1709 Bridgeway, Sausalito, CA 94965; (415) 332-4681; FAX (415) 332-7460.

Ocean Voyages was founded sixteen years ago to provide participatory educational sailing programs throughout the world. Programs are open to sailing enthusiasts of all ages. Most programs run from one to four weeks in length. Ocean Voyages works with educators and institutions to design customized programs for youth participation.

Ocean Voyages works toward preserving the maritime heritage of the United States and providing opportunities for people to gain sailing education and seafaring experience. Coastal and inter-island programs are available in addition to offshore passagemaking opportunities. Program areas include Hawaii, California, the Pacific Northwest, Galapagos Islands, Aegean Sea, Caribbean, French Polynesia and New Zealand, as well as Pacific and Atlantic Ocean crossings.

Ocean World Institute, Inc.

Robert Keith, Ocean World Institute, Inc., 831 South Bond St., Baltimore, MD 21231; (410) 522-4214. *(Minnie V.)*

Operation Sail

Operation Sail, Inc., 2 Greenwich Plaza, Suite 100, Greenwich, CT 06830; (203) 629-4600, fax (203) 629-1992.

Operation Sail, Inc., a non-profit organization, is dedicated to serving the cadets and others who man the wonderful tall ships of the world. Our mission is not only to bring these ships and fine young people together, but to support and nurture the continued existence and proliferation of sail training.

Operation Sail is the oldest tall ships organization in the United States. Our first Parade of Sail took place in New York Harbor on July 4, 1964; since then, in 1976, 1986 and 1992, thousands of sailing ships, their cadets and crews, have participated in OpSail events. Since its first gathering of tall ships, Operation Sail has continued to encourage international awareness of the great maritime traditions that are such an important part of or country's history. As our nation's flagship tall ships organization, we take great pride in the fact that, since or founding in 1961, the number of large sailing ships around the world has more than doubled.

Operation Sail's Tall Ships® Information Bureau was created to serve the tall ships community; its mission is to assist, inform and answer questions concerning tall ships and sail training. Since its formation in early 1993, the Tall Ships® Information Bureau has received and responded to a great variety of inquiries in such areas as liaison with government officials, customs and immigration, transportation, port facilities, environmental regulations, educational programs, current and historical ship information, ship schedules, reference works, tall ship events, et.

On July 4, 2000, Operation Sail will again assemble the great fleet of tall ships and the vessels of navies from around the world in New York Harbor. With this huge gathering of sail training, private and naval craft, we will unite young people from around the world in the ongoing appreciation of the maritime heritage common to us all.

Orange Coast College Sailing Center

Orange Coast College Sailing Center, 1801 West Coast Highway, Newport Beach, CA 92663; (714) 645-9412; FAX (714) 645-1859. *(Alaska Eagle)*

Orange County Marine Institute

Daniel T. Stetson, Director of Maritime Affairs, Orange County Marine Institute, 24200 Dana Point Harbor Dr., Dana Point, CA 92629; (714) 496-2274; FAX (714) 496-4296. *(Pilgrim)*

Oswego Maritime Foundation

Henry Spang, Vice President and Education Through Involvement (ETI) Director, Oswego Maritime Foundation, McCrobie Building, 41 Lake St., Oswego, NY 13126; (315) 342-5753. *(OMF Ontario)*

Out o' Mystic Cruises, Inc.

Rita Schmidt, Out o' Mystic Cruises, Inc., 88B Howard Street, New London, CT 06355; (203) 437-0385. *(Mystic Clipper)*

Pacific Northwest Passages

Pacific Northwest Passages, PO Box 485, Langley, WA 98260; (206) 321-4840. *(Sunderland)*

Pennsylvania Historical and Museum Commission

Capt. Walter Rybka, U.S. Brig *Niagara*, Pennsylvania Historical and Museum Commission, 164 East Front St., Erie, PA 16502; (814) 871-4596. *(Niagara)*

Philadelphia Ship Preservation Guild

Karen H. Love, Executive Vice President, Philadelphia Ship Preservation Guild, Penn's Landing, Chestnut St. at Delaware Ave., Philadelphia, PA 19106; (215) 923-9030, (215) 928-1819; FAX: (215) 923-2801. *(Gazela of Philadelphia)*

Pilgrim Packet Company

Capt. Gary Kurtz, P.O. Box 491, Kendall, NY 14476; (716) 682-4757. *(Schooner Pilgrim)*

Plimoth Plantation, Inc.

John Reed, Plimoth Plantation, Inc., PO Box 1620, Plymouth, MA 02360-1620; (508) 746-1622, x250; FAX (508) 746-4978. *(Mayflower II)*

Pride of Baltimore, Inc.

W. Bruce Quackenbush, Jr., Executive Director, Pride of Baltimore, Inc., World Trade Center, Suite 222, 401 East Pratt St., Baltimore, MD 21202-3045; (410) 539-1151; FAX (410) 539-1190. *(Pride of Baltimore II)*

Project Sail, Inc.

Paul Pennoyer, Executive Director, Project Sail, Inc., 23 Gramercy Park South, New York, NY 10003; (212) 439-8084.

Project Sail works with a number of youth groups throughout New York City, including the East Harlem Maritime School, Hostos Community College and three Sea Explorer Ships of the Boy Scouts of America. Project Sail offers shore-based training in maritime-related skills including navigation and piloting, marlinespike seamanship and rowing, with the aim of preparing them for extended sailing voyages. Project Sail works with a core group of about eighty-five teenagers using facilities on the Harlem River and at the State University of New York Maritime College at Fort Schuyler, the Bronx.

Pueblo Mariners of New Mexico

Capt. William Young, CWO, USCG (ret.), Coordinator, Pueblo Mariners of New Mexico, 1688 Plum Road, NE, Rio Rancho, NM 87124; (505) 891-2474.

Rebel Marine Service, Inc.

Rebel Marine Services, Inc., 1553 Bayville St., Norfolk, VA 23503; (804) 588-6022. *(Norfolk Rebel)*

Sail Adventures In Learning, Inc.

David or Arden Brink, Sail Adventures In Learning (S.A.I.L.), Inc., 99 Commercial Street, Bath, ME 04530; (207) 443-6222. *(Discovery)*

Sail and Life Training Society

Capt. Martyn J. Clark, Executive Director, Sail and Life Training Society (SALTS), PO Box 5014, Station B, Victoria, British Columbia V8R 6N3 Canada; (604) 383-6811; FAX (604) 383-7781. *(Pacific Swift, Robertson II)*

Sailing Crafts, Inc.

Capt. Jeff Crafts, Sailing Crafts, Inc., P.O. Box 131, Southwest Harbor, ME 04679; (207) 244-7813. *(Rachel B. Jackson)*

Sail Martha's Vineyard

Nancy Hoffmann, P.O. Box 1998, Vineyard Haven, MA 02568-1998; (508) 696-7644
In fall of 1994, Sail Martha's Vineyard began a program, with the cooperation of the public schools, to provide free sailing programs for Martha Vineyard's public school children.

Saint John Port Corporation

Peter Clark, Saint John Port Corp., 133 Prince William St., PO Box 6429, Station A, Saint John, New Brunswick E2L 4R8 Canada; (506) 636-4809; FAX (506) 636-4443.

San Francisco Maritime National Historical Park

San Francisco Maritime National Historical Park, Ft. Mason, San Francisco, CA 94123; (415) 556-3002.

The San Francisco Maritime National Historical Park has *Alma, Balclutha* and *C. A. Thayer* as part of their living history exhibits. The Park's program provides insights into the life of mariners and the history of the sea, with an emphasis on understanding through experience and doing. Overnight stays aboard the vessels introduce school children to life aboard ship and the role of the seaman, and through the experience, help them relate the past to themselves. The ships are open to visitors during the day. The *Alma* also makes visits to ports around the Bay as part of tall ships events and sail training experiences.

Sausalito TALL SHIPS® Society

Alice C. Cochran, President, Sausalito TALL SHIPS® Society, PO Box 926, Sausalito, CA 94966 (415) 331-1009.

The Sausalito TALL SHIPS® Society is a non-profit organization dedicated to education in nautical skills and the operation and preservation of traditional sailing vessels, particularly tall ships. The Society's goals include promoting tall ships in San Francisco Bay, providing shore-side education, providing sails and shipboard education for members, sponsoring scholarships for sail training cadets and collaborating with other maritime organizations.

In the last three years the Society has sponsored scholarships or provided access to sailing experiences for over 50 people on the tall ships *Californian* (California), *Concordia* (Canada) and *Kaisei* (Japan). *Pacific Swift* (1994), *Lady Washington* (1993), *Kaisei* (1992), and *HMS Bounty* (1991) have each been the featured vessel in our annual Vintage Boat Show, a fund-raiser for sail training scholarships. Last year all of our members had an opportunity to sail on a square rigged ship (*Hawaiian Chieftain*) or on a barkentine (*Concordia*) or on a square topsail schooner (*Tole Mour* and *Pride of Baltimore*) in the tall ships parade.

Schooner AMERICA U.S.A., Inc.

Schooner *AMERICA* U.S.A., Inc., 100 North Union St., Alexandria, VA 22314; (703) 683-4654. (*AMERICA*)

The Schooner Bluenose Foundation

The Schooner *Bluenose* Foundation, Suite 303, Xerox Building, 1949 Upper Water St., P.O. Box 34009, Halifax, Nova Scotia B3J 3N3 Canada; (902) 429-8100, fax (902) 429-8633. *(Bluenose)*

Schooner Exploration Associates, Ltd.

John P. McKean, Schooner Exploration Associates, Ltd., "0" Lily Pond Dr., Camden, ME 04843; (207) 236-8353, (800) 233-PIER (summer); PO Box 4114, Key West, FL 33041-4114; (305) 296-9992 (winter). *(Appledore II)*

Schooner Heritage of Miami Inc.

Capt. Joseph A. Maggio, Schooner *Heritage of Miami* Inc., 3145 Virginia St., Coconut Grove, FL 33133; (305) 442-9697. *(Heritage of Miami II, William H. Albury)*

Schooner, Inc.

Karl Rosenbaum, Executive Director, Schooner, Inc., 60 South Water St., New Haven, CT 06519; (203) 865-1737. *(Quinnipiack)*

Schooner Pilot Trust

Mr. E. N. Paulsen, Schooner *Pilot* Trust, 1220 Rosecrans Street, Suite 308, San Diego, CA 92106; (805) 686-4484 (phone/FAX). *(Pilot)*

Schooners Foundation

George L. Maxwell, Schooners Foundation, 53 East 66th St., New York, NY 10021; (212) 988-1057; FAX (212) 988-1257.

The Schooners Foundation is a private non-profit organization which promotes sail training in the United States and Great Britain by increasing the number of people who participate. The foundation provides funds to programs and trainees, and its activities include fund raising and the consideration of grant applications.

The Schooners Foundation is affiliated with the Sail Training Association (STA) Schooners, *Malcolm Miller* and *Sir Winston Churchill*, and publicizes the opportunity to sail aboard these 150' topsail schooners to interested individuals in the United States. The STA schooners offer a program of three to twenty-one day cruises in British and European waters for teenagers and adults. In addition, the schooners offer special programs geared towards management training for companies. Information on the STA schooners may be obtained by contacting the Schooners Foundation.

Schooners Foundation funding is normally provided as matching grants to sail training programs seeking to expand participation. In the past, grants have been made for the purpose of increasing the size and scope of programs and as financial assistance for individual trainees. The foundation does not restrict itself in the types of programs it considers for funding, however it is mainly interested in on-the-water activities geared towards young people conducted by the STA schooners and ASTA member vessels and organizations.

Grant applications may be made at any time to the Schooners Foundation secretary. In applying for a grant, please do so in writing and provide specific information about the activity or individual for which funding is needed, the amount requested and how it will be spent, and the source of matching funds. General information on the vessel and program is also important and applicants will be contacted if additional information is necessary.

Sea Education Association (SEA)

Sea Education Association (SEA), Inc., PO Box 6, Woods Hole, MA 02543; (508) 540-3954, (800) 552-3633; FAX (508) 457-4673. (*Corwith Cramer, Westward*)

Sea Exploring, BSA

Commodore Bill Sills, Sinnissippi Squadron, Sea Exploring, BSA, P.O. Box 106, Springfield, WI 53176-0106; (414) 249-1709, fax (414) 249-0106.

Sea Explorer Ship 303

Lenny Damaso, Sea Explorer Ship 303, Otetiana Council, Boy Scouts of America, 4185 County Line Rd., Fairport, NY 14450; (716) 377-5683. *(Lotus)*

Seaport '76 Foundation

Marvin Ronning, Executive Director, Continental Sloop *Providence*, PO Box 76, Newport, RI 02840; 401 846-1776, FAX (401) 848-0360. *(Providence)*

Sea Scout Ship No. 1

Sue Larkin, Skipper, Sea Scout Ship No. 1, Sea Exploring, BSA, PO Box 100, Zenda, WI 53195-0100; (414) 249-0225; FAX (414) 249-0733.

Sea Scout Ship No. 97

John E. Kelly, Sea Scout Ship 97, 5271 Forty-fifth Ave., S.W., Seattle, WA 98136; (206) 932-0971. *(Yankee Clipper)*

Small Ships

Mr. John Millar, Small Ships, Newport House, 710 South Henry St., Williamsburg, VA 23185-4113; (804) 229-1775.

Sound Experience

Sound Experience, PO Box 2098, Poulsbo, WA 98370; (206) 697-6601. *(Adventuress)*

SoundWaters

SoundWaters, Four Yacht Haven West Marine Center, Washington Blvd., Stamford, CT 06902; (203) 323-1978. *(SoundWaters)*

Southern Windjammer, Ltd.

Capt. Robert Marthai, Ph.D., Southern Windjammer, Ltd., 2044 Wappoo Hall Rd., Charleston, SC 29412-2057; (803) 795-1180. *(Pride)*

South Street Seaport Museum

Don Birkholz, Jr., Director, Maritime Operations, South Street Seaport Museum, 207 Front St., New York, NY 10038; (212) 748-8600. *(Lettie G. Howard, Pioneer)*

Square Sails School

Bob Booth, Square Sails School, PO Box 3216, Newport, RI 02840; (401) 842-0647. *(Land's End)*.

State University of New York Maritime College

State University of New York Maritime College, Fort Schuyler, Bronx, NY 10465.

St. George's School

St. George's School, Newport, RI 02840; (401) 847-7565. *(Geronimo)*

Student Ocean Challenge

Student Ocean Challenge, PO Box 631, Jamestown, RI 02835; (401) 423-3535; FAX (401) 423-2877.

Sydney Harbour Ports

George Wheeliker, Executive Director, Sydney Harbour Ports, Regional Development Board, PO Box 248, North Sydney, Nova Scotia B2A 3M3 Canada; (902) 794-4631; FAX (902) 794-8824.

Tabor Academy

Capt. James Geil, Tabor Academy, Marion, MA 02738; (508) 748-2000. *(Tabor Boy)*

Tall Ship Bounty Foundation, Inc.

Tall Ship *Bounty* Foundation, Inc., P.O. Box 990, Fall River, MA 02722; (508) 673-3886, fax (508) 675-6592. *("HMS" Bounty)*

Texas Maritime Academy

Texas Maritime Academy, Galveston, TX 77553; (409) 740-4400.

Texas Seaport Museum

Texas Seaport Museum, 2016 Strand, Galveston, TX 77550; (409) 763-1877. *(Elissa)*

Thompson Island Outward Bound Education Center

Mr. Peter Willauer, President, Thompson Island Outward Bound, PO Box 127, Boston, MA 02127; (617) 328-3900, FAX (617) 328-3710.

T. J. Enterprises, Inc.

Timothy L. Jones, President, 4556 Starcher Court, Suffolk, VA 23434; (804) 255-0096.

    T. J. Enterprises, Inc. is a special events consulting agency, specializing in maritime festivals and tall ships solicitation and hosting. Timothy Jones has 22 years of experience with the city of Norfolk, Virginia, and currently contracts with the City of Norfolk, and Norfolk Festevents, Ltd. as Director of Ships. T.J. Enterprises also produces Bass Expo of Virginia, a bass fishing trade show exposition at the Hampton Coliseum, Hampton, Virginia.

Toronto Brigantine, Inc. (TBI)

Gordon Laco, Toronto Brigantine, Inc., 283 Queens Quay West, Toronto, Ontario M5V 1A2 Canada; (416) 203-9949. *(Pathfinder, Playfair)*

    Like many good ideas, Toronto Brigantine was founded by happy coincidence. During the Christmas holidays in 1960, a Toronto businessman, J. Garfield Lorriman, and his wife Mary, were impressed by a film about the great Norwegian sail training ship *Christian Radich*. When the Lorrimans and a group of their friends set about researching the possibility of building a sail training vessel for Toronto they discovered the *St. Lawrence II*, built in Kingston and sailed in part by the Royal Canadian Sea Cadets since 1955.

    The group, headed by the Lorrimans, was determined to put together a sail training organization in Toronto. They located Francis Maclachlan, the designer of the St. Lawrence II, and commissioned him to build another tall ship.

    After two years of fund raising and building, the 60' brigantine *Pathfinder* was commissioned in 1964. Over the next few years the sail training program grew to include a 37' foot cutter and a shore base. In 1972, Toronto Brigantine built its second ship, *Playfair*, to accommodate its increasing number of program participants. *Playfair* was named in 1973 by Her Majesty, Queen Elizabeth II.

    Over the years, the program has progressed from its Sea Cadet/military training style and now emphasizes responsibility; the operation and sailing of the ship is placed in the hands of the 14 to 18-year-old crew. The core philosophy remains the same; Toronto Brigantine believes sail training for youths builds character through adventure.

    Today, more than 6,000 young men and women from all over the world have participated in the program.

Traverse Tall Ship Co.

Traverse Tall Ship Co., 13390 S. West Bay Shore Dr., Traverse City, MI 49684; (616) 941-2000. *(Malabar, Manitou)*

Urban Harbors Institute

Madeline Walsh, Urban Harbors Institute, UMASS, 100 Morrissey Blvd., Boston, MA 02125; (617) 287-5570.

The Urban Harbors Institute conducts multidisciplinary research on urban harbor issues ranging from water quality to waterfront development. The Institute sponsors workshops, symposia, and educational programs. It also publishes reports and proceedings; provides technical assistance to community and business leaders, and the general public; and maintains a resource library.

The Institute is associated with the University's programs in environmental sciences, geography, and management. Its core staff, senior associates, and researchers have expertise in public policy, coastal resource management, marine law, economics, waterfront planning, international coastal zone management and education.

USA Services, Inc.

USA Services, Inc., 1111 Ingleside Rd., Norfolk, VA 23502; (804) 855-2233.

U.S. Coast Guard Academy

U.S. Coast Guard Academy, Commanding Officer, USCG Cutter *Eagle* (WIX 327), New London, CT. 06320; (203) 444-8595; when away from port: Lt. Cdr. Graham, *Eagle* Support Branch, (203) 444-8279. *(Eagle)*

U.S. Merchant Marine Academy

Sail, Power and Crew Squadron, U.S. Merchant Marine Academy, Kings Point, NY 11024-1699; (516) 773-5396.

U.S. Naval Academy

Director of Naval Academy Sailing, U.S. Naval Academy, Robert Crown Center, 601 Brownson Rd., Annapolis, MD 21402; (410) 293-2885.

Every Navy and Marine Corps graduate of the Naval Academy must demonstrate competence aboard sailing craft. To this end, the Director of Naval Academy Sailing operates what is arguably the nation's largest and most comprehensive sail training program. The program utilizes over two hundred fifty sailing dinghies and service craft and thirty offshore vessels to provide each midshipman with leadership, seamanship, navigation, meteorology and marlinespike training. The sail training program at the Naval Academy consists of four parts:

• Basic Sailing: All members of the entering class (approximately 1,100 students) are required to learn to sail. This is accomplished in the summer before the first academic year. Each midshipman receives twenty-four hours of underway instruction in

Lasers, 26' Knockabouts and the Navy 44' sloops.
 • Command and Seamanship Training: Approximately thirty-five percent of each class of midshipmen participate in a summer cruise aboard one of the Navy 44' sloops. Crews consist of eight midshipmen and two instructors. The boats cruise in groups of six to ten to Bermuda or New England and return to Annapolis after a month.
 • Varsity Intercollegiate Team: One of the twenty-nine varsity sports at the Naval Academy, the Intercollegiate team consists of forty midshipmen sailing in Lasers, 420's, FJ's and J-24's. The Academy has won the National Championship for college sailing three times recently, 1991, 1993 and 1994.
 • Varsity Offshore Team: This varsity team has over one hundred midshipmen who compete in offshore one-design and handicap racing. While the crews compete in short "round the buoys" races, the team's forte is blue water, offshore racing. Academy boats are regular contestants in the Marblehead to Halifax, Annapolis to Newport and Newport to Bermuda races. A midshipmen crew won first-in-fleet honors in the prestigious Annapolis to Bermuda Race aboard the Navy 44, *Vigilant*, in 1994.

U.S. Navy

Robert L. Howe, Executive Director of U.S. Naval Sailing Association, Naval Station Annapolis, 58 Bennion Rd., Annapolis, MD. 21402-5054; (410) 293-2130.
The United States Navy, through its Navy Sailing Program, maintains an active fleet of sail training vessels at bases, colleges and universities throughout the country and around the world to support an active program of sail training for personnel. The program uses a specially developed and standardized curriculum to assure Navy "sailors" are qualified—and eligible—to sail at any of the thirty-two sailing centers that the Navy maintains. Each of these centers maintains its own fleet of small boats; some centers also have large boats, which are used for both training and recreational sailing.

Vessel Zodiac Corp.

Karl Mehrer and Tim Mehrer, Vessel *Zodiac* Corp., PO Box 322, Snohomish, WA 98290; (206) 483-4088, (206) 325-6122. *(Zodiac)*

VisionQuest National, Ltd.

VisionQuest National, Ltd., PO Box 447, Exton, PA 19341; (215) 458-0800. *(Bill of Rights, New Way)* See also *Tole Mour*

Voyager Cruises

Capt. Frank Fulchiero, Voyager Cruises, 73 Steamboat Wharf, Mystic, CT 06355; (203) 536-0416. *(Argia)*

Williams College-Mystic Seaport Maritime Studies Program

Anna Fitzgerald, Admissions, Maritime Studies Program, Williams College-Mystic Seaport, 75 Greenmanville Avenue, PO Box 6000, Mystic, CT 06355-0990; (203) 572-5359; FAX (203) 572-5329, E-Mail: AnnaMSM@aol.com.

Williams College and Mystic Seaport Museum unite to provide an academic adventure in maritime studies. The interdisciplinary program offers students of all majors the opportunity to spend a semester on the study of the sea. Twenty-two undergraduates each semester are selected from the nation's top colleges and universities to spend a semester living and taking courses at Mystic Seaport in Mystic, Connecticut. The core curriculum of the Maritime Studies Program incorporates Maritime History, Literature of the Sea, and Marine Science (Oceanography or Marine Ecology). Academics are enhanced by hands-on training aboard the Mystic Seaport's many ships as well as by maritime skills classes in boat building, sailing, wood carving, sea chanteys, and climbing aloft on a square-rigger.

Williams-Mystic students also participate in three field seminars each semester, as part of their curriculum. The fall semester voyages offshore for two weeks in the North Atlantic and the spring semester to Bahamian water aboard *SSV Westward* or *SSV Corwith Cramer*. This two-week expedition involves intensive student participation in sailing the vessel as well as primary involvement with the ships' oceanographic research mission. Students learn to hoist and strike sail, man the helm and the bow watch, and maintain the ship as they take shifts in the twenty-four hour watch system. Scientific research also occurs around the clock, with students deploying sampling equipment overboard, retrieving and analyzing samples, recording data, and presenting their findings to their professors and classmates.

In addition to the two week offshore voyage, the students also travel to Nantucket and New York for a short field seminar and to the Pacific coast, California and Oregon for an exciting eight day field seminar, comparing maritime topics between regions and coasts.

Students return to Mystic where they apply the knowledge learned in their field seminars toward their on-going research projects in history, marine science and marine policy. The resources available to them at Mystic Seaport and in the surrounding coastal communities are unmatched on any college campus. A full semester of credit is granted through Williams College. Financial aid is available.

WoodenBoat School

Rich Hilsinger, Director, WoodenBoat School, PO Box 78, Naskeag Rd., Brooklin, ME 04616; (207) 359-4651; FAX (207) 359-8920.

The WoodenBoat School is located on a 64-acre waterfront campus in Brooklin, Maine. Founded in 1981, the school's twin focus is on wooden boat building and sailing instruction taught by experienced sailors in cutters, friendship sloops, ketches and more than 20 assorted small craft ranging from a 7'6" Nutshell sailing pram to a 28' Friendship Sloop. A majority of the course offerings, which last no more than two weeks, teach various aspects of boat building and woodworking. Instruction in related crafts such as sail making, marine surveying, marine mechanics and electronics, rigging/handwork, and painting and varnishing is also offered.

Yankee Packet Company

Capt. Mike and Lynne McHenry, Yankee Packet Co., Box 736, Camden, ME 04843-0736; (207) 236-8873. *(Angelique)*

Youth Adventure, Inc.

Ernestine Bennett, P.O. Box 23, Mercer Island, WA 98040; (206) 232-4024

International Sail Training Associations

There are hundreds of sail training programs around the world. Compiling and maintaining comprehensive and up-to-date addresses for the ships involved would be a massive undertaking. The following organizations have functions corresponding to those of the American Sail Training Association and can help supply some information about sail training opprotunities in their respective countries.

Australia
Mr. Malcolm C. Hay, Chairman, STA of Western Australia, PO Box 1100, Fremantle 6160, Western Australia, Australia.

Canada
Chris M. Bagley, Canadian Sail Traning Association, PO Box 709, Station B, Ottawa, Ontario K1P 5P8 Canada; (705) 728-8265.

Finland
Sail Training Association Finland (STAF), c/o Kotkan Satamalaitos, Laivurinkatu 7, 48100 Kotka, Finland.

Germany
Sail Training Association Germany (STAG), D-2850 Bremerhaven F, AM Hollwerk 1, Germany.

Japan
Sail Training Association of Japan (STAJ), Nanyo-do Building 2F, 1-14-4 Hongo, Bunkyo-ku, Toky 113, Japan; (03) 3818-6272; FAX (03) 3818-7816.

Netherlands
Sail Training Association Netherlands (STAN), Postbus 55, 2340 AB Oegstgeest, Netherlands.

Poland
Sail Training Association Poland (STAP), Gdynska Fundacja Zeglarska, al. Zjednocczenia 3, 81-963 Gdynia 1, Poland.

Portugal
Aporvela, Caleada Palma de Baixo 4-8F, 1600 Lisbon, Portugal.

Russia
Sail Training Association Russia (STAR), St. Petersburg Engineering Marine College, Kosaya Line 15a, St. Petersburg, Russia.

United Kingdom
Sail Training Asociation (STA), 5 Mumby Rd., Portsmouth PO1 3PT, England, United Kingdom; (0705) 586-367; FAX (0705) 584-661.

United States
American Sail Training Association, PO Box 1459, Newport, RI 02840; office: 365 Thames St., Newport, RI 02840; (401) 846-1775; FAX (401) 849-5400.

Rig Identification

Full-Rigged Ship
(3, 4- or 5-masted)

Bark
(3, 4- or 5-masted)

Barkentine
(3, 4- or 5-masted)

Gaff Topsail Schooner
(2, 3- or 4-masted)

Brig

Brigantine

Square-Topsail Schooner
(2, 3- or 4-masted)

Gaff Schooner

Yawl

Ketch

Sloop
(gaff-rigged)

Sloop
(Marconi or Bermuda rigged)

Notes:

Notes:

BOWEN'S WHARF CO.

NEWPORT, RI

Historic Waterfront District with over 40 Retail Shops, Restaurants & Marine Businesses

⚓ 1995 Maritime Arts Festival*

May 19, 20, 21. A Maritime Feast of Music, Entertainment, Art & History Exhibits Special Performances & Open House Aboard Select ASTA® Tall Ships®
*A portion of the proceeds directly benefit ASTA®.

⚓ 1995 Newport International Boat Show

September 14, 15, 16, 17. Host site of the Maritime History and Sail Training Exhibits and Programs.

⚓ 1995 Bowen's Wharf Waterfront Seafood Festival

October 14 & 15. Our 5th Annual Celebration of New England and the Bounties of the Sea, including Maritime Exhibits, Live Entertainment, Children's Activities, Lobster Races & More!

For information on Bowen's Wharf, Dock Space Availability, Seasonal Events or Shops & Restaurants, please call: (401) 849-2243 or (401) 849-2120 or write to us at P.O. Box 60, Newport, RI 02840.

TREWORGY YACHTS

#1 BUILDER Of U.S.C.G. Certified 40' to 100' Custom Steel PASSENGER CARRYING VESSELS:

"Inland Seas"
Science Ship
"Appledore IV"
"Appledore V"
"Liberty"

Awlgrip®

Building Futures Since 1976
For More Information Call:

(904) 445-5878

Mark & Toni Treworgy
5658 N. Oceanshore Blvd.
Palm Coast, FL 32137

CUSTOM BOAT BUILDING
Treworgy
PALM COAST, FL.

Can anybody make a difference helping one tall ship a year?

Yes.

The great ships of the great legends rarely survive beyond a museum glimpse of a distant era.

But on those great occasions when these vessels survive and sail again, they rekindle a spirit that awakens an entire heritage of independence, individuals and adventure.

To see one tall ship, full sail at sea, is somehow enough to renew this spirit forever.

To this end, Cutty Sark has established and endowed the Tall Ships Foundation™, to help one ship each year move nearer to the open sea.

Once each year, beginning October 1994, the Cutty Sark Tall Ships Foundation will select one tall ship to receive $25,000 to aid in the raising of funds for restoration.

Cutty Sark and the Foundation will also create programs to raise awareness—and greater funds—for the cause.

Is this too little, too late?

It is never too late, and there is never enough. And each year, one more tall ship will sail again.

Because that's all it takes—one more commitment, one more ship.

Then one more believer, forever.

CUTTY SARK®

For more information write to the Cutty Sark Tall Ships Foundation
P.O. Box 110231, Stamford, CT 06911-0231

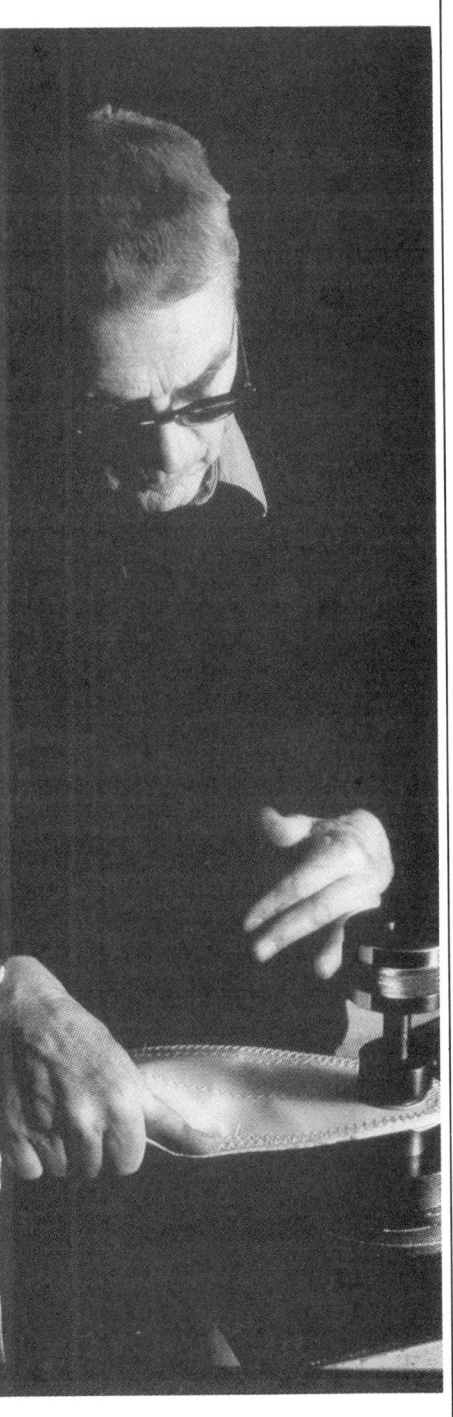

No Additives.
No Preservatives.
Just Hood Quality.

The best sails begin with the best components. Hood's secret to producing great, long lasting cruising sails begins with the cloth. You see, at Hood we produce our own cloth, insuring that it's the best you can buy. Hood pioneered the use of Dacron and we are still the only sailmaker weaving our own cloth. And, we guarantee worldwide service on all Hood products.

Our Dacron cloth is woven tighter. It's not dependent on resins for shape retention. For its weight, Hood sailcloth is more pure yarn, so it's soft, manageable, and will withstand even the harshest elements. Hood now offers cruising sails made from Ultra Spectra - our Dacron reinforced with Spectra® - for added strength and longevity.

The pride we have in producing our cloth is carried into the design of your sail. Our HoodNet software links Hood cloth characteristics to sail design, laser cutting, and manufacturing. This advanced technology assists us in creating the correct shape for your cruising sails.

Quality is the backbone of our craftsmanship. Every seam is stitched with our trademark ultra violet resistant brown thread. Corners are reinforced with either Hood rings or hand-stitched leather clad patches. Each batten pocket is fortified from the inside out with extra layers of fabric.

Hood sails have cruised more miles around the world than any other brand of sails. Our commitment to quality service has been our trademark in sailmaking since our beginning. Hood lofts are located in every corner of the world, to service you and your sails, wherever you cruise.

Hood sails are controlled from the first fiber to the final hand-stitch. Pure quality. No additives. No preservatives. That's why Hood remains the most trusted name in sailmaking.

The Trusted Name in Sailmaking.

HOOD
SAILMAKERS

International
200 High Point Avenue
Portsmouth, RI 02871

For more information, call
1-800-688-4660

HOOD SAILMAKERS WORLDWIDE
ANNAPOLIS, MARYLAND 301-268-4663; STAMFORD, CONNECTICUT 203-325-4663; COSTA MESA, CALIFORNIA 714-548-3464
GROSSE POINTE, MICHIGAN 313-822-1400; FORT LAUDERDALE, FLORIDA 305-522-4663; HONOLULU, HAWAII 808-537-4884
SAN DIEGO, CALIFORNIA 619-223-1249; SAN FRANCISCO, CALIFORNIA 415-332-4104; ST. PETERSBURG, FLORIDA 813-823-3392
BARBADOS 809-423-4600; TORONTO, ONTARIO 416-364-9111; TORTOLA, BRITISH VIRGIN ISLANDS 809-494-2569
VANCOUVER, BRITISH COLUMBIA 604-875-0360; ARGENTINA, AUSTRALIA, ENGLAND, FRANCE
GERMANY, ITALY, JAPAN, NEW ZEALAND, SPAIN.

PRIVATE VACATION
VILLAS

The Caribbean's Finest

INTIMATE SMALL
HOTELS

St. Barthelemy, St. Martin, Anguilla, Barbados, Mustique, British & U.S. Virgin Islands, Saba, Nevis, South Of France

For Brochures, Rates And Reservations

WIMCO
West Indies Management Company

28 Pelham Street, Newport, Rhode Island 02840

Fax: 401-847-6290   Tel: 401-849-8012

1-800-932-3222

UK: 0-800-89-8318   *France:* 05.90.16.20   *Germany:* 01.30.81.57.30

WIMCO is proud to support the mission and goals of the American Sail Training Association.

·A·CHINA·CLIPPER·DROPS·ANCHOR·IN·NEWPORT·HARBOUR·

Courtesy Newport Historical Socirety

Tall Ships® Visits Since 1525!

When Giovanni Verrazzano sailed into Newport
he had to create his own event
but you can call us
to schedule your ship's port visit

Newport, Rhode Island
America's First Resort!

- Tall Ships® Host for 1976, 1982, 1986, 1992
- 3.5 Million Visitors Annually
- Natural Deep-Water Port
- Home of the Newport Music, Jazz and Folk Festivals

May 19 - 21, 1995
Maritime Arts Festival at Bowen's Wharf

Newport County Convention & Visitors Bureau
23 America's Cup Avenue, Newport, RI 02840-3050
1-800-326-6030 or in RI 401-849-0921; FAX 401-849-0291

The HARVEY GAMAGE Sea Education Voyages serve student groups of all ages. Operated in partnership with schools, colleges, research organizations, museums, and other educational institutions, programs include academic studies in marine science, literature, arts and humanities, math and history.

Individuals or institutions who desire information about HARVEY GAMAGE Sea Education Voyages should contact: Program Director, Sail Adventures in Learning, Inc., 99 Commercial Street, Bath, ME 04530 207-443-6222.

S.A.I.L., Inc *is pleased to introduce the Ocean Classroom program - a fully accredited high school term at sea. Offered in the fall. Call for information.*

Explore the world. Discover yourself.

Sail aboard the schooner HARVEY GAMAGE. Pass your wake across the sea and mark yourself for a true life explorer.

SAIL MAINE

SCHOONER MARY DAY · CAMDEN · MAINE

The Classic Windjammer Vacation
SCHOONER MARY DAY
Outstanding Sailing
Great Food, Wild Islands, Snug Harbors
Seals, Eagles, Whales, Puffins

Capt. Steve & Chris Cobb
Box 798 Camden, ME 04843
800-992-2218

free brochure

FILM TELEVISION
Marine Coordination
Locations
Boat Wrangler

All types of ships and boats for
Sets
Support
Safety

Marine/film professionals. Experienced in feature, documentary, commercial. Recent credits include *Interview With a Vampire, Gambler V, Craftsman Tool*

contact: **Steve Cobb**
C.N. Co. Film Service
(207) 236-8489

SOUTH STREET SEAPORT MUSEUM
celebrates the 100th Anniversary of the launching of the 1893 Gloucester Fishing
Schooner
LETTIE G. HOWARD

Following a landmark restoration, the Lettie G. Howard will be operational and available for educational programs in Spring of 1994.

COME JOIN US, BY LAND OR SEA.

For information call:
(212) 669-9400, or write us at
207 Front Street,
New York, NY 10038

Wayfarer

Need Parts FAST?

Whenever . . . Wherever
Call Wayfarer Worldwide Parts
—your personal parts agent

For big parts or small
—emergency or not—
we'll put the pieces together for you.

It's our specialty!

1-800-229-4378
207-236-4378
FAX: 207-236-2371

WAYFARER MARINE CORPORATION
Your Full-Service Repair & Storage Yard
P.O. Box 677 • Sea Street • Camden, Maine 04843

We will be happy to give you a guaranteed quote on any parts or service you need. May we send you our brochures?

S·E·A·H·A·W·K

The coast is clear and 7 times closer.

Swift's Armored Sea Hawk delivers tremendous light transmission under minimal conditions and a sharp, bright image to guide you home.

Driving rain won't ruffle the feathers of this nitrogen filled, waterproof glass and its shock resistant rubber armor is ideal for mariners, duck hunters and birders.

753 SEA HAWK (Armored)
7x,50 I.F. - (393 ft.)
42 oz. - R.L.E. 84.2

SWIFT

Swift Instruments, Inc.
952 Dorchester Ave., Boston, MA 02125
In Canada: Vision Canada LTD., Pickering, Ontario L1N 3S1

PRODUCERS OF SAIL BOSTON 1992

"We at Conventures want you to consider us as your friend, host and resource in Boston."
Dusty Rhodes,
President

Join us for the Second Annual Boston Seaport Festival
August 18-21, 1994

Conventures

250 SUMMER ST. • BOSTON, MA 02210 • (617) 439-7700

HALIFAX

Good Sailing and Fair Winds from the historic Port of Halifax, celebrating its 250th birthday in 1999, and Nova Scotia, home of the Bluenose. Remember 1999!

Tourism Halifax
P.O. Box 1749, Halifax
Nova Scotia B3J 3A5
(902) 421-8736

Adventures in Ocean Studies!

Educational programs for:
high school students
undergraduates
teachers

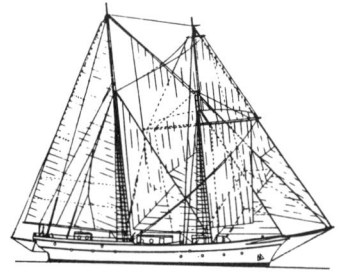

S·E·A
Explore the ocean environment from aboard a tall ship!

Sea Education Association
PO Box 6 · Woods Hole, MA · 02543
800-552-3633

· CAPT. G. W. FULL & ASSOC. ·
· MARINE SURVEYORS ·

**SURVEYORS
of
SAILING SHIPS**
**46 Cedar Street
Marblehead MA 01945**
Telephone (617) 631-4902
Fax (617) 631-8450

Smooth sailing to ASTA from the city of Providence at the headwaters of Narragansett Bay

If shore leave allows you the time, come visit our outstanding zoo at Roger Williams Park.

Vincent A. Cianci, Jr.
Mayor of Providence

NEW YORK HARBOR

OpSail™

OPERATION SAIL, INC.

Tall Ships® Information Bureau™
203-629-4600 Fax: 203-629-1992
2 Greenwich Plaza, Suite 100
Greenwich, CT 06830

A Non-Profit Organization Dedicated to Sail Training and Good Will Among Nations. Established 1961

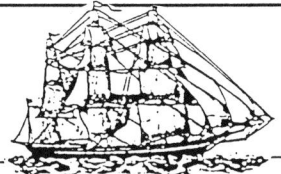

Captain's • Cove • Seaport

on Historic Black Rock Harbor in Bridgeport, CT

Lat. 41° 09' 40" Long. 73° 12' 48"

Always a berth for a visiting Tall Ship!

Home port of *"HMS" Rose, Black Pearl,* & *John E. Pfriem*

Phone (203) 335-1433   Fax (203) 335-6793

Listen to official NOAA Weather Radio Marine broadcasts of your choice from any National Weather Service station nationwide.

BOAT/U.S.
WEATHER WATCH

Provided by the Weather Radio Network, Nashville, TN. $.98 a minute.

1-900-933-BOAT

LIRAKIS

Hang out with the Best!

Catalog $2.00

Lirakis Safety Harness Inc.
18 Sheffield Ave.
Newport, RI 02840 USA
401/846-5356 Fax 401/846-5359

The Great Chesapeake Bay Schooner Race VI
Oct. 11 thru Oct. 15, 1995

The largest collection of traditionally rigged Schooners on the East Coast will race from Baltimore to Norfolk. Help "Save the Bay" and foster traditional sail training. JOIN US!

For an entry form & race details contact:
Captain Lane Briggs
Schooner Norfolk Rebel 1553 Bayville St.
Norfolk, VA 23503   804-588-6022

A FED. NON PROFIT CORP.

BOX 71   TEL. (207) 633-5071

NATHANIEL S. WILSON
SAILMAKER
EAST BOOTHBAY, MAINE
COTTON & DACRON SAILS

LINCOLN STREET   EAST BOOTHBAY, MAINE 04544

Builders of the Pride of Baltimore II   *Builders of the Lady Maryland*

PEREGRINE WOODWORKS

PAUL POWICHROSKI   GARY SUROSKY   G. PETER BOUDREAU

YACHT & SHIP CONSTRUCTION AND REPAIR
PHONE: 410-727-7472   FAX: 410-727-1396

Notes:

Notes...

Sign On With ASTA Today!

The American Sail Training Association is a non-profit, tax-exempt 501(c)(3) organization registered in the state of Rhode Island and Providence Plantations. Membership is open to all interested individuals, non-profit organizations, communities, and corporations committed to furthering the goals of sail training. All contributions are tax-deductable to the extent permissible by law. There are five membership categories.

Student/Trainee membership – $15
Open to regularly enrolled academic students and to shipboard trainees. Student/Trainee members receive *Running Free*, the ASTA newsletter which gives news of interest to ASTA members, including listings of job openings and program opportunities. Student/trainee members also receive an ASTA decal and a membership card. (Note: Student/Trainee category members do not receive ASTA *Directory*.)

Regular membership – $35
Open to all individuals and families. Regular members receive all benefits described above, as well as *ASTA Directory of Sail Training Ships and Programs*. Regular members are also entitled to a discount if they attend the annual ASTA Sail Training Conference held each fall.

Organization membership – $125
Open to all sail training groups, corporations, cities, and other interested organizations. Organization members receive benefits as listed above, plus a certificate of membership suitable for framing. Organization members are also entitled to full descriptive listing in ASTA *Directory of Sail Training Ships and Programs*.

Supporting membership – $250
Open to individuals and organizations who wish to demonstrate their additional support for ASTA through increased dues. Supporting members receive all the benefits of a regular member.

Life membership – $2,500
Life membership enables an individual to provide vital support to ASTA and, as a one-time payment, entitles him or her to all benefits of regular annual membership for the remainder of the member's life.

Please fill out and return form on next page...

To join ASTA...

simply cut or copy the form below and send it to ASTA, PO Box 1459, Newport, RI 02840 or FAX to (401) 849-5400. Payment may be made by personal check or money order, or charged to either VISA or MasterCard. Members outside of the United States, please add $10 to the applicable rate for your membership category. If you have additional queries, please call ASTA at (401) 846-1775.

ASTA Membership

Please enroll me in the following membership category in the American Sail Training Association. (See next page for gifts for your friends and yourself.)

U.S. funds please. Outside the United States, add $10 additional

☐	Student/Trainee	$15
☐	Regular	$35
☐	Organization	$125
☐	Supporting	$250
☐	Life	$2,500

Dues are payable annually with membership in effect for one year from date of payment (except for Life which is a one-time payment).

All ASTA members except Student/Trainee will receive the *ASTA Directory of Sail Training Ships and Programs*

NAME _____

ORGANIZATION _____

STREET ADDRESS _____

CITY/STATE/ZIP _____

PHONE NUMBER _____

☐ Check Enclosed   ☐ VISA   ☐ MasterCard

Card Number _____ Expires _____

Signature _____ Date _____

ASTA, PO Box 1459, Newport, RI 02840

More from ASTA

Billet Bank (crew listings, for members only) — $5

As a service to members, ASTA maintains a Billet Bank through which experienced sailors (licensed or not) can be put in touch with ships in need of a crew.

ASTA Gift Items

ASTA Directory of Sail Training Ships and Programs $8.00

ASTA Syllabus and Log Book $4.25

Guidelines for Educational Programs under Sail $6.00

The Sailing Experience, VHS format video, 9 min $18.00

Ceramic Coffee Mug with ASTA logo $6.00

Pin, ASTA logo in oval, pin back; pewter or copper finish $6.00

Flags, blue field with white ASTA logo and letters, nylon with tape/grommets. Suitable for flying from your ship, home or office: ....

..................................2'X3'+$20., 3'x5'=$25., 4'x6'=$30., 5'8'=$40.

ASTA Blazer Patch (magnetic flap) $33.00

ASTA Blazer Patch (pin back) $30.00

Ties, navy blue with white, woven ASTA logo $24.00

Prices include 1st Class postage and handling.

Please send me the following items(s):_____

_____
_____
_____

NAME _____
ORGANIZATION _____
STREET ADDRESS _____
CITY/STATE/ZIP _____
PHONE NUMBER _____

U.S. Funds please.

Check Enclosed_____ VISA _____ Mastercard_____
Card Number _____ Expires _____
Signature _____ Date _____

ASTA, PO Box 1459, Newport, RI 02840

Notes:

Notes:

Notes:

Notes: